ALEXA

PETER STOTHARD is the editor of the *TLS* and the author of two previous books of diaries, *Thirty Days* (2003) and *On the Spartacus Road* (2010). He is a classicist who has spent most of his life as a political and literary journalist. From 1992 to 2002 he was the editor of *The Times*. In 2012 he was chairman of the judges for the Man Booker Prize. He was knighted in 2003.

More praise for *Alexandria*:

'If I have any quibble with the book, it is based on wanting to spend more time with Stothard; to hear him on topics not discussed in the book ... Others can praise Stothard's journalistic precision but what impressed me more is the Classical self-knowledge ... The book is full of such won wisdom; and although not ostensibly there to report on the first stirrings of political change in Egypt, his glancing observations tell us more about a paranoid, fractious state than countless more column inches ... and all of that shot through with a supremely humane intelligence' Stuart Kelly, *Scotsman*

'Wonderful, surprising ... This is an uplifting book – a constant reminder that life is far more richly layered and mysterious than we realise' *Daily Mail*

ALEXANDRIA

The Last Nights of Cleopatra

PETER STOTHARD

GRANTA

Granta Publications, 12 Addison Avenue, London W11 4QR

First published in Great Britain by Granta Books, 2013
This paperback edition published by Granta Books, 2014

Image on pages 1, 255 and 379: Georg Scholz, *Weiblicher Akt mit Gipskopf* (Seated Nude with
plaster Bust) 1927 © Vereinigung der Freunde der Staatlichen Kunsthalle Karlsruhe e. V.
Image on pages 87 and 381: Elizabeth Taylor's profile on DVD cover of Cleopatra © 20th
Century Fox/Everett/Rex Features. Image on page 275: Bust of Lucius Munatius Plancus ©
The Art Archive / Musée de la Civilisation Gallo-Romaine Lyon / Gianni Dagli Orti. Image
on pages 315 and 322: Jan de Bray (c.1627–97), *Banquet of Mark Antony and Cleopatra*, 1652.
Oil on canvas. Supplied by Royal Collection Trust / © HM Queen Elizabeth II 2012.

Map on pp. x–xi copyright © Leslie Robinson and Vera Brice, 2013

A CIP catalogue record for this book
is available from the British Library.

1 3 5 7 9 10 8 6 4 2

ISBN 978 1 84708 704 1

Typeset by M Rules

Printed and bound by CPI Group (UK) Ltd, Croydon, CR0 4YY

MIX
Paper from
responsible sources
FSC® C020471

i.m.

RJMG (1951–2010)

In the new year of 2011, on the eve of
the Arab Spring, I was in Alexandria to complete
a book about Cleopatra. With me were the remains
of seven previous attempts. This time
there had to be an end.

CONTENTS

ALEXANDRIA

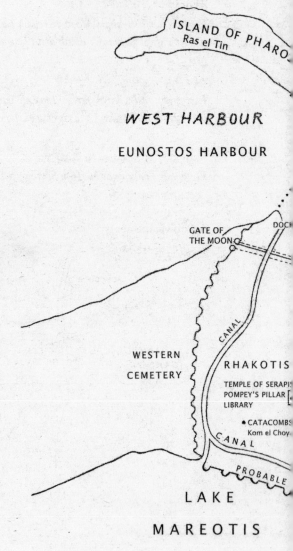

ISLAND OF PHARO
Ras el Tin

WEST HARBOUR

EUNOSTOS HARBOUR

GATE OF
THE MOON

DOC

CANAL

WESTERN
CEMETERY

RHAKOTIS

TEMPLE OF SERAPIS
POMPEY'S PILLAR
LIBRARY

● CATACOMBS
Kom el Choy

CANAL

PROBABLE

LAKE

MAREOTIS

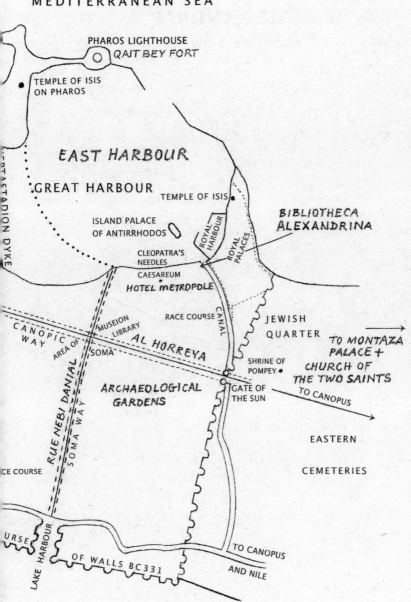

MEDITERRANEAN SEA

PHAROS LIGHTHOUSE
QAIT BEY FORT

TEMPLE OF ISIS
ON PHAROS

EAST HARBOUR

GREAT HARBOUR

TEMPLE OF ISIS

HEPTASTADION DYKE

ISLAND PALACE
OF ANTIRRHODOS

BIBLIOTHECA
ALEXANDRINA

ROYAL
HARBOUR

ROYAL PALACES

CLEOPATRA'S
NEEDLES

CAESAREUM
HOTEL METROPOLE

CANAL

RACE COURSE

JEWISH
QUARTER

CANOPIC
WAY

MUSEION
LIBRARY

AREA OF
SOMA

AL HORREYA

TO MONTAZA
PALACE +
CHURCH OF
THE TWO SAINTS

SHRINE OF
POMPEY

TO CANOPUS

RUE NEBI DANIAL
SOMA WAY

ARCHAEOLOGICAL
GARDENS

GATE OF
THE SUN

EASTERN

CEMETERIES

CE COURSE

TO CANOPUS

LAKE HARBOUR

OF WALLS BC 331

AND NILE

31.12.10

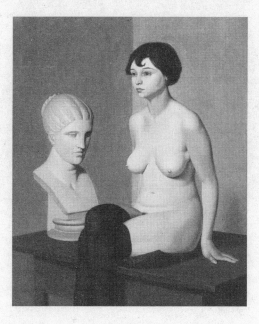

Hotel Metropole, Place Saad Zaghloul, Alexandria

This is precisely the eighth time I have begun to write this book. I am certain of that. It sometimes seems the only certainty. Here in Room 114 of the Metropole Hotel there is written evidence of all the other seven attempts, long pages and short scraps, bleached and yellowed, each piece patch-working into the bedcover as though they had always been here. I have unpacked them as carefully as though they were ancient history itself, more carefully than I packed them in London yesterday. There is no order yet. The first are not even my own words. They are Maurice's. I have not read them for forty years, not since we were at Oxford together and I first followed his florid dictation. I have not yet unpacked anything else.

There was a red tent within a red tent within a red tent. That was what Frog said. The walls behind were grey-green and damp but in front of the canvas slit that led to the sanctuaries were dry roses. Inside the first encircling corridor the floor was warm leather. Through a second slit into a second circle there was a different carpet, silk or satin, light enough to show the outlines of the limbs that lay bodiless beneath.

These limbs were lower legs, both right legs, the soles of their covered feet fixed upwards, the faint shape of the sweating toes visible beneath the cloth. The higher parts of the thighs were out of sight inside the final red tent on the floor of the innermost chamber. There was no opening by which to pass through and see why two women, probably women, were lying face down in the hidden heart of this strange construction; or why one of each of their legs was stretched outside into the corridor as though for some reason surplus to requirements.

The only instruction was on a pink card secured by a jewelled brooch, carrying words in Greek, 'veiled in the obscurity of a learned language' as Edward Gibbon once noted on a similar occasion: 'Menete! Nereidais Kleopatras Palaistra' *('Wait Here to Wrestle with Cleopatra's Mermaids').*

Maurice's story of the Red Tents was part of my fifth Cleopatra, perhaps one of the less respectable attempts. It was wilfully mysterious, a mingling of geometry, classics and pornography, as though in parody of a school curriculum. It was a shock at the time (I was easier to shock back then) but I recorded it in clear, round lettering, in a college room at Trinity, as accurately as the fumes of sherry and Old Spice allowed. At some point in the coming weeks I will try to remember more.

Maurice is the longest-serving character in this story. He was my oldest friend. We shared little in common, he the smooth one, I the rough, he the pale-faced, I the freckled, he the teller of jokes and tales, I the listener. But without always liking each other, we knew each other from the age of four. We shared primary and secondary schools, children's parties and sports fields, college rooms and student stages. We also, for a short while, shared a passion for a dead queen of Egypt.

This was not always the same passion. Maurice's thoughts were mostly theatrical, sensual, sexual. Tarpaulins, tapestries and human tangents were the props of a drama that lasted all his life. My thoughts were more often literary, 'just a bit too boring' he used to complain. In 1971 we each thought the other a bit confused. He was a man of the modern. I was the student of classical times. We argued. He is dead now, but we still seem to be arguing. By the end of this journey I want some of those arguments to have ended.

My hotel bed is becoming crowded. The papers do not form easy categories or files. Each lies flat and alone. The earliest words are from fifty years ago, the first efforts of an Essex schoolboy; the latest from the 1980s from a classicist finding some sort of success as a journalist. Between these beginnings and ends, which show uneven patterns of progress, there are pages written in Oxford between 1969 and 1971 and at an oil company desk in London in 1976 and in the Calthorpe Arms, a crepuscular pub beside what once were the offices of *The Times*.

It is not a clear pattern. But I can already see debts that need to be paid, to V, an Essex schoolgirl when her contribution began, to a troubled boy called Frog, to two types of Oxford mermaid, to a grey mistress of the petroleum industry, to Margaret Thatcher and to Her Majesty the Queen, as museum-keeper as well as monarch.

There will be others to thank, an athletic schoolmaster, a not at all athletic Oxford authority on ancient plagues, a long-distance swimmer, a hero of the Anzio landings, a cancer-stricken newspaper editor and Maurice himself who also died of cancer, just before this journey, and without whose dying memories it would not be happening as it is. Tonight, on the eve of this new decade, the eve of the year in which I will be sixty years old, every remnant of my past Cleopatras is a different patch, in a fraying quilt, on a bed, beside an iron balcony, before a view over the bay where her palaces, ships and libraries used to be.

From the year 1960, when Maurice and I were nine years old, only a book title survives, *Professor Rame and the Egyptian Queen*. The earliest pages are from around 1963, Sellotaped in yellow stripes, an account which began, with naive confidence, at Cleopatra's birth, in a room not far from this hotel, and with her father, King Ptolemy XII, known to obedient subjects as Dionysus, the drunkard god, and to the disobedient majority as Old Fluteplayer, the drunkard musician.

Most of my surviving words are handwritten. Only a few of the later parts are typed. Many other pages were lost entirely, left in desk drawers of abandoned jobs and buildings. But that hardly matters. At this New Year in Alexandria, there will be new words each day as though in a diary, the only reliable way that I know I will write at all. This book is not going to be a reconstruction. It is a new start and this time there will be an end.

This time there is also an instruction from the Queen herself, a signed order, the only surviving autograph from any classical figure whose life story has flourished beyond life. This document was unknown in 1985 when the last page was closed on my seventh Cleopatra. It was found at the turn of the new millennium among Roman office papers reused for stuffing mummies, Cleopatra's single word, her last word as I intend to see it, written in her own first language, in Greek, in neat, small, upward-sloping letters, *ginestho*, let it be done, do as I command, make it happen.

The *ginestho* papyrus is of no special kind. The ink is dull. The order is securely dated like any proper product of a well-run office. The date is February, 33 BC, as we now designate our months and years, the prelude to the most dramatic time in even as dramatic a life as Cleopatra's. The order, dictated to a secretary and presented in a fair copy for signature, is that one of her most loyal protectors should be freed from certain taxes. She takes up her pen at a forty-five-degree angle, routinely, relaxedly, running the last four letters together in a single fluid stroke, and writes the *ginestho* on the decree that Mark

Antony's general, Publius Canidius Crassus, and his heirs in perpetuity, may export each year from Egypt 300 tonnes of wheat and import 130,000 litres of wine without paying tax to her or to her children.

This is a tax exemption for the far future from the Egyptian head of a great Greek family who has entered Rome's civil wars, world wars then, with every intention of being on the winner's side. Her man, Canidius, commands the greatest army of the time. She herself commands the most massive personal treasury. The odds are that her lover, Mark Antony, will soon defeat his rival Octavian for the leadership of the Roman world, the legacy of her earlier lover, the assassinated Julius Caesar. She may even choose to exert that leadership not from Rome but from her own palace here – where tonight the cars honk ceaselessly in the square, the birds and beggars scratch on the beach, and the Nile waters still mingle, more sluggishly now, with the Mediterranean sea.

'Make it happen,' she wrote. Her word went out into corridors of bureaucrats and bandits, corrupters and corrupted. Her fellow Alexandrians would never be as admired as much as the 'classical' Greeks from Athens who lived four hundred years before. Nor would they be as feared as the Romans who conquered and followed them. But Cleopatra's people were bureaucratic pioneers, masters of the catalogue and file, inventive manipulators of myth, model office workers as well as models for much else in the ways of life they exported to the future. Although Cleopatra signed orders for music and poetry, wars and executions, medical experiments and monumental theatre, exempting a man from taxes was in no way a smaller matter than these. Revenue made things happen; or stopped things happening.

Of course, this *ginestho* soon became an unnecessary concession. Within two years Cleopatra was dead. The Romans took all Egypt for themselves. Her promise had become a bribe that she need not have made, a few words on a fragile piece of papyrus, a part of the rubbish used to fill the space between a body and a coffin. For the next two thousand years it would cushion an unidentified cranium against a painted piece of wood, a lesson in recycling from an age resourceful in the arts of reuse. Only in the last ten years has it become a thing of resonance once again, one of those rarest of objects, a direct connection between a great queen and those of us who have so long tried to make her our subject.

I.I.II

Hotel Metropole, Place Saad Zaghloul

After clearing the bed of old paper, I have had a long and dreamless sleep. After a short walk around the square, I am back in Room 114 with the latest news from here that for most Alexandrians is no longer new. Indeed I must be one of the very last people in this city to know that persons unknown, at least one of them no longer knowing, breathing or anything, have marked the arrival of 1.1.11 on their electronic watches with a bomb, detonated thirty minutes after midnight, a mile or so away outside a crowded church.

It was Mahmoud who told me, a young man from here at the Metropole Hotel. His message was of tense reassurance. He stared hard, tugged down the lapels of his tight business suit, and spoke with minimal opening of his mouth: there was 'nothing to worry about'; everywhere in the world there were 'suicidists'; the media should not make so much of twenty-three deaths that happened to have happened in Egypt.

He had an older, unshaven, workman-trousered colleague who mildly disagreed. Socratis was from the Cecil, the rival colonial refuge on the sea side of the square. He was more relaxed but gave a sharper warning: today, he said, 'might not be the best day to visit Pompey's Pillar or the Library'; even in the early hours there was 'agitation, alarm and the police are checking papers'.

This Socratis seemed the senior of these gentle quarrellers. I first noticed them when I arrived last night. They were waiting like bored cab-drivers beside bags of horse-feed beneath my window. In the dark I did not ask myself, or anyone else, who they were or why they seemed relieved to see me. In the dirty morning light I was more curious.

Our brief conversation about the bomb did not provide many answers. Mahmoud slicked down his hair, kept his lips taut and his words as if from a clipboard. Socratis growled noisily, dribbled from the left side of his mouth and pulled pointlessly at the curls around his ears. Neither appeared to listen to the other.

'Why are you here?', asked Socratis. 'Nothing comes to Alexandria in the winter except birds to the lake, most of them when they have lost their way.' I explained my business and we kept on talking. He too was 'a man of business', he claimed. 'A bombing is very bad for all business.' I sympathised. 'Old Zaghloul is not getting any visitors at all,' he hissed, pointing to the police who waved away anyone approaching the giant striding statue that separates the hotels in this square that bears his name.

I nodded. I was still finding my way. 'Who was Old Zaghloul?' I asked. Mahmoud looked impatiently towards the sea. Socratis answered, but grumpily, like a speaking guidebook: 'a very modern Egyptian, a father of our country, a hero who in 1924 survived many years in prison but only a single year as Prime Minister'. He smiled and pulled again at a spring of hair that would not be kept down.

Old Saad Zaghloul, he added, as though in afterthought, was one of those who thought 'wrongly' that he could do business with the British occupiers of Egypt, while the British thought 'just as wrongly' that they could do business with him. 'Yet all the time,' said Socratis, 'things were going on that first gave us Colonel Nasser and now something much, much ... the same.'

He hesitated and swept his right hand from side to side, palm down like a cricket umpire signalling a boundary. Maybe Socratis is a professional guide – with one or two unofficial opinions. Mahmoud may perhaps be a guide too, even though he has the complexion of an office-dweller rather than a man of the outdoors. Perhaps he is an organiser of guides, shrinking back nervously from the restless, blinkered horses.

Or perhaps he is not frightened of the horses but of something else. 'Careful, careful,' Mahmoud whispered to both of us with warmth and a threat: 'Zaghloul, Nasser, Mubarak, all of them good men.' Socratis, unmoved and mud-eyed, suggested that we all meet later in a place he called 'my cafe'. First he had to make some hospital visits.

I too need to pause. Before I begin this last Cleopatra, the one that this time I will finish, I want to describe myself a little, to try to see myself as I see Socratis or Mahmoud or as I see the past, revealing first what is easiest to reveal.

So what do I see?

First: a sixty-year-old man, settling into his room, as tall as a wardrobe, as broad as a pillow, hair the colour of a greying sheet, stubble like a scratchy blanket and a long horizontal scar across his stomach like the crack in the door.

What else?

In order to write I have my back to the sea. The view of the steely Mediterranean is desirable but distracting. This is a cramped and crowded room – with a high ceiling, generous wall space but little accommodation for another chair. I have not yet rearranged the furniture. I am standing upright, scribbling in a notebook with a pen pressed against the door as though it were a desk.

A closer observer – if suitable surveillance were installed – would see me writing quickly, almost as though I were talking. Just occasionally my jaw moves in emphasis or amplification, a movement made clearer on unshaven cheeks.

I have no need to look respectable. Twenty-four hours ago I left London unexpectedly, and no one I know will see me here. I could have fixed to see writers or politicians or critics, the contributors to the newspaper that I edit. I might have brought crisp, clean clothes, linen suits and a laptop computer. Instead, I am wearing frayed jeans, scuffed suede shoes and am pushing out words on a notepad against a thin panel of wood.

This is not how it was supposed to be. For the last weeks of my fifty-ninth year, I had a suitcase packed for a different trip, to the winter sunshine five thousand miles to the south. But Christmas was frozen. The London airports were iced for many days; and when the ice melted there were too many travellers for South Africa and not enough planes. Egypt was an easier ticket to buy – from Hampstead to Cairo, to the fluorescent checkpoints of the desert and the Metropole Hotel, to a tiny, tall room with a balcony overlooking the sea.

Rue Nebi Danial

Socratis gave me instructions about where I should be going next. The walk was short. The directions were simple: right on Al Horreya, left on Nebi Danial, past the bookshops and piles of trousers where the two streets meet, the Piccadilly Circus of Alexandria, as the guidebook says; past the lives of Fidel Castro and Richard Burton, catalogues from JCPenney and the Modern Dining Centre, past dozens of purple overalls, an advertisement for a discussion about

Jean-Paul Sartre in 2002, a brown-and-white radio mast in Eiffel pattern and a tightly shuttered home for French missionaries.

I was told to sit in the cafe by the fountain, the 'Sea Fountain' I think he called it. Just before Nebi Danial ends in a bus station there is a low, iron fence around a sloping, green-marble slab broken by grass. Above a watery-coloured rock sits a concrete swirl of foam speckled by golden mosaics and on the foam, riding erect, or as erect as anything could ride on so toppling a tower, is a winged woman with claws, part angel, part sphinx, pushing out a conch shell from which water, powered by a hanging electric flex, may once have flowed. A Sea Fountain? Yes, this must be the place that he meant.

That was about an hour ago. How long do my new friends expect me to wait? And what do I know about them to make me wait? The answer is still almost nothing except that they share an interest in one of the very few tourists in town. This interest may be official or entrepreneurial. It is hard to say. What they cannot know about me is that waiting with paper and pen at a table is what I am here to do. I am writing about Cleopatra for the last time.

If, as Socratis suggests, this needs to be a day of caution lest al-Qaeda has begun an Egyptian campaign, there is no harm for me in that. A break may be useful. To write beside a busy street, with the constant hope of interruption, is the best way for me to write, sometimes the only way. If there are to be no tourist destinations today, there is time for a reminder of my very first attempt on Cleopatra, for going back fifty years to *Professor Rame and the Egyptian Queen*, to a place in every way different from this L-shaped room of languid waiters and tiny tables that Socratis called 'my cafe'.

His cafe? I doubt it. He also says that the Cecil is his hotel. He may not even come. He is right, however, that a grey-haired Englishman with a few old papers, a pad of new paper and an Arabic guide to classical sites seems unlikely to be disturbed as long as from time to time he buys a Lipton's tea, the pale yellow brand name that must have been on these unwashed walls for fifty years at least.

CLEOPATRA THE FIRST

Once upon a time there was a Professor James Rame, an ageless, characterless male who knew Cleopatra personally. He loved her. He loved her because she was beautiful, bold and smelt like my mother. This professional alien, space traveller and hero of a long-lost adventure at the courts of Alexandria, was my first and only fictional creation. I was ten years old.

Professor Rame and the Egyptian Queen, a fantasy of golden hair and blue skies (or so I like to think), was written in what my parents used to call a 'box room', almost square and about the size of this cafe alcove. A near-perfect cube, it contained a high wooden desk and it doubled as a home for water tanks and staircase support. Just as in Room 114 at the Metropole, it was easiest to write there while standing.

The rest of the little red-brick house was filled with radio noises, *Mrs Dale's Diary* and the permanent hum of a Hoover. But in the windowless box room there was silence. The bare plastered walls, pink as a story-book pig, were protection against invasions from beyond.

Outside in the garden there were other walls, solid mounds of what my father called Essex clay. To him it was dead, inert, inevitable wasted earth abandoned by builders in a hurry. To a child it was like living flesh or warm plasticine that I could punch, climb, cut, try to mould, try not to offend. Half a century ago, behind the back doors of semi-detached houses on the Marconi works estate, a mile from Chelmsford, were hundreds of slimy-sided cubes of this clay, newly cut by machines, soft but indestructible, leaden red by day and looming brown by night, garden obstacles that at a child's bedtime might become an Egyptian temple or an ancient Roman face or a Russian.

My first Cleopatra was a phantom, a dream in the dark. When she joined Professor Rame's Egyptian adventure she became a bit more than a mud-red face, more than a mouth, a nose and a neck. She had a name. She did things, felt things and made things happen. I am sure she did. But I cannot remember any of them or anything of how I imagined her.

I can guess that Professor Rame's hostess had some of the finer female characteristics, those that went with perfume and jewellery, not with oven-cleansers or Kilner Jars, with my mother's ambitions not her insecurities, with my sister's bright blond hair not her noisier toddler habits. But I can only guess. I would give much now for a few sentences of how Cleopatra and the professor first met, that first clash of other worlds. But the name is all there is. Sometimes one just has to accept the absence of memory as better than the pretence of it.

There is nothing so very wrong in remembering only a name. Much of what we know of antiquity are names, the names of lost people, plays, histories, the names of learned treatises, works on medicine, on how to prevent slaves escaping and how to apply make-up. My own Cleopatra (as I saw her then), the seventh woman of her name to rule in Egypt after its submission to the Greek generals of Alexander the Great, wrote a treatise about make-up. Or maybe she had her name attached to someone else's lipstick tips: librarians and booksellers even then believed that a work was more likely to be read under the name of a celebrity. If history had happened differently, mascara might have been all we knew about her. Instead, she became the lover of two great Roman generals and, as some came to say, changed the history of the western world. On Cleopatra's name there is space enough to pile a mountain.

Professor Rame's own name was different. It was invented as a disguise, a suggestion of what I was supposed to become. My professor wore an adult form of school uniform, National Health pink-rimmed glasses and was a master of engineering science. He had to be. He could hardly be a professor of anything else if he were to travel in space and time.

Imagination of the ancient world was a luxury in 1959. Engineering was the necessity, in our case radar engineering. For my father and the men who lived around us, seeing the invisible was a profoundly practical matter. Max Stothard was a designer of military machines that made us safe.

In our house there was no time for the nonsense of any history older than the century. Ours were homes built in anxious haste, dug out of a butcher's farmland below a giant steel aerial mast that had been erected against the Communists as soon as the Nazi threat was past. The mobilisation of men and material to watch for Cold War missiles was as urgent as in the hot wars – from Crete to Alamein – in which my father and his engineering friends had learnt their craft. In former fields, beside a town that already boasted the title 'Birthplace of Radio', we were the families whose fathers understood klystrons, tweeters and 'travelling-way tubes' for the long-distance radar that kept the enemy at bay.

Every man on the estate knew either about the transmitters that saw things faraway in the dark or about the various electric valves that powered a radar's eyes. They worked at benches, not at desks. There was a wartime spirit still. The interest was not the Korean War, the one that filled the headlines of the *Daily Telegraph* of 28 February 1951, the issue my mother kept in the sideboard because it marked the day of my birth. Still less did it stem from the Suez War, a nasty disturbance that might as well have happened in Cleopatra's Egypt for all the concern it created for us. Our war was the war with Moscow.

The Soviet threat was an evil. But, like everything in that hopeful time, it was also a good. As well as defending British prosperity against the great Red menace, we were supposed to share in it, creating a haven of high education, a science park, even an Essex garden community in which the clay cut to make the foundations of 51 Dorset Avenue might one day grow cabbages, fruit trees and flowers. By 1960 Mr Churchill's England had become Mr Macmillan's – with only the barest distraction from Mr Eden's debacle in Colonel Nasser's Egypt. Life was going to be fine.

There were many advantages for us on these company streets. Almost every family had a TV set, assembled during our fathers' lunch-breaks rather than bought in a shop. We had miniature radios when most of the country still kept the BBC in big wooden boxes: Professor Rame's career began with the bedroom sound of science fiction, bluff Englishmen bringing their voices to Mars and the Moon.

Books, by contrast, were rare. There were just five of them in 51 Dorset Avenue, the brightest coloured being a sky-blue edition of S.T. Coleridge, the title printed in such a way that for years I thought that the poet was a saint. Next to this sat a collected Tennyson, in a spongy leather cover. On the shelf below was a cricket scorebook in which someone had copied improving philosophical precepts; and beside that, *The First Test Match*, a slim, slate-green hardback. This was the one of them that looked read and reread.

The fifth book is the only one that is with me in Alexandria fifty years on, my Nottinghamshire grandfather's copy of the second half of Virgil's *Aeneid*, Books 7–12, with the name B. Stothard, in a firm, faded script, inside the flyleaf. The first owner of this red Loeb edition, English and Latin on opposite pages, was a family mystery. My father refused ever to offer anything beyond a set of not quite consistent facts: that Bert Stothard had been a farmer who had lost a fortune thinking there was oil beneath his farm, that he had been a miner, a mining engineer, a Methodist preacher, a manager of the parts department at a maker of stone-crushing machines. Every description was of some other existence. In 1956 he died, leaving behind a secretive son and the second half of a Latin epic poem.

In the two thousand years since the time of Cleopatra this *Aeneid* has been the most famed of all writings in Latin. It has been the book of empire-builders, the story of how a young Trojan prince escaped the fires of conquered Troy and sailed away to found the far greater city of Rome. Its first half tells how Aeneas put imperial duty before his love for a foreign queen (there is more than a touch of Cleopatra in Dido), and how he visited his dead father in the underworld to get divine instruction for the task ahead and endured various adventures of varyingly entertaining sorts. Its second half is more gruelling, for Aeneas, his men and for readers, a story of military struggle through Italy, the defeat of hostile tribes and some vengeful killings that even Virgil's greatest admirers wished he had omitted.

There must be many other two-volume sets of the poem where Part One is borrowed (and never returned) and Part Two is never borrowed at all. Those who begin with the seventh book of the *Aeneid*, the first book of the *Aeneid* in the library of Dorset Avenue, take an unusual route into the story. They know nothing of Troy or Dido, nothing of sex and cannibalism in caves. They begin with the military struggle, the shrugging-away of the Trojan past so that the Italian future can begin.

There is also, at the very start of Book Seven, the question of ending, of memorial, of what part of us is remembered and how and whether any memorial is worthwhile. In the first sentence of Latin I ever saw, Aeneas has just buried the woman who nursed him as a child in Troy. Her name is Caieta. His father is dead; his lover, Dido, is dead. His mother, the goddess Venus, while as alive as she ever was, has shown divine inattention to childcare. So Caieta is an important part of the hero's past and one of his last connections to it. He buries her on a coastal hill near Naples and builds a monument. *Tu quoque litoribus nostris, Aeneia nutrix:* You too to our shores, nurse of Aeneas.

Caieta may seem an odd character to appear at the beginning of a book about Cleopatra. She is almost unknown. Most students have read the Aeneid without registering her at all. Her name begins with C and ends in A but that is not the reason she will play her part in this story. She will be there because she was the first Latin name I knew when it began. This final version of my Cleopatra, whatever it becomes, will be most of all a book of chances.

Professor Rame's adventure, my own first Cleopatra, owed a little to Bert Stothard's *Aeneid*, but more as an opening to an ancient world than a guide to what was in it, more as an object than a text. I could not make sense of Latin yet. My professor owed much more to radio and its infant child, TV. Electronics were about to banish the printing press even then. On our estate of clay we were proudly in the fore-front of that change. Our tiny transistor radios may have lacked the smartest cases; our televisions had often no cabinets at all, their twinkling glass valves strung out along the picture rails and around the back of settees. But we were surrounded by science. When we wanted a better picture, the contrast of our blacks and whites was improved from the first principles of the cathode ray. To make the most of the Coronation, the *Billy Cotton Band Show* or even *Mrs Dale's Diary*, a massed expertise could be deployed, from as far afield as Noakes Avenue, the outer limit where Marconi-land ended and Essex farming returned.

The houses were so alike, and the food in their cupboards so absolutely alike, that it hardly mattered where on the estate we fed our pet pond creatures or ate our tea. Most boys and girls had the same-shaped box room for their den, the same cube within a cube. A sawn-off end of a radar tube was so perfect for newt-keeping that every boy who braved the 'bomb-hole' pond in the 'rec' had one of his own. Break the glass screen and there was always a replacement the next night. We all had field glasses, relics of our fathers' wars or second-hand from the army surplus stores; we knew the names of every swooping, hovering or merely hopping bird. All groceries came from the same dirty-green, single-decker coach of 'Mr Rogers', a silent ex-soldier who piled his fruit and vegetables on either side of the aisle where the seats had been and twice a week toured the avenues from Dorset to Noakes to sell cereals, sugar, flour and everything that the gardens might one day produce but did not yet.

Ours was a community of algebra and graph-paper. Mathematics was the language of choice. Contract bridge was the nightly recreation. Prizes for success in this sport of the mind fell tumbling from our sideboard doors whenever they were opened too roughly, uniformed knaves on ashtrays, unsmiling queens on decanters, aces on miniatures of port and brandy whose liquids had long dried away but whose evidence for victorious rubbers remained. My curly-haired, smiling father had a brain for numbers that his fellow engineers described as Rolls-Royce. Notoriously, he did not like to test it beyond a purr. In particular – and this was unusual in a place of intense educational self-help – he did not care to inculcate maths into his son. This was a task that he had recognised early as wholly without reward. Max Stothard would occasionally attack the mountain of clay in his garden but never knock his head against a brick wall. He much preferred to be relaxed.

Like most of our neighbours, he had learned about radar by chance, in his case after lying about his age, volunteering for the navy and spending most of the war becalmed off West Africa. He had wanted to fight but did not. On a ship called HMS *Aberdeen*, he had stayed three thousand miles from the desert-rat fights of Libya and Egypt. He sent home red-leather-bound knives to his mates back in the Nottinghamshire mining lands. He sent postcards of Dakar's six-domed cathedral to his strictly Methodist mother. But he never fired a hostile shot except at a basking shark.

In his infinite leisure hours he studied the many curious ways that waves behave in the air above the sea. That was how he spent most of the rest of his life, in the south of England instead of the north because that was where the radars were made, quietly reasoning through his problems on his high chair in the Marconi Laboratory and in an armchair at home, spreading files marked Secret like a fisherman's nets.

Life on our estate was based on a bracing sense of equality and a grateful appreciation of peace. Although most of our fathers felt they had a part in this great military project of the future, rarely can so massive a martial endeavour, the creation of air defences along the length of Britain's eastern coast, have been conducted in so calm a spirit. My mild mother competed gently for influence against other mothers – in studied unconcern for what the Marconi estate was for. The fighting war was absolutely over. The Marconi tower was a lightening conductor as well as a controller of missiles. The new business was civil, work that would keep us safe and increase our prosperity as the politicians promised. And because everyone was in it, everyone was in it together.

That was the determined message of Miss Leake (her name seemed perilously amusing from the first time I heard it), our headmistress at Rothmans School, whose doctrine of excellence-and-equality, delivered in her severest voice, was adapted only slowly to the advancing evidence of differences around her. My younger sister and I were peculiarly different. Jill was sharper, wilder, a primal force. I was quiet and accepting.

There were girls with superior proficiency at maths to any boy. There were boys who could barely count but who designed the most beautiful fighter planes to crash the female enemy down to earth, exchanging sketches that would today attract close attention from the police. For our first two years our teachers reassured us repeatedly that we were all much the same. But eventually, inexorably and certainly by the time that we had reached the age of nine, those of us who multiplied well were divided from those who did not.

Streaming was the name for the separation. Maths was just the start. Those, like Maurice and I, who could not sing were called 'groaners' and kept outside the classroom door during music lessons. That was when I first properly noted his pale face and wit. Those who preferred Aeneas to algebra were allowed to write fiction for our homework, as long as it was science fiction.

Miss Leake was the high mistress of these rules. We rarely saw her and wondered sometimes how she could exert such power when the polished brass nameplate on her door was her only regular presence. My father came to see her only once. He was not at all worried about my being a 'groaner' (he listened to little music himself bar the songs of the American mathematician, Tom Lehrer) but he was faintly sad about my absent number skills.

Jill would sometimes join Max and the gramophone in singing Lehrer's version of 'We'll All Go Together When We Go', 'The Periodic Table' and 'Poisoning Pigeons in the Park'. I could not and did not sing. My mother could sing well but did not. None of that mattered. Numbers on the Marconi estate were the key to advancement. Euclid, the Alexandrian 'Father of Geometry', was the best and only Greek. Physics was the first step to a working future, a future in paid employment in a world which itself worked well.

Many Rothmans pupils with no aptitude at all for figures – who could draw a dive-bomber but never do equations – were pummelled onto numerical paths. Jill resisted. To my mother's frustration she was a brilliant resistor, an early lesson to me of female will. But how possibly, asked our neighbour on the other side of the clay mountain, could anyone pull themselves up by any other route than mathematics? My father agreed, but he did not force me and he could not force my sister. He did not argue the superiority of science or anything much else, except bidding conventions in hearts and spades and the best way to see threats low in the sky.

My mother had bigger worries than innumeracy. She had heard from rival mothers that I had damp eyes when stories were read in class, not necessarily even the saddest stories. I was much too open to the world around me, absorbent almost: she put this failing in different words at different times. Professor Rame and his Egyptian queen were among many bad influences. It was better that I spent more time outside. In the real world everything would always be fine.

My mother was a shy connoisseur of small improvements and distinctions. She was born in the city of Nottingham, not 'the sticks', the phrase with which she dismissed Bert Stothard's fields and stone-crusher factories. When she met my father after the war, she had been a secretary at John Player's, a clean job in tobacco, and she had her eyes on a place in a silk shop or Raleigh Bicycles. She was always alert to social distinction. Were the engineers' families of Rothmans Avenue, Dorset Avenue and Noakes Avenue truly quite the same? Did the more brilliant scientists live in Rothmans, the more managerial in Dorset, the more clerical in Noakes? Were they richer in Rothmans and rather poorer in Noakes? Who took a daily newspaper? Who took the *Daily Telegraph*?

At the very edges of the bus routes that served the school were money-men and accountants, some of whom farmed chickens (for their eggs or maybe their tax efficiencies), whose sons and daughters we could visit at birthday parties. Did these 'Millionaires' Row' houses really have four bedrooms? With attention we could find out. Whose kitchen had less Fablon and more Formica? Should Marley floor tiles be polished? Did parquet flooring have always to be made of wood and was it harmed by sledging across it on cushions? My father played Tom Lehrer's mutually assured destruction song 'We'll All Go Together When We Go' when guests came for a drink. But was this acceptable or not? Why was Jill not playing with Sophie? Why was Peter not out with Maurice, the bank manager's son? Why was he always stuck in that box room? And where exactly did everyone go on holiday?

Summer was the great unequaliser. On the North Sea coast, only thirty-or-so miles away, the skies were known equally to all masters of air defence and to their sons who watched wheeling gulls and weightless terns above cold brown waves. But the beaches beneath were crisply divided. Clacton, Walton and Frinton were significantly different. We always went to Walton-on-the-Naze, the middling one of the three, which had the widest concrete esplanades where children could ride bikes. Clacton-on-Sea had slot machines and candyfloss booths where 'other people' could waste their money. Frinton-on-Sea had no candyfloss, no caravans (we always stayed in a caravan), no fish-and-chip shops, not even a pub, just jubilee gardens and what was known, only by warnings not to walk on it, as 'greensward'.

Maurice's family went to Frinton. Did Rothmans Avenue families prefer Frinton too? By the time of my eleventh birthday in 1962, it sometimes seemed that they did. Our Marconi estate was small, confined and had only one entrance to the world. Once inside it we could always roller-skate through the class lines. On the coast, it was an

27

impossible walk, and even an awkward drive, between three neighbouring towns that seemed built deliberately to show how apart from one another we could be.

My father was a typical Marconi engineer of his time in every respect except one: he rejected the right to insist that there was only one right path. That was his grace and glory. He never stopped me preferring stories about science to the understanding of what science actually did. He did not invade the box room. If lumps of clay looked to me like anything other than lumps of clay, that was not a problem for him. He did not much like the Coleridge and the Tennyson being on hand. But he did not take them away.

He read the fiction that I wrote about my manufactured hero, Professor Rame. He even praised it. There was 'no future in it' but he was never much concerned about the future. I wish I could say that he had first introduced me to Cleopatra. But there was only a short consultation a few years later (he consulted me, which is why I remember it) about whether ancient names would be suitable for Marconi weapon systems. Would *Caesar* or *Cicero* be better than *Blue Streak* or *Blue Steel* for the weapons guided by our great metal tower, the one that protected the estate from electric storms and the British state from communism? How about *Cleopatra*? Absolutely not, he said. A missile could not be named after a woman, even a queen.

Alexandria became much later a favourite city. But the only place here that he ever mentioned was one called Settee Street. Maybe it is here still. He knew that Cleopatra's capital, stretched out between a lake and the shore, had once had a great lighthouse, a radar mast in reverse, a tower aiming to be seen rather than to see, an exchange of particles and waves, the line on which my father made his world.

Once the Cold War was over he had to switch his interests to foreign and smaller customers. Once the Russian warships had left Egypt's biggest harbour, there were opportunities here both for arms-dealers selling modern radar dishes and for archaeologists uncovering ancient lighthouse parts. Alexandria hosted a navy which needed help against its enemies and that was the kind of place my father sought for the rest of his life.

In 1960 he much approved of the schoolteacher who told us vicious war stories from ancient myth to illustrate the virtues of modern deterrence. After I brought to class his family *Aeneid* he was pleased to learn that he owned the final half, the books of marching through Italy, not of loss and doomed love. My father liked to see people as electro-machinery, as fundamentally capable of simple, selfless working. His own mind was closed to the communications of religion or art. He had a peculiar intolerance of violins and the soprano voice. He most of all loved jet-streams in the skies over air shows.

A decade after we left Dorset Avenue, for a bigger house with an orchard and a cellar, the whole estate began a slide into another age. Miss Leake retired. The Marconi families moved away. It was no longer a place where every house shared the same business. There were no longer newts, nor anything but grass, in what was once the mysterious 'bomb-hole'. The great clay statues were cleared from the gardens, leaving only a few lumps behind.

Bibliotheca Alexandrina

An hour ago Mahmoud sent a message to the Sea Fountain cafe ('Dead Fountain' would be more accurate) telling me to meet him here at the Alexandria library, 'anywhere close to the catalogues'. His neatly written message, in an envelope from the Metropole, was delivered by a driver in a stiff plastic suit. It contained a map and directions and an apology from Socratis who needed 'to visit his mother'. Surprisingly obedient (I am not quite sure why) I gathered my papers, paid my bill, stretched my legs and left. The cable in the mouth of the Dead Fountain's sphinx gave a swaying farewell.

I went back down Nebi Danial and along Al Horreya, this time trying to imagine how it might have looked in Cleopatra's time, with Corinthian columns instead of French china shops. I took a left turn at the Roman fort and floral clock, the old city gateway, and walked on to the new Alexandrian library, invisible until it is reached, a shallow bowl of glass by the sea.

Waste paper was swirling in the wind. The hot-chocolate cafes were empty. An armed guard of anxious young soldiers waited and watched as though for a visit from unusually senior officers. The only welcome came from headscarfed school students scampering through the sculpture park between a green stone tornado, a green crescent moon and a grey head of the great Alexander.

There was no mention in Mahmoud's note of any specific time to meet. But a change of seat was anyway overdue. The peacock pattern of the cafe furniture is still imprinted on my flesh. This new chair is a luxurious contrast, designed for keyboard-tappers in the new glory of the very newest Alexandria, a library built at Greek billionaires' expense to remind Egyptians and their visitors that Greeks made this city, and that there is more to history here than pyramids and Pharaohs.

The shelves are designed to evoke Cleopatra's family library, the most ambitious book collection ever attempted. Today, whether because of terrorist bombing or excessive security, it is almost empty, evoking only to the very few. What do I do while waiting for the promised arrival of my guides? First I ask myself to forgive my own vanity. Secondly, I seek my own name in the catalogues and ask – only idly – what, if anything, of me has survived this far?

After Professor Rame's adventures there was no further fiction. So I have no need to look among the novels. In my life as a newspaper editor and reporter I must have written millions of words of journalism. Most of them were anonymous 'leading articles' on now forgotten issues of lost days. But there might perhaps be traces here of my foreign correspondent's life.

In the print catalogue there is a French translation of my first book, *Thirty Days*, a daily diary which covered my time spent with Tony Blair and George W. Bush during the Iraq War in 2003. This *Trente Jours* will possibly impress Mahmoud. But to use the 'electronic archive of the world's press' demands more technical skill than I can muster. The screen shakes and so do I.

Is it worthwhile ordering any other books? Two desks away there is a huge pile of Latin classics awaiting an absent reader's attention, each one tagged with its own ticket. The *Aeneid* is in a single dark-blue volume. Its requester may not come. If he or she does arrive, I can politely return it or wait to see if its absence is noticed. To begin at Book Seven with Caieta has always been a good introduction, however little I understood of it fifty years ago. I can go there again.

The *Aeneid* was the epic that Rome's first emperor, Octavian who called himself Augustus, hoped would expunge the memory of Cleopatra, a figure whom he made a symbol of everything he was against. The Egyptian queen was, in this version, a seductress, an oriental, a capricious autocrat who melted pearls in wine. Her conqueror intended Virgil's poem as a victory speech, proof that Alexandria had been defeated and true Roman virtues made triumphant.

But immediately I am bidden to stop. A librarian appears as though to take back the book for its rightful borrower. There is a thudding behind her. Mahmoud and Socratis are finally here, waiting impatiently by the catalogues, not allowed further entry because it is too close to closing time. They are gesturing at me to come out. I point to my watch. I will be with them in a few minutes. There are limits to being led by unknown guides.

So, to take a breath and end where I began, with Book Seven of the poem: Aeneas and his followers have newly arrived in Italy after their troubled odyssey from Troy. With good reason the sailors are anxious about their futures, reluctant to let go of their past. Some of them have already set fire to their ships in order that they might stop somewhere, anywhere.

Dido of Carthage, Cleopatran temptress and corrupter, has burnt herself to death. Aeneas has also buried his father and now, as he bids farewell to Caieta, wonders whether his nurse will ever be remembered by anyone else. He doubts whether there is truly any glory in having a name attached to a tomb; but he labels her bones nonetheless.

> *Tu quoque litoribus nostris, Aeneia nutrix,*
> You too to our shores, Caieta, nurse of Aeneas,
> *aeternam moriens famam, Caieta, dedisti;*
> have given eternal fame by your death,
> *et nunc servat honos sedem tuus, ossaque nomen*
> and now your honour marks this place,
> your name these bones
> *Hesperia in magna, si qua est ea gloria, signat.*
> in great Hesperia, if that is any glory.

That has to be the last line. Socratis is scowling. The driver, his suit a sickly mix of yolk and mud, looks as though he will break the windows. Yes, there was some glory for Caieta. She is still remembered two thousand years on, especially by readers who begin the *Aeneid* in the wrong place. Biographers want the dead but they have only the living. We must work with the tools that we have.

2.1.11

Hotel Metropole, Place Saad Zaghloul

It is now four in the morning by the clock in Room 114, ten hours since Mahmoud and Socratis arrived together at the library. I have had more than enough time to establish how little I know of them.

Mahmoud was bright-eyed like a boy on his first day at work. He brought with him a pack of Cleopatra cigarettes, a Cleopatra Ceramica catalogue of modern bathroom furniture and a DVD of last season's Ramadan TV series starring an Egyptian queen who looked a little like my ancient Miss Leake. He quickly noted the existence of *Trente Jours* and said with a studied sincerity that, if he were ever to write a book himself, he would undoubtedly make a journey to this most famous of libraries so that he could read it here.

At the same time Socratis merely smirked. His face, like a mask of mud, cracked in only the finest lines. Either he doubted that Mahmoud would ever write a book or he despised my motives in reading my own. This older, calmer man was careful not to betray himself too much. He kicked one workman's boot against the other and tugged at the belt of his soft wool trousers.

But there was also a third man, a squat and square-faced driver who had no such qualms, a laugh like an idling diesel engine and a confident look – as though he knew he represented the true views of both his bosses. Mahmoud was displeased by this mockery. He became almost embarrassed. His cheeks glowed to match his brown

37

polished shoes. He scowled. Excessive laughter was improper behaviour, he seemed to suggest, unacceptable rudeness, the response of a yes-man who said 'yes' far too loudly. The driver took no notice. He pushed out his stomach against his soil-stained plastic jacket. When he could inflate no more, he exhaled with a grumbling sigh.

It was as hard as before to gauge exactly what was going on or even who was in charge. Socratis commanded the chauffeur. But maybe both of them were there to look after Mahmoud. Does some part of Egypt's tourism department employ drivers who dress like their car seats? The guidebooks, which say a good deal about the badges on state uniforms, have no guidance on that.

Eventually Mahmoud tapped his Cleopatra cigarettes against his Cleopatra Jacuzzi pictures. He looked sleek and serious again. Socratis froze his fissured cheeks into a frown, forcing his man in the upholstery suit to apologise. 'The wretch', he said, expressed 'the sincerest sadness.' He did, indeed, look chastened – as though the worst possible thing had happened to him, as if he had lost his car, as if his parking assistant (an ubiquitous breed in Alexandria) had driven his Mercedes out across the Corniche, down into the harbour and out among the drowned ruins of Cleopatra's palace.

After these peculiar pleasantries were over Mahmoud suggested dinner at our hotel. It was possible to eat well there, he said, as long as one was with him. Socratis thought that I would prefer Monty's bar at the Cecil, where the alcohol was more reliable, where there was wartime memorabilia of Desert Rats and where faded British grandeur might be more comforting in troubled times than the French kind.

Socratis was the victor. He said smilingly that he would choose the restaurant and Mahmoud would pay the bill. Mahmoud did not complain. These men had surely to be team players. Each man had some sort of connection to his hotel although neither seemed to work there or anywhere, or had yet asked specifically if I required his services or had said what this would cost. I did not press them. This is not journalism. There is no need for certainty or haste. The driver, cheerfully smirking again, was sent to bring round the car. The doors closed and we were out again past the green moon and the stone tornado, waiting at the place where the library's great slope of glass slides into the street by the sea.

Eleven hours on, that all seems an age ago now. On the cloudless, windswept balcony of Room 114 it is almost morning. It has not been a good night in the hotel where, as the brass key fob boasts, 'the temple of the great love of Cleopatra and Antonio was born'. I am staring drowsily at golden lights, a green tower, lines of red underscored by white neon. There is a deafening dawn chorus of musical cars and whinnying horses. But at least, inside this tall tube-like, golden-wallpapered room, the hours of poisoning are almost past.

Before dinner, as we sat in the Cecil bar, Socratis asked again why I was here, why I was spending winter weeks in Alexandria when other tourists, the seasonally knowing and the temporarily terrorised, were not. I told him the truth. If it were not for unseasonable Christmas snow over the British skies, I would not be here. I would be somewhere warmer and further away, toying perhaps with my Cleopatra story but, as before and so often, not seriously writing it. He seemed disappointed to hear that. He wanted me to want to be here (he said so several times) even though the assault on his fellow Copts meant that I had to be careful where I went. He very much wanted me to have a successful trip.

This was new information. Socratis is a Copt, a man of the world's

39

most ancient Christian church. Mahmoud is the man of Islam. Both like to stress continuity, differences that should not be exaggerated, a past that little changes.

My own knowledge of Egypt does not go back much before the conquest by Alexander the Great or forward beyond the last Romans. All I know about its religion is that in the unimaginably long pre-Alexandrian history of this country men worshipped dogs and kings among many gods, except for a brief revolution in the fourteenth century BC when there was just one. After the failure of these first one-god believers, all the many holy beasts rapidly returned, mingling with Persian and Greek gods when different conquerors came, multiplying for more than a millennium until the Jews and Christians again brought 'one god' to Alexandria and until the Muslims did the same.

In old Zaghloul's idea of a modern Egypt, forged in prison and in power a hundred years ago, religious differences were not supposed to

matter. Now they matter more, to foreigners as much as to the Egyptians themselves. British bishops, while patronising about primitive Coptic beliefs, have anguished over the bombs and persecutions. British politicians have supported President Mubarak, especially when he has hunted down Muslims of an equally primitive kind – and promised to keep the worst of them in jail.

The three of us sat down for our first course of oily squid and parsley. There was nameless fish and minced meat ahead. Socratis seemed content but quietly so. Mahmoud took charge although he looked as though he would much prefer to be elsewhere, sometimes as though most of him was elsewhere, leaving behind little more than a puritan stare above a menu.

When Mahmoud spoke it was as though from the standard handbooks of public relations. He blamed all reporters who threatened national solidarity and the tourist trade. Novelists and poets, he added, could be even worse. Too many artists came here when they would rather be in a different place, looking for something that had disappeared or never existed and then complaining when they could not find it.

He particularly deplored the Cecil Hotel bookshop which year after year promoted E.M. Forster's First World War guidebook to Alexandria, 'a work whose author would rather have been in India' and who called his subject 'the spurious east'. And there was always and everywhere Lawrence Durrell's *Alexandria Quartet*, which, 'for anyone who could finish it', made the city out as a place of prostitutes, plutocrats, drunkards and primal religion. Of all the foreigners who had ruled Egypt, he said, 'the English were forever the most foreign'. Socratis nodded sagely at that.

As we ate and drank, I was sympathetic to Mahmoud – or tried to be – denying the slightest ambition to bewail a city of dreams that had somehow died. I have no nostalgia for the sexual invention and cosmopolitan beauty that Lawrence Durrell and E.M. Forster so longingly describe. I have not arrived with half-admitted hopes of the city being what it used to be at some other time or something or somewhere other than it is. I am not looking for souls of poets dead and gone. I may try to imagine the colonnaded streets of Alexander the Great's successors but that does not mean I yearn for them or despair of what came next.

Afterwards Socratis took us upstairs to 'after dinner at Monty's bar'. Vodka arrived. Socratis and I drank it. Mahmoud, a dutiful man of his faith, did not. On the other side of the dark-wood, low-ceilinged room, a group of tropically dressed military men, Australians, Americans and a Spaniard, were more seriously enjoying their alcohol. There was not a woman in sight. We were running out of things to say.

Suddenly, sensing a failure of hospitality, Socratis took over responsibility for the night. He pushed down, as ever vainly, on his bouncing curls. He said all would have been much better if his mother had been with us. He blurted this out, as though this had been his secret all along. His mother was the one who knew about Cleopatra. She had talked about her often when he was a child. She knew all about Alexandria's leaders, King Fuad, King Farouk, Colonel Nasser, Anwar Sadat and everyone.

To his mother these were 'all good men', just as Mahmoud had said. She knew about the great Alexander of Macedon, who had been here so short a time, and Queen Zenobia of Palmyra, whose short reign as a conqueror of Alexandria is sometimes forgotten, as well as Queen Cleopatra whose life and death are remembered so well.

Mahmoud looked anxious – as though he had heard this all before and knew we were heading for bad places. After a third round of toasts, Socratis, fatter faced and softer eyed, seemed to be mocking his absent mother. Or was he repeating dutifully her views of rulers' virtues? If only, he said, she had been able to meet me and speak for herself. If only she were not still so upset by the bombing of her church.

Her church? So it was her own church that had been bombed? Had she been inside with the doomed New Year celebrants of St Mark and St Peter of the Seal? Well, no, Socratis admitted. But she had heard the blast. She had said so, and her son believed her. She had immediately visited the scene. Or maybe not. She had claimed to have done so. Socratis was doubtful. It hardly mattered. The old lady, he said, had vivid descriptions, 'gnarled green cars and blood-sprayed walls, bodies wrapped in newspaper, women who could not piece together their husbands, fathers scrabbling for each lost limb of a child', and other horrors that she would not and could not relate. And she had questions. What happened to the souls of people who when they died were not whole people? It was 'a curse on Alexandria. If only Jesus had never come here.'

Mahmoud and I stared at each other across a plate of sagging biscuits. The balance of our talk had changed. The teams had changed. The conversation was becoming ridiculous. I said carefully that I would like to have met Socratis's mother. I would have liked it very much, more than to have heard this peculiar version from her son. That was when I first felt the grip of poison, indigestible words and foods together.

Mahmoud's reaction was, as ever, to blame the newspapers and television reporters, those who had made her see what she had not seen. The media was the message, he said proudly. My own best effort was to say, with due hesitance, that I did not know of Jesus ever visiting Alexandria. The Saviour had come here in his 'missing years', Socratis replied, not quite meeting my eyes and flicking shreds of olive towards the portrait of General Montgomery on the Monty's wall. 'Where else would he have come than to the greatest city there had ever been?'

Mahmoud sagged again. He circled a forefinger around his ear to signal a mockery of this madness. He pulled air from his mouth in a silent blah-di-blah. All this Jesus and Cleopatra was the sound of the mother speaking through the son and Mahmoud had heard it too often before. 'And HE is still here,' Socratis added with capital emphasis. If Jesus is still here, I asked, does your mother think that Cleopatra and King Farouk are here too? He showed no sign of taking offence. 'The monarchs are only sometimes here', he replied firmly, 'but they never go away far.'

I looked away. I feared I was going to laugh. Mahmoud began to reply but stopped and decided to settle the bill instead, looking mournfully at the vodka tax, the expensive vice of others. I offered to pay but was dismissed with a sweep of hands from both men. Mahmoud did not drink a drop of spirit but at that moment he looked drunk, a reluctant debauchee, whose last act at the table was to light up a Cleopatra. He asked if I would have preferred him not to smoke? No. Mahmoud picked up his credit card receipt, inhaled deeply and followed his friend from the room.

This was all over by ten o'clock. Since then I have had two hours' sleep. Perhaps the cause of the food-poisoning was a particularly damp bread roll, a slice of mollusc cooked too little or too long ago. The conversation did not help. Whatever the cause, a peculiar lightness of stomach or the perpetual lights of trams and cars, the prospect of further wakefulness seems assured. On the narrow strip of carpet between the bottom of the bed and the thin French desk lie accusing scraps of Cleopatras from the past.

3.1.11

Hotel Metropole, Place Saad Zaghloul

It is 6.17 a.m. on the electronic clock, too early for the Metropole breakfast. I have had a coffee and a sugar cake outside. For the second time this week, this year, I have completed my early morning round of the seaside square, slowly down the red staircase, quicker through the lurid stained-glass light of the hall, out away past dozily guarded doors and tall pots for sand and cigarettes.

This time there was no more news of bombs. There was only the constant roar of cars and drivers on the walk down to the open grey water, an easy circle back among the horse-drawn traps, and a dash across the road to the closest cafe, once part of the Metropole itself, probably the best part, with darkened windows opening directly onto the widest pavements. Now I am back inside the hotel again, past the security men who do not register my existence in any way. The thin-lipped receptionist welcomes me with a smile to the hotel of 'Antonio and his Queen'.

In Room 114 the first page of Cleopatra the Second is waiting on the freshly smoothed counterpane. I pick it up and, for the first time in more than forty years, begin carefully to read.

CLEOPATRA THE SECOND

The main street of her city was mapped in a long, low cross. Between the Gate of the Sun and the Gate of the Moon stretched the Canopic Way, lined

with columns connecting the two heavenly protectors of the city. The much
shorter vertical axis was called Body Street and ran from the last mass of Nile
marsh before the sea to the causeway that led to the world's greatest light-
house, the world's tallest building, on what had once been an island. On one
side of Body Street was the theatre, the temples for torch-lit processions and
the first true library and on the other the city of the dead. Along the shining
white harbour front stood palaces and military encampments and behind
them ...

These opening lines are on pages from a school rough-book. No
one uses paper like that now. It is lined like a ploughed field and only
a little smoother. It is beige tinged with pinks and blue as though any
coloured dye would do. But it has survived well enough. Although in
1963 'best books' were intended for the best work, 'rough' did not
need to mean 'second best'. A rough-book at my second school was
more than merely a cheap thing made from the barely processed bark
of bristling bushes and held together with staples. It was a pupil's own
private book, a place for rough work, for mistakes, guesses, imagined
things that might be pornography (often) or poetry (less often), or
maps copied dutifully from other books, anything that need never be
seen by anyone else.

This first passage of street directions seems to owe something to
Mahmoud's *bête noire*, E.M. Forster, who researched his Alexandria
guide during the First World War when he was enjoying his first
homosexual affair, cataloguing the wounded of the Dardanelles campaign and wishing he were in India. The fat bulk of Forster's *Pharos and
Pharillon* is still in the Cecil shop, annoying local sensitivities. But I am
sure I never saw it in my rough-book days.

I could flatter myself to think that the torch-lit temples and celes-
tial gates came from Achilles Tatius, an Alexandrian novelist of the

second century AD who vividly thus described them. But his romantic description of Alexandria, embedded in fantastic tales of tortures and sexual yearning, is deep in *Leucippe and Cleitophon*, Chapter Five, an unlikely destination for a teenaged boy. At the beginning of the 1960s I was newly arrived at a 500-year-old school, red-bricked, golden-gated, darkly grassed, where fluency in Greek was valued almost as much as Association Football. But I knew nothing yet of the Greek novel.

Perhaps I was copying a comic book, or a romantic novel written by someone who themselves had read Forster or Achilles Tatius. No master at this Brentwood School would ever have checked in a rough-book for plagiarism, or studied in any way these Cleopatra pages which, fifty years on, show an unchanged surface of flakes and furrows and dried, inky pools. With royal-blue Quink and a fat pen and nib from the Parker Company, my second Cleopatra story began. On the back of the first page are trial workings for maths problems, as insolv-able then as now. On the front is the beginning of an imagined journey, a list of street names with an ancient map, followed by 'the birth of Cleopatra in 69 BC, the second daughter of the man who at that time called himself King Ptolemy of Egypt'. His other names, I wrote, were the New Dionysus and the Fluteplayer and all of his rights and titles were owed originally to Alexander the Great, the man who gave the city its name and whose body gave its name to Body Street.

It is a modest start. All the letters are large even for a rough-book in which small letters were always likely to become an ink smudge. The name, the date, the phrases 'second daughter' and 'called himself King Ptolemy' are larger still. To place a birth so early in a book seems a simple act of a teenager seeking something he could securely and truthfully say, a reminder now of the peculiar desire of biographers, until we are trained out of the habit, of beginning with what we cannot possibly know or what we are likely to know of least.

It would have been better and simpler in 1963 to have continued with the map and described the road from the shores of Lake Mareotis into the city, passing by the Dead Fountain cafe on Rue Nebi Danial, as Body Street is now called, and turning right, halfway to the sea, to the Floral Clock, once the eastern gate of the city, known then as the Gate of the Sun. But perhaps information was scant. Today there are guidebooks and a broad agreement among their writers about where the ancient city stood. In Brentwood in the sixties, the last Essex suburb before London began, my Alexandrian street directions, copied from who knows where, did not perhaps convince me even when I was copying them.

The date of birth, 69 BC or maybe late 70 BC, is still the best that anyone has. It is based on the assurance of Plutarch, the biographer of Cleopatra's last lover, Mark Antony, that she was thirty-nine when she died and that she and he shared the same birth month. But the scepticism of my rough-book phrase 'who called himself King' is excessive. Although Ptolemy XII was a bastard, a successful pretender and bankrupt who had made himself wholly dependent for this throne on the military power of Rome, he did not merely 'call himself king'.

Or, at least, he was not alone in doing so. The Romans called him King Ptolemy, as did the neighbouring descendants of Alexander's other generals, even when they were trying to add bits of his kingdom to their own. So did the people of Alexandria, almost always known by later writers as 'the mob', who either accepted his unusual desire to be the Greek god 'Dionysus' or abused him as the 'fluteplayer' or 'massage parlour musak man'. He was an autocrat. His subjects' choice of name for him probably depended on whether he was listening.

Ptolemy XII was a fat bastard in every commonly used sense today. But, at the time of Cleopatra's birth, the Romans could call him 'our fat bastard' and so, more or less cynically, could almost everyone else. He was the latest in the twisted line of succession from Alexander's general Ptolemy, an artful conqueror who had taken the throne of the Pharaohs some 250 years before and imposed his Greek rule on people who, even then, were 'the ancient Egyptians'. Every Macedonian king of Egypt, however disputed his descent, was called Ptolemy.

This Ptolemy XII had at least five children whose names are known. The phrase 'second daughter' also represents a reasonable rough-book effort, a likely truth, although my Cleopatra may have been Ptolemy's third female heir. Failure to mention a mother may have shown some appreciation of the uncertainty about who precisely the mother was. Most probably she was the king's wife and sister, also called Cleopatra. The Greek Ptolemies were enthusiastic adopters of the incestuous practices of the Pharaohs. Every honest book on this subject has drowned its readers in a gene pool of Ptolemaic doubt.

Her grandmother, for example, was some sort of concubine, a royal mistress, someone else's wife, sister or mistress, possibly another Macedonian Greek who traced her lineage to one of Alexander's camp-followers. Or maybe, as hopeful African–American scholars have suggested, she was an Egyptian, even a very black Egyptian from the Nubian parts of the country that are now Sudan.

If Cleopatra's parents were brother and sister, she would have had only one set of grandparents, an idea that has attracted psychoanalytic writers as much as genealogical ones. But, from the surviving rough-book evidence here, it seems as though my Cleopatra the Second was on course to avoid such literary perils – either through teenage igno-rance or an early developing journalist's sense of when a topic induces sleep.

There follow teenaged scribbles on Alexandria as it was when Cleopatra was born. I may have chosen this as some kind of classroom project. I have no surviving best-book evidence or memory. I can now see these pages only as in a direct line from the faces of Essex clay.

This first description of Alexandria was respectable, certainly no disgrace. Being five thousand miles from the city in the 1960s did not make it impossibly harder than being inside the city now in 2011. Alexandria in the modern age is not like Athens or Rome: almost none of its ancient buildings survive as monuments or memorials for others. There is little easy tourism. The sites are mostly invisible. Its palaces, libraries and lighthouse are wrecked beneath sand and water. Its best known relics, the needles named after Cleopatra, which once stood where the Metropole stands now, have decorated London and New York for more than a century. To be a dissatisfied tourist is easy. To an optimist the neat lines of the ancient street map are not so much a show of what has disappeared but of a city still waiting to be found.

Alexandria is never far away wherever we are. Useful ideas were its best exports – the universal library, straight streets with addresses and post codes, astronomy and gastronomy, Greek columnar architecture in forms that people could live in rather than merely worship or admire, 'the pen' and 'the wine-press', new names that still survive for newly identified parts of the brain, and one of the greatest of all human dramas, the story of Ptolemy XII's second daughter herself. From Alexandria came also poetry as experiment, surprise as a virtue, word pictures of painted pictures, style for style's sake, so much adaptation from classical Greece which, without this city, would have died. Without the Alexandria of the Ptolemies, there would have been a very different Virgil, Tennyson and Coleridge, to begin only with the restricted contents of my Dorset Avenue library.

Bibliotheca Alexandrina

I am back at my polished modern desk, reluctantly for my ambitions but successfully for my health. It is good to be out of Le Metropole. The hotel on the site where 'the great love of Cleopatra and her Antonio was born' makes no boast of hygiene. It luxuriates in its old dust and glory. It seemed a nauseous place when I arrived, its staircase lit by a stained-glass French garden, yellows, reds and greens stirred with grey. Last night's poisoning has passed – but is not quite forgotten. So on this sunless day, the third of the year, I am back in the glassy, grey successor to the first great library of the world.

This Bibliotheca Alexandrina is clean enough to be a hospital, one of those Middle Eastern hospitals of the rich where there are the finest operating theatres and very few patients. It is tasteful, broad and low. Its roof is a tilted sundial. Its terraces are filled with sculpture. Its rows of desks cascade down towards the sea. It is like an elaborate ornament to a garden. It does not contain many books. It may not be much of a library at all.

A subversive thought: if the New Year bomb had exploded here instead of in Socratis's mother's church, the needles of glass and granite would have been a splendid sight. There would have been fewer deaths and a beach of shining fragments from here to the sea. Letters would litter the pavements. On the walls and windows are imprints from hundreds of different scripts, Egyptian hieroglyphics and Celtic runes, Minoan Greek and Times New Roman, Arabic, Turkish and Chinese. Once the blast had blown, there would have been alphas and abjeds, diphthongs and digammas everywhere. Investigators could have spent their days dividing Linear B from Latvian, Old High German from Apache. Every syllabary would find its semi-vowel.

There would have been louder international outrage. This library cost $250 million to build. More than a thousand architects competed to design it. Greek ship-owners and Arab sheikhs all paid their part. This wonder of the modern world is especially loved by President Mubarak and his wife. Or so Mahmoud told me. So it might be unwise even to speculate on its transformation into a seaside sky of letters, glittering in the bomb blast of a New Year night.

Is it even polite to contemplate such destruction? No, it is not. Not even in light-headed revenge for having been so sick. Or I should shroud my contemplation in code. But I do not have a code. Maurice used to have one. He liked to mix letters and numbers for the school-boy thoughts and hopes that in schooldays needed disguise. And he continued doing so well into his Oxford days, maybe beyond.

Just before my old friend died last year he tried to explain his code to me. There were a few bits of script left but he was weak by then and we did not make any progress. I read him his account of the Red Tents and he smiled at the memory of Cleopatra's mermaids. That bit had survived because I had written it down from his dictation. But he could no more understand his juvenile school jottings than can scholars understand so many scratches on old walls, pots and plates.

This place where Cleopatra once sat would be wonderful as a sky full of glass. No. Stop it. I regret the thought but can no more stop myself thinking it than stop myself vomiting. This would be a new destruction. 'Destruction' is always the word that accompanies 'Alexandrian Library' in books. The first library here has long been famous for its death even though no one can agree precisely how that death began – or ended. Some blame Cleopatra's first visit from a careless Julius Caesar, the spread of flames from ship to shore. Others blame the Christians or the Arabs or other vandals. Last night I readily agreed with Mahmoud that excessive nostalgia is an Alexandrian curse, that it is absurd for visitors constantly to compare his city with what once it had been and what it has lost. But this new library is an incitement.

The first library of the Ptolemies was an extraordinary creation of the human mind, the definer of learning itself. Here was the first collection that aimed to hold all books from everywhere. Other kings had built collections to show that they and their kingdoms were great. Alexandria celebrated the greatness of everything its rulers could borrow, steal or buy. No one knows what the first library looked like or how large it was. But we do know what was done here.

Yes, I know. I should stop complaining. I need to feel more positive before I write much more. I am merely sick and discontent. What does this library have that no other library has? Nothing very much. There are 500,000 remaindered books from France, some records of how the French made fools of themselves in the Suez crisis. The French, it seems, have been generous in their gifts. There are a few Islamic collections, all of them carefully filleted so as not to incite or offend. Or so it is said.

I do not know if that is true. A library can certainly be a dangerous thing. When Mr Mubarak keeps Egypt calm and bland, many seem grateful to him. I too should be more grateful. It is warm here. It is clean. It does not make me sick. I am going to start this Cleopatra day

with something modest, with her indexes and lists. It may seem wrong to have come so far and to be spending hours at a desk beside electronic catalogues. But since this is the birthplace of the index and the book catalogue, it is not perhaps so very wrong.

The Greeks of Egypt loved names. They loved lists of names. Their names had meanings as ours once had meanings. Cleopatra meant 'famed for her father'. There were Cleopatras who had lived and those whom the living had imagined. Fiction on one side, fact on another: that is common enough in a library. Separating those two groups of Cleopatras was one of the first purposes of a librarian.

Fiction was defined through lists of names, the names of characters, as we call them. Yes, there was sometimes room to doubt. There were hard cases. That was what scholarship was for. The Greeks knew well that there had been many past confusions, that gods and heroes, different types of beings, had once wandered among humanity on earth. But that was then. In Alexandria's library truth and the fiction might usefully, and most of the time, be kept apart.

There was also a substantial history section. And history, like fiction, was also defined by lists of names. The classical Greeks had invented chronology by listing the annual magistrates of Athens by their names, the holders of priestly offices, the winners of the Olympic games. That was how they separated the years for those who saw themselves as Greek.

Catalogues were the key to existence, to a man or woman having existed and continuing to exist. Inclusion in the first Olympic lists became a key, a kind of membership card, for belonging to the history of the Greeks. When one of Alexander's ancestors wanted to compete in the games, he was rejected as not Greek enough. As soon as Macedonians were accepted for the running races and their names were on the winners' list, they became part of measured time. They were members of the club. They were part of civilisation. In Alexandria's library many membership lists became permanent, a source of reference for ever.

Dead bodies needed to keep their names. Preserved bodies especially needed names. Otherwise what was the point of the preservation? Many of the biscuit-coloured bundles under the streets here were once called Cleopatra. In life that had been their name.

After death a corpse might be dried, drenched in scent and wrapped in linen. The coffin might be marked with a thousand messages to the gods, surrounded by water pots lest its occupant needed a drink, and leaves of bronze and berries of clay lest it needed some reminder of other life. None of that was enough. There was nothing as important for survival as a person's name.

In an ordered society lists are made to last. Alexandria was the first society ordered in what we can recognise as a modern way, ordered for women as well as men, for small households as well as large ones, for the classes that we can for the first time describe as 'middle classes'. After a death a permanent label would securely be tied where it could not decay or fall, a red pottery tag on which lines of letters would forever undulate, up and down and up, as though the hard clay were still the soft scrap of cloth by which living men gave names to their ordinary possessions, to their travel trunks, laundry and dogs.

In a library, as in a graveyard, life is fixed. I should be moving on now to love affairs and banquets, the stuff of history's romances, most especially for histories of Cleopatra. But all in good time. I have not quite finished with the librarians. For the moment they are making me feel better. I can hardly remember now the colours of last night at the Metropole. The spewings and explosions have almost passed.

For Alexandria's ancient cataloguers of the imagination, the greatest subjects were the classical Greek plays. The Ptolemies wanted the best texts of tragedies and comedies more than anything that entered their harbour. They bribed and cheated for them. The dramas of the Athenians, written a century or more before the age of Alexander the Great, were a means of maintaining life itself in upstart Alexandria when Athens was past its prime. In little lidded library boxes, where papyrus scrolls were stored, there were many plays, many more than survive today. In those plays there were many names of mythical heroes and heroines, many mythical Cleopatras.

Who were they? Before I begin the rest of the day I will choose just one. Among the tens of thousands of boxes that once lined the walls here, there was once only one truly celebrated character called Cleopatra. This was not a living Egyptian queen or even a dead one but an Athenian, a daughter of a human woman and the divine North Wind, a mixed parenthood that rarely did a child any good.

This Cleopatra lived in Thrace, as far north in the Greek world as Alexandria was south. She was a respectable granddaughter of the founder of Athens, married, a mother, cast out by a barbarian husband and his new wife. Her fate was to watch the blinding of her two sons – and then to die with them, of hunger and thirst, inside a cold, dark cave.

There were many plays from classical Athens that told of this Cleopatra. If anyone would have known exactly how many it would have been one of the men who ruled the Ptolemies' catalogues. Only here in the new Greece, on the delta of the Nile, could a studious reader discover all the many ways in which King Phineus of Thrace had married, unmarried and remarried; and how his second wife had blinded the children of the first with the sharp shuttles of her weaving loom.

Sophocles, the greatest dramatist of Athens, three times told this same tale of the trials faced by his heroine in a distant wilderness, twisting the elements of the plot this way and that way in order to show the whole in all its horror. He also used the story in a fourth play, *Antigone*, one of the rare plays that still survives, one of the best known of all Greek plays, the tragedy of a Theban princess, the daughter of Oedipus, the noble daughter who defied the law to give her rebel brother a sacred burial banned by the state and is condemned for that to a prison cave and death by starvation.

So we can still read about the ex-celebrity Cleopatra of Athens and Thrace. But, like so many classical subjects, we have to see her though her likeness to someone else, the now famous Antigone of Thebes. The doomed Cleopatra of the North Wind is one of the examples shown to Oedipus's own doomed daughter by her chorus of sympathetic attendants. The message is that many other royal women have stood, inevitably briefly, against inescapable fate. Antigone, starving in darkness for giving her brother a decent burial, is supposed to be comforted by that.

It hardly seems a great deal of comfort. This most ancient Cleopatra, born in a cave of the winds, died under the earth where there was no wind, no air and no children who could see her die. Sophocles's heroine, facing the same fate, hears of her example and knows that she is not alone – in past or future. That is how drama is deepened and widened – by reference to other names and other stories, some of which we still know, many that we do not, the past that is forever now, the now that never stops.

Sophocles's *Antigone* is incomplete. It is corrupt, as scholars term a text altered by the errors of scribes. But that has never much mattered. The global inheritors of Greece have kept it as much for its argument as its poetry. It has been a good place for a lost Cleopatra story to hide. A matter of chance perhaps, but then survival, even in the best-catalogued library, owes often much to chance.

Antigone teaches moral argument. It shows the conflict between obedience to man's laws and the requirement (higher or not?) to obey the laws of the gods. In the classroom the decision of Antigone to die for her beliefs seems a wonderful thing, civics, politics, a whiff of future hopes. Antigone is brave and right. She stands up to state power. She poses questions which are with us still. Whose side are we on, the obstinate woman who sticks by her principles or the legitimate ruler who demands obedience to himself?

As Brentwood schoolboys we most certainly were on Antigone's side. Or we said we were. When we read *Antigone* with our teachers we always knew where we stood. In theory there was no contest. Of course, if a real choice like that been ours, we would probably (no, certainly) have left the body unburied and obeyed the king. Sophocles understood that even if his young readers did not.

Just occasionally in class, not often but all the more remembered for that, the arguments fell back and the modern parallels disappeared. What was left was the poetry, the Greek in all its alien difference. One dark Brentwood afternoon, revelling in the foolish delight that the language of tragedy, like calculus or a crossword, was so unreasonably difficult, I asked one of our teachers, the most elderly and often the least inspiring, what was the most challenging piece of Greek he knew.

It was cheek as much as anything. I did not care about this man's opinion very much. We were not generous to our teachers, certainly not to the occasional ones, not to this man who was eccentric, antique, who rarely had his full complement of pipe, teeth and books – and sometimes, it seemed, not even his mind. But I feel generous to him now – for this one lesson that I still remember when so many others have gone.

It was October. It was 'last period'. Satchels were packed and piled for boarding house or home. There were wet leaves steaming on hot pipes, a biology experiment. There was the oily smell of paint. Half the classroom, probably half the school, was close to sleep. The old teacher's response to my question came in a sudden torrent, the fourth choral ode of *Antigone*, sung in Greek with a whistle as though forced through his false teeth and fetid tobacco. It was a shocking sound, the first time that the Greek language, the language of Cleopatra and her library, sounded to me as though it had ever been used.

What did it all mean? Eventually I got my answer in English, with stars to mark the absent words, the holes in a text that no one will ever securely fill.

. . . are the shores of the Bosphorus **** *and Thracian* ***** *Salmydessus*

where neighbouring Ares saw with cruel joy the accursed wound blinded against two sons by a wild wife bringing blackness to eyes seeking vengeance smashed by bloody hands and the sliding needle from the loom ...

The Greek lesson had ceased and Greece had taken its place. This was a rare lesson from the classroom, raw cruelty in the language of reason.

Altar fires die. Fat no longer burns ...

These were words without rules. A home of philosophy and debate becomes a home of maddened birds, whirling, screaming, prophesying the worst of things, pecking at the diseased and dead, shitting back poison from unburied bodies.

A wild wife bringing blackness to eyes.

This way, that way, this way, that way, in and out, in and out, needles and beaks: the fate that faced the oldest Cleopatra in Cleopatra's library.

4.1.11

Rue Nebi Danial

This is becoming a book about me. That is not what I intended. Perhaps I can steer it elsewhere, noting that there are many ways to write a memoir, some we choose, some we are expected to choose, and others that follow their own path.

If I were able I would choose to write about the people who have meant the most to me over my sixty years, so very few people. If I were to meet expectations I might write about Margaret Thatcher, who made the politics of my own time dramatic for a while, or about her successors who never did so quite as much; or about *The Times* and the *TLS* which I have edited for so long.

But I have written too many words about those politicians and in those papers. Most have sunk deservedly deep beneath the library sea. A memoir must be more than a regimented repetition. I could write a memoir of the year 2000, my memorable millennium, when the doctors said that I was about to die. I could describe the peculiar pancreatic cancer that could not, they said, be cut away or cured. I could describe the cut that eventually came, the banned drugs that saved me and the sights that they brought up from my mind. But I have already written much of that and locked most of it away.

There are so many threads in our lives that can be tugged. We are like old bags for wine or shopping. Draw a different string and the bag will take a different shape. I am in Cleopatra's city and this is

Cleopatra's thread, a story of failure for the most part (mine not hers) but no less a memoir for that. It already connects more than I expected it would. I cannot see the final shape but I am confident that it is there to be seen.

Back in Socratis's cafe in the early morning, the one he called 'my cafe', I have not yet seen him in his proprietor's place. Beside the dead fountain there are the usual tiny tables, yellow teas and the views over a sea creature with an electric flex in her mouth. Low in the sky the sun is in eclipse.

Outside in the road this is a morning for the men in grey. There are vans with covered windows, military men, men with guns and men with merely shrugs. The coffee-drinkers watch the soldiers as though they are nothing to do with them in any way. Their studied inattention is as notable as if they were screaming out in protest.

No one glances at the sky where, for the past ninety minutes, a large bite of the early sun has been gradually obscured by the passing moon, a partial eclipse, now at its fullest extent. Horses, waiting for tourist hire, have stamped their hooves as though there was something untoward in the air. Grey-backed crows, accustomed to use these early hours for gutter-feeding, have found the skies a temporarily safer home. But no coffee-drinker has even looked or paused as the sun has become moon-shaped and the tracing paper sky above the tenements and palm trees is drawn, redrawn and drawn again in hazy shades of brown.

I should not be shocked. These are people of reason. It is fine for me, a visitor, to fix my mind in the age of the first horoscopes. That is what a tourist likes to do. Perhaps their anxieties are as hidden as is half of the sun. Or maybe they genuinely do not care. The Egyptians who lived before the Greeks came did not worry about eclipses. Their priests were men of science who arrived early at the knowledge that these bites out of the sun could be predicted. Far from proving man's subservience to the heavens, they showed his power over it. As for arbitrary arrests, those too were as common as light.

If Socratis were here I would tell him that Plutarch, one of the liveliest sources for the life of Cleopatra, came to Alexandria once (yes, unlike Jesus, he probably did come) and gave the best description of an eclipse in all ancient literature. Why does that matter? Any accuracy about events that we can still see ourselves is a useful test of writers from the past. I will need Plutarch if I am going to say very much that is colourful and characterful about Cleopatra. If I can trust him about the sun, I may trust him about a queen.

Socratis is supposed to be here soon. When he arrives, I will also ask him what today's eclipse means to him and to his mother. Anything? Encouragement? Encouragement too, I will say, for Cleopatra's story, even though I am still only skirting its contours.

Why did I begin my rough-book version? A grateful sixty-year-old will often credit good teachers. But in the frozen flatlands of Essex almost half a century ago, in the hardest British winter for four hundred years, it was a bad teacher who had the best claim, a Mr G, a peculiar man even among a staff of some very peculiar men.

My second school, in a low, redbrick town called Brentwood, was founded as a sixteenth-century penance. In the reign of Bloody Mary (as we new Elizabethans were taught to call her) Sir Anthony Browne, a local worthy, had ordered a Protestant boy burnt at the stake. Our founder never thought the boy would choose to die, an Antigone of his time, when he had the chance to recant and live. But like many worthies he was wrong. Sir Anthony Browne became repentant. When the regime changed, there was added need for repentance – and thus for building a school that survived cautiously behind an old red wall (the name of our school song), a mysterious Latin motto (*Incipe*: Begin) and a foundation myth of a child charred for love of the gospels. Brentwood's national renown was for football. Its Latin and Greek were prized too.

At Rothmans Miss Leake held Brentwood in especially high esteem. Maurice's parents were very anxious that their son should be a Brentwoodian, mine only slightly less so. It was the place to which the wealthiest of the area were destined to go and to which the poorest, thanks to the youthful science of social engineering, could sometimes go too. It offered equality in its own way.

Miss Leake would never have met the robotic, rubber-hosepipe-wielding Mr G. She believed that her scholarship boys would be taught by the earnest, slender, slightly socialist young men who visited her from time to time, asking if she had anyone who might excel at soccer or Cicero. This was an honest mistake. Behind Brentwood's Martyr's Memorial many eccentric instructors lay hidden, including Mr G, an ex-soldier of cement-mixer voice and stature, a survivor of a war which had been unkinder, it seemed, than the one experienced by my father and his floating radar-engineers.

Mr G had not fully survived. Explosions still plagued his mind. The clattering of desk tops could drive him maddened from any classroom. Often the noise of classes with Mr G could be heard for hundreds of yards around, the crash of wood on metal interrupted by yelps from boys whose entertainment had been temporarily spoiled by the lash of his rubber hose.

This damaged pedagogue preferred to read than to teach us. This was his privilege since his function was not to take responsibility for any particular subject. Instead, he filled the gaps left when regular teachers were away. If he could be cajoled into telling stories of the Himalayas (which he pronounced with a long second syllable as though gargling sand) or his war among the Pyramids, that was fine with us.

Thus on a January morning in 1963 (the rough-book has the month but not the day) Mr G began to read to us from a battered library book. There had been the usual riot as he arrived. At least two unfortunates were still imprisoned under the master's desk, crushed and bent together in the common manner of the time. And, at some point not long afterwards, I must have copied out some of the words. Presumably Mr G left his text behind as he escaped.

All this I discerned at a glance. Then I looked upon the face, the flawless Grecian features, the rounded chin, the full, rich lips, the chiselled nostrils, and the ears fashioned like delicate shells.

I imagine that the lesson began smoothly enough. On this occasion he had an exotic story to tell. Maybe we were quiet for a while.

I saw the forehead, the crisped, dark hair falling in heavy waves that sparkled in the sun, the arched eyebrows, and the long bent lashes. There burnt the wonderful eyes that seemed to sleep and brood on secret things as night broods upon the desert, and yet as the night to shift, change, and be illumined by gleams of sudden splendour.

The words 'forehead' and 'splendour' would have been rolled out like fresh asphalt, the 'bent' and 'yet' clipped like gravel. That was how he always spoke. There was probably some modest clattering of desks already. But some of us were listening.

It was not in these charms alone that the might of Cleopatra's beauty lay. It was rather in a glory and radiance cast through the fleshly covering from the fierce soul within. For she was a Thing of Flame.

A THING OF FLAME. This phrase appealed so much that I wrote it in capitals, twice.

Even when she brooded, the fire of her quick heart shone through her. But when she woke, and the lightning leapt suddenly from her eyes, and the passion-laden music of her speech chimed upon her lips, who can tell how Cleopatra seemed?

By now the clattering would have been brutal. I do not record it. But it was always brutal, bringing with it either retreat or retribution.

In her met all the splendours that have been given to woman for her glory, and all the genius which man has won from heaven. And with them dwelt every evil of that greater sort, which, fearing nothing, and making a mock of laws, has taken empires for its place of play. In her breast they gathered together, fashioning that Cleopatra whom no man may draw, and yet whom no man, having seen, can ever forget.

Regular punishment came from the master's rubber hose, a vicious beast. It was perhaps as an additional penance that these rough-book words were written, though that would have been unusual. Without modern internet searches I would have never discovered their origin in *Cleopatra*, a tomb-raiding adventure from 1889, by the novelist Rider Haggard, best known for his character, She Who Must Be Obeyed.

They fashioned her grand as the Spirit of Storm, lovely as Lightning, cruel as Pestilence, yet with a heart; and what she did is known.

There ended the lesson. Last year Maurice told me that he too still remembered it well. He was the smaller of the two prisoners bent in the hollow where the master's desk had been forced against the classroom wall. The larger boy had spent the period with a broken nib in hand, tattooing *A THING OF* high on Maurice's thigh.

Cleopatra the Second, like much else at that ice-bound time, made slow progress. This eighth Cleopatra, resumed now in sunshine that is merely cold, has rather more on which to build its story. There is not only my greater age and knowledge (of some things at least) but other fresh encouragements, not in new readings of Cleopatra fictions but in new possibilities of fact.

Since 1963 much new has been learnt about Alexandria. Great piles of papyrus have appeared from rubbish tips and coffins. New ways of unrolling and deciphering papyrus have emerged, rediscoveries of marbles and bronzes from shipwrecks and sand, new advances most of all in ways of thinking about this Greek city in Egypt, this ever fragile city of thought built on the coast of colossally pyramid-filled plains.

There are thousands of ways to put together the pieces, now the most numerous from any time or place in the ancient world. This is not a jigsaw. There is no picture to be completed. The slivers of the newly found can merely force us to look again at the old. But that in itself is a new power.

73

I must be confident. Alexander and Cleopatra are two of the figures that float through that history, linked by lesser men, famed in their deaths but never themselves quite dead. The city's spirit has evaporated but it can better now be collected. Alexandria has become a million virtual things blown away to everywhere, hard to catch and keep but peculiarly modern for just that reason. In all the ways that she can be remembered and has been, Cleopatra has become that spirit.

Back in Brentwood, back in 1963, my rough-book continued with details of obelisks, the gold-and-bronze-tipped granite needles that for thousands of years captured for Egyptians the power of their sun. At dawn the first beams brought old friends up from the underworld; at dusk the reddened rays took them back. The obelisk caught the points of change, the rising and the going down, a function forgotten when imitators travelled further north. All over the Essex that I knew there were sunless obelisks squeezed between shops and offices, stones that satisfactorily commemorated wars without ever casting even a shadow.

Faraway antiquity was grounded in what was near. On the next three crumbling pages came a detailed description of buildings in an Alexandrian landscape, one which might have come from classical texts or guidebooks but much more likely grew from sights closer to home, infinite flat space interrupted by monuments and threats, long avenues, endless fields punctuated by wooden posts and running tracks, Brentwood's own sad obelisks, panelled halls built to remember both world wars, narrow corridors of crumbling brick and rotting clothes, temporary stages and a temple.

After that came a giant V sign, not an expression of abuse but the rough shape of Africa. Attached to the north-eastern coastline is a smaller V, representing the shape of the Nile as it spreads out from Cairo, west to Alexandria, east to Suez. A third V stands as code for the only girl's name in the book.

V, like Maurice, was there from the very beginning of this story, one of the few primary-school friends who remained a friend as we moved on. She was one of those clever girls whom the less clever boys most resented, one of those against whom the sons of missile designers designed missiles of wishful thinking. She was difficult, abrasive, often mocking, sexy, I suppose in retrospect, although I did not much suppose so then. Like Maurice, she was influential only from time to time. But hers were important times.

There is also a large W, marked out in blue. Mr W was a teacher, as unorthodox in his way as Mr G but more useful, the kind that Miss Leake expected from Brentwood School, tall, classical, scholarly, athletic, the son of a 1948 Olympian. He had a thin face filled with powerful stubble, a long blazer that on his junior pupils would have reached the floor, and a passion for libraries, the Greek and Latin languages, and fast running. He was a man of sibilantly hissed views – on classical and political controversies – all of them the more fiercely and freely expressed the further he could distance himself from authority.

Mr W was the first to set out for me what soon became one of the strongest of the reasons for writing about Cleopatra: that the queen was important because Alexandria was important. She and her city have hung together for 2000 years. She is the face on ancient coins – and on film-posters, sanitary ware, cigarettes and T-shirts here too. If picturing Cleopatra was helpful for understanding Alexandria, that was fine with Mr W. He was the first man who told me anything about her that was more than a name, a clay sculpture, a space-traveller's friend or a fictional fantasy.

Mr W taught sprinting and the high jump as well as classics. On track and field I was the opposite of what an athletics trainer should want, running fastest and jumping highest at the beginning of the season when everyone else was awaking, then falling back through the ranks as other competitors improved. Training made me worse, certainly comparatively worse, but such was Mr W's hostility to progressive ideas of all kinds that my lack of progress was almost a vindication, something attracting only a few hisses of disgust and occasional wry words of praise.

The best-known W-hiss was rarely heard on the athletics field, being one of ritual abuse against those misguidedly studying German instead of Greek, especially when they failed to leave his classroom fast enough in what were known as 'split-periods'. Greeks vs Germans constituted one of many much-loved lines of difference in a school that could turn any difference at all into sport, theatrical competition and other forms of barely repressed violence. In that respect it was not so unlike Alexandria, having few ideals beyond respect for power and the encouragement of only such creativity as was properly approved.

Brentwood was about twenty miles of Essex road away from my Rothmans–Marconi estate. These were miles that I travelled in a bright green bus, in that first winter through the thickest snow, the iciest for centuries. The fish froze in the school ponds. Dead birds clogged the drains. The Sixth Form weather club, which had its own wood-slatted measuring cage by the cricket pavilion, recorded twenty degrees of frost. The kindlier teachers told us that it would not always be like this.

The daily effort of arrival and return was deemed a privilege. The school offered free places to boys from many distant parts of the county whose minds might benefit from a classical education and whose tolerance for bus travel was high. It educated some proficient classicists (who could use their journeys to learn almost any quantity of grammar), as well as some even more proficient footballers and sons of footballers, all of us crammed into a string of brick buildings along enormous tracts of fields, ponds, white-marked pitches and unmarked wilderness.

Cleopatra's family, the Ptolemaic autocrats of Egypt, were in the 1960s only at the edge of classical studies. Lessons in Athenian democracy and Roman republicanism were the core. As Mr W explained in one of his bloody-minded moods, there was something strange in that priority. In the hanging-around times of spring athletics he argued that Alexandria was much more important as well as more useful than Athens, that the much-vaunted Athenian democrats of the fifth century had destroyed themselves by their ideals, that Alexander's little-studied, non-democratic Greeks had been the successful exporters of reason and beauty around the world.

Democracy was a word overused and little understood. Its syllables were Greek but that did not mean there had ever been a Greek democracy, not one that we would recognise as such today. Cicero's Republican Romans, so beloved by the head of the classics department, had quickly been replaced by Rome's emperors, the first of whom gained decisive victories, as well as much of their ideas, inspiration and money, here in Alexandria. Some of Mr W's views, I later found, had been much more crisply expressed by Oscar Wilde. But the first exposure to an old thought is a wonderful thing.

Consider, for a start, he said, King Ptolemy I. That is what we call him now. Ptolemy the Saviour was what he called himself.

There is a scuffle underneath the broken French street lights by the cafe door. Socratis's driver has arrived. So has a large brown dog. So have two policemen with the logo 'Tourist and Antiquities' on their uniforms, policemen employed to manage foreigners, the least alarming of the many forces that keep law and order around the bus station.

Rather than coming in to collect me, the driver looks through the windows and walks towards the next door along the street. I am hoping to go to Pompey's Pillar, one of the biggest ancient sites on my map, one of the sites of Cleopatra's library, probably the longest-occupied site in the whole of the city. Perhaps he is going to be or bring my guide.

The driver stops where I can still see him. He waits outside beside a bower of naked cherubs and a poster of two men in sunglasses advertising suits. His dog disappears first. The policemen follow. They could be with or against each other, all on the same side or all on different sides. Finally the driver is gone. There is tinny laughter, the clump, clump, clump of yelping and tumbling down basement stairs; then silence.

I could go to Pompey's Pillar on my own. I have the directions. But it seems more polite to wait.

There was only one occasion when I hit another boy so hard his eyes bled. I never did anything like it again.

The trouble came when Mr W first lined up every new boy to see who could run the fastest. The result was not supposed to be in doubt. Those who were good at football were also good at cricket and tennis and running. A sportsman was a sportsman. There was no more to be said.

I did not want to run. Maurice was beside me. He did not want to run either. We were in the centre of the line, the worst place to be unnoticed. On either side stretched a stream of aertex shorts and shirts in varying shades of white.

To the horror of the football captain, no one else's progress over the playing field dash was faster than mine. For the last twenty yards I could see and feel that I was in front. Perhaps I appeared triumphant. Certainly a red-headed centre-forward took his defeat badly. He hit me and I, inexperienced in the art of hitting, smashed the bridge of his nose – and the septum too, as I recall the shouted word whose meaning I did not know.

There ensued a series of unpleasant scenes. I was shocked that I could cause such damage to the division between someone's nostrils. I was shocked that I could want to. Mr W made a case for self-defence. Maurice said that he was always getting hit, that everyone was always hurting or getting hurt. I have never hit anyone since. I try hard not to raise even my voice. I do not like being in a cafe when something violent is happening in the basement next door. There are yelps from man and dog – and unpleasant laughter.

In 1963 there was no immediate result of my nose-smashing except that for a few months I was left alone. The running track became a refuge. While running, I could repeat dates and verbs and spellings and all the many things that needed to be repeated.

In the rough-book, under the sign of the W, is a list of a dozen men called Ptolemy. Theirs is a story that a good teacher makes seem simple even though its truth is not simple at all. This gene pool is swamp. But the misidentifications, missing links and murdered nieces can all come later. At this stage of the Cleopatra story there is nothing wrong with a little simplicity. Just consider, as Mr W used to say, the man who became King Ptolemy I.

He was a new boy on the block. When Alexander the Great first ordered the building of Alexandria, the man who would be its first king was miles away. While Alexander was defining his city boundaries – making long lines of barley in the ground that marsh birds, to the horror of the soothsayers, as quickly stripped away – there was no Ptolemy in Egypt.

When Alexander died in Babylon in 323 BC, after eleven years of founding many Alexandrias throughout the greatest empire then known, the first Ptolemy was just one of the Macedonian generals. He was also the son of Alexander's father's mistress. He had a nose like the beak of an eagle.

He also showed himself to be eagle-eyed. With Alexander dead he saw the main chance and grabbed it. If Egypt was to become his personal inheritance, he needed some proof that this was the will of the gods, the fates, the dead king himself or whatever else had wishes which might help him. Like a master conjuror, he seized what he said was Alexander's body – and then he brought it to the city that he said was his share of the spoils. It was a spectacular coup.

Alexander had predicted an Olympic festival of backstabbing after his death. And so it came about. The generals fought among themselves and Ptolemy was one of the biggest winners. Ptolemy saved himself, saved his Alexandria (who now remembers any of the other Alexandrias?) and saved a civilisation too. Did he genuinely save Alexander's body? Maybe. But whatever the body in the casket, it was a magnificent symbol of power.

Many came here to see it. Some say that it might now be in St Mark's Cathedral in Venice, Alexandria's most revered bones being mistaken in 828 for those of St Mark himself, taken away when the Venetians thought that they were getting the relics of their favourite evangelist. Alexander's tomb has long been sought here as though it were the Holy Grail. It has never been found except by fraudsters of various faiths and none.

When Ptolemy placed his eagle-standard in Alexandria he won himself an extraordinary prize. Egypt may not have been as wealthy in the fourth century BC as a thousand years before; but it was a miraculously constant generator of wealth. Those who measured the flood waters were the first bureaucrats to be able to predict accurately what tax they could expect the next year. Little was more important than that.

No conqueror could carry away the power of the Nile to fertilise and feed. None could destroy the faith of the people in the gods they held responsible for their magic river and the Pharaoh who was the living embodiment of those gods. In three thousand years there had been wars and invasion but also a stability exorbitant in length and scale that allowed the building of monuments, unmatched before or since, to prove just how exceptional it had been. Egyptian rulers had sometimes held sway far beyond Egypt's borders. To be king here meant much more than being a king of Egypt alone. But the Nile was always the spine that supported the whole.

Ptolemy's son and successor, Ptolemy II, was obsessive in concentrating the written wisdom of the Greek world alongside that of the Egyptian ancients. He brought books and writers to a library that would in one place, his own place, be there to answer every question that could ever be asked. This Ptolemy Philadelphus, the brotherly lover, developed a long Alexandrian marriage between learning acquired elsewhere and a people who classified that learning. He sought the secrets of medicine and encouraged doctors who dissected the living and the dead.

Experimental science did not follow as future historians thought it could and should have done. The second Ptolemy did not find as many deep thinkers as he found exploiters and showmen. Perhaps he did not seek them. He did not build pyramids. He did set new standards for the organisation of knowledge and theatrical illusion. When he commanded a street carnival, one of the floats was a wine skin made from thousands of dead leopards, 30,000 gallons of wine, drawn by 600 men, with drinking fountains at the sides for those who walked and watched. Or that was how his sycophantic fantasists wanted it to seem.

Ptolemy III, Euergetes, the Good-doer, was most famed for his queen, Berenice, whose first husband had been his mother's lover. When a lock of her hair disappeared from an altar, the librarian and poet Callimachus dutifully found it in the stars, noting in his verse the neatly coiffed shape of the new constellation in the sky and how, down on earth, the sun set over a favourite obelisk.

Century by century one Ptolemy dissolved into another, marrying and murdering, taxing and exempting from tax, as dynasts do. An emergency tax deal between Ptolemy V, Epiphanes, Man of Light, and the priests of Memphis became the text of what we call the Rosetta Stone, one of many concessions, like Cleopatra's *ginestho* decree, aimed at buying support, maintaining calm, spreading happiness and discouraging insurrection.

The Ptolemies of Alexandria sponsored poetry but not poetry that changed politics. They preferred revolutionary Greek examples from the past. Fifth-century Athens was famed for tragedy, sixth-century Lesbos for poets. Alcaeus of Lesbos had famously rallied his fellow islanders with '*nun kre methusthen*" ('now is the time for drinking') when an especially hated autocrat was ejected from power in the town of Mytilene.

This Alcaeus wrote poems of love and alcohol, seabirds and the sea. He also coined the phrase 'ship of state' and worked to influence the direction in which it sailed. Not much of his work has survived as he wrote it; much more has survived in imitation. Cleopatra ruled a library where there was very much more Alcaeus, a massive presence from the past, massively influencing art while making the minimum difference to life.

The political story became one of decline. The Greek Pharaohs paid mercenaries to fight their neighbours' armies. Ptolemy VIII, a second self-styled Good-doer, became best known for trying to make elephants drunk enough to trample on Jews, for killing his sister's son on his wedding night and for the diaphanous gowns on his famously fat body. Ptolemy X – or maybe it was Ptolemy XI, the 'scarlet bastard' – needed to meet a temporary shortage of cash to pay his creditors and melted down the golden coffin of Alexander the Great, making the relic just a little less attractive to future looters.

Soon Alexander's body, the *soma* of the city, even the pretence that it was there, had gone. The founder became merely a *sema* in Greek, the city's sign, a vowel shift of 'o' to 'e', a shift of meaning to something merely semantic, a sign that would survive only in the pages of library books. Few thought that Alexander himself would have disapproved – or done any differently with so precious a casket. A favourable place in history is not the prime aim of a king when creditors, claimants and killers loom. This bankrupt Ptolemy was the only

Greek before Cleopatra's *ginestho* appeared whose handwriting had survived. *Erroso* was his message to posterity; take care, he wrote.

Socratis's driver emerges from the basement, with his yellow jacket over his arm, sweating nonetheless. The Tourist Police follow, one shaking out his arms as though after exercise, the other checking the state of his fists. The dog comes last, unchanged by whatever exertions have taken place down below. I want to ask Socratis what has been going on but he is still not here. He surely cannot be far away. Having waited so long, I can wait a little longer. Mr W's tour of ancient Alexandria is almost complete.

So consider the last Ptolemy. Mr W always wanted matters to be 'considered'. It was one his favourite words.

After a century and half of decline, Cleopatra's Fluteplayer father ruled an empire that had lost territory to east and west but he could pretend that this was not so. Pretence was his reality. When marrying off his daughters, he consigned his eldest to a man who pretended to be the heir to the Syrian throne and, when that failed, to a chancer who said he was the son of another king. And yet in the sixties BC, through dynastic manipulations and the carefully managed support of Egypt's ancient priesthoods, he could still gamble the country's riches – and its debts – on his staying in command.

Like all rulers of Egypt for the past millennium, he had no great army of his own. Roman power was encroaching on all sides. But the Romans seemed happy enough to accept payment for protection. To find a way to link the boundless Roman ambition with the more modest, but still significant, ambition of the Ptolemies was a reasonable way forward. That was the policy of Cleopatra's father in the year of her birth and the twelfth year of his rule – and no one has ever realistically suggested that he had an alternative.

Mr W thought that judgement and realism were two of the greatest gifts that classical study could impart to his pupils. Ptolemy XII was not a master of government, by any standard then or now, but it did not benefit students to look at beacons of virtue alone or even, when Mr W was at his most frank, to study them at all.

The two most important words in Greek prose were *men* and *de*, 'on the one hand' and 'on the other hand'. It was impossible to write the first language of thought without these words. There were always two sides. Worship of a single purity, he said, produced the purest trouble. Chance governed all. Virtue was occasionally rewarded, more often not. Religion was risible. Purity was confusing as well as perilous for the young. Fabricated purity (and was there really any other kind?) was worse. Democracy was a delusion. Showmanship, pragmatism and shallow thought were the dancing partners of our time.

That was the W doctrine. It was useful for schoolboys to look at figures in ancient landscapes as murky as our own. We might only then turn our attention to current questions of politics. It was a shame that Harold Macmillan had gone. Sir Alec Douglas-Home was not perhaps the ideal Conservative Prime Minister for the coming election. Mr Quintin Hogg would have been a better choice. But a Labour victory would ruin everything. Those local hooligans who had painted 'Tories Must Go' on the Queen's Building's bright new brickwork were wholly wrong. The headmaster had been quite right to offer junior boys 6d per letter for scraping the offensive words away as fast as possible. Mr Harold Wilson was the sort of socialist who might end Greek and Roman history for ever if the country was foolish enough to give him a chance.

At home, all talk of politics was banned. Politics suggested choices and there were really no choices. On the Rothmans estate the power of reason would always prevail. I tried the choice between Alexandrians and Athenians but that distinction, to my father, was especially foolish. Evil bastards would appear anywhere from time to time. He and his new colleagues would make the missiles and the anti-missiles that, by mathematical certainties, would deter them. That was all the truth that was required. And that was when, accurately but quite unfairly, I started calling him an arms salesman.

5.1.11

The Roman Theatre, Sharia Yousef

My mother much approved of my father's advancement from laboratory bench to office desk, from designer of radars to seller of them.
This was promotion. He was making more money. He was distinguishing himself (and therefore her and us) still further from the
technicians and factory workers in the lower reaches of the Rothmans
estate. An arms salesman was more like a bank manager. We were
approaching closer to the status of Maurice's family and leaving
behind V and the Noakes Avenue neighbours.

Maurice and I were both at Brentwood. V was at the Chelmsford
High School. Even if there had been a free Brentwood School for girls
(which there was not) she would not have been there. That was a disappointment to me but not to my mother, who said she 'dressed like
a shop girl'. Her mother 'talked too much' and her father (she had
heard this from a man playing bridge) had 'a Ford Popular mind'. A
Rover mind was good. A Rolls-Royce mind was the best. It was very
common on the Rothman's estate to liken minds to cars.

This morning I am alone at the Roman Theatre, one of the main tar-
gets on my tourist map, only fifty yards from the Dead Fountain cafe
but hidden from it behind a beehive of bustling security police and
soldiers. When he left me here, Socratis said that it would be a quiet,
safe and 'inspiring' place for me to write about Cleopatra. I was not in

a mood to argue. His driver, unusually, was nowhere to be seen. I wanted to ask what had happened in the cafe basement yesterday. But I did not.

Cleopatra herself never saw this theatre, a tight semi-oval of sixteen rows of stone, one of the type known as an 'odeon', more a small concert hall or council chamber than a place for plays. It is the only one if its kind in Egypt and a tiny reminder of Rome's architectural legacy to Alexandria, probably a gift to the city in around 200 AD from Septimius Severus, the first African emperor of Rome. Severus was born in Libya, a permanent traveller and one of the most assiduous emperors in attempting to understand the British. In his theatre today, in a cheerful kind of homage, two young sisters from the north of England are making the best of a surreptitious picnic. Perhaps they had been promised a winter beach holiday by parents who had not asked sufficient questions of the travel agent. One girl kicks a plastic bottle. The other dips a paper plate in a puddle of rainwater and tears it to pieces with her hands.

This odeon is now a theatre within a theatre, one antiquity within another. The highest seats are where the divers in the eastern harbour have brought some of the newly discovered statues and ornaments that were once a part of Cleopatra's city. These pharaohs and sphinxes, their features worn by so many centuries under the sea, now sit on the edge of the outer theatre, as though watching the watchers below, all of us in permanent rehearsal. I can sit here between them.

There is an eyeless granite globe, with no definition left beyond what a large bird might leave on soft clay, but shaped unmistakably as a head. Beside it sits a second mass that might be a man, with deep eye-sockets and the extremities of a lip. On one side of these is the upper body of a woman, tightly waisted, with full breasts held by rounded lines of drapery; and on the other a torso, no more than the shape of a giant bone, the knuckle where the legs might part.

These discoveries are often seen as declining figures, feasts for nostalgia, their faces a flat shadow of their past. But that is not the only way to see them. They can also be about to come alive, taut as though holding their breath, palpably present in the furthest rows from the stage. It is as if they have not yet been carved, their eyes still in the mind of the sculptor, their clearer future still to come. These are images that have not been imagined yet. In our own theatres we might also say that they were seated in 'the gods'.

V was once the only person who knew about me and Cleopatra. In the pitted paper of my rough-book pages, there is a picture of her as some sort of recognition of that fact – or rather interrupted parts of her, black parallel lines representing hair, belt and patent shoes. She looks respectable, restrained, albeit in slices. Maybe her black skirt was

too short for my mother's taste, her hair too fringed, her belt and shoes too shiny. She was a year older than I was, an important year older. A search of old photographs revealed just one of us both together, aged about eight or nine, me behind the ears of a rocking horse more suited for a much younger child, her on the grass behind. The whole image, framed by a white border like a mosaic tile, was barely three square inches. My hair stood up like a brush. Hers fell down over her nose.

That rocking horse park was where we most often met. Occasionally I visited her house. It was full of model roundabouts that her father made from balsa wood, low tables filled with soft, smooth cars and windmills twirling from meat skewers. I was not invited in far. Though scholarly in spirit, she preferred a solidarity with those she perceived as her fellows, fifteen-year-olds in general, fifteen-year-old girls in particular, those whose parents were more political than mine, were aligned a little with the Left, and could never be described as arms sellers.

Cleopatra was a piece of common ground. V's heroines were Virginia Woolf and the Pankhursts. She admired female struggle. This was 1964. My Egyptian queen could have been a good example, she said, if her storytellers had not been obsessed by sex and fashion shows. The custom of inbreeding brothers and sisters, whatever its social and genetic drawbacks, was excellent for gender equality. What did I think about that?

And how had Cleopatra spent her teenage years? Did I not know? I should find out. If I did not want to know how she had spent the years that we ourselves were living through, what was the point of studying a life at all?

There was no kind of answer in the new film, she said suddenly and coldly one day. Elizabeth Taylor was much too old. V knew about films when I knew only the stories for films. At Chelmsford County High School she already belonged to a more social set than that to which a young Brentwoodian might belong, citing from time to time the opinions of university students, boys who had jobs, men who rode in cars and paid for drinks in pubs.

She had seen *Cleopatra* in London quite a few months ago, she said, but would be happy to see it again with me in tow, making her point as though this were a rare generosity. In the meantime I could trust her that it did not include the queen's teenage years. There the conversation, like so many of the ones we had, abruptly ended.

When Cleopatra was ten, her father lost his job. Even kings could lose their jobs, particularly kings who had a family like the Ptolemies. In 59 BC there was a palace coup and her elder sister, Berenice, was suddenly the Queen of Egypt. Ptolemy XII was suddenly no more than a former monarch, one whose only hope of restoration was help from Rome, from foreign generals, Pompey, Julius Caesar and their various surrogates and rivals.

So late in 58 BC, when Cleopatra was eleven, the ex-king travelled to Rome, via Rhodes and Athens, to plead his case. There is a commemorative inscription from Athens that mentions a daughter travelling with him, imperfect evidence that Cleopatra accompanied her father on his trip but enough for me now.

Berenice's rival Alexandrians swarmed on Rome at the same time. Their task was to profess the superior loyalty and generosity of the new monarch, poisoning the reputation of the old and promising stability, the word which in Greco–Egyptian meant commonly the liquidation of junior alternatives. The fate of Cleopatra herself was at high risk – but less so in Rome perhaps than in the basements back home.

Cleopatra did not speak Latin but she had already proved herself a student. She was an asset for her father, a healthy young heir for presentation to bankers and other sceptics. Neither of the Alexandrian factions had an easy case to make in Rome. How Egypt should best be ruled was a topic on which many Romans held a view, not merely a matter of how much wealth could be stolen for the Republic but which of the Republican leaders should steal it. The treasure was colossal. But for ambitious generals such as Pompey and Caesar, themselves nearing the brink of civil war, it was much worse that their rival scoop the prize than that the prize stay in Ptolemaic hands.

There was little sentimentality at Rome over any particular Egyptian monarch, merely a preference that, if the king were to be replaced by a queen, the switch should be made with Roman consent. At first Ptolemy struggled. He had less money. His Egyptian enemies dined and bribed on a massive scale. It took almost a year – of incurring debts and making promises, of troublesome oracles and other inducements unknown – for Ptolemy to win his argument and be promised a Roman army that would put him back in power.

What would Rome have looked like to an Egyptian princess? Familiar? Yes. Unfamiliar? Also yes. A foreign city then was like a past city now. To travel is to see what is the same and what is different. The study of ancient history is a never-ending negotiation between what has never changed and what has changed utterly. We are not looking at parallels between old and new, always deceptive, always false. We are looking into the space between the lines.

In 58 BC Rome was larger than Alexandria, but it was not as grand. Romans paid much less tax than Alexandrians and were much less governed. Rome had no army of bureaucrats, merely armies that rifled the treasuries of others. The Roman constitution allowed dictators but not permanent dictators.

Rome was also becoming much more like Alexandria than later Romans liked to think. Egypt was becoming fashionable around the Roman Forum. The fastest-growing city in the Mediterranean, whose ground plan was already being ripped apart by the competitive instincts of Pompey and Caesar, was at the beginning of a cultural thrall to the power that was in decline.

Fewer Roman houses displayed marble or the most obvious luxury of Alexandria. But the piles of varyingly veined and coloured stones awaiting erection suggested that this would soon change. There were new statues of gods in gold and ivory, making the older ones look their age. Some of Rome's finest houses were decorated with scenes of the Nile. Crocodiles and hippos gaped alongside crested cranes and cobra.

Isis, Cleopatra's personal goddess within the pantheon of Egypt, was so fashionable that she was a political issue. Should she or should she not be banned? There was a new Senate order to dismantle the shrine of Isis on the Capitol. Amid the clatter of masons constructing and reconstructing memorials to military triumph, there was also some serious damage to Egyptian religious rites. But the bar on Isis worship, like most senatorial attempts to change personal behaviour, was inconsistent. From Cleopatra's personal perspective Egypt was, at least, what everyone was talking about.

Some of Rome's religion was wholly alien to an Alexandrian. Worshippers were allowed in the most intimate parts of the temples, places where only the Egyptian elite ever entered. There was a peculiar reverence for Vestal Virgins and no one seemed to believe in the afterlife. But her Isis cult was ubiquitous. Cleopatra's goddess was twinned here with Fate and Fortune. She had a sanctuary at the foot

of Rome's most south-easterly hill, protected there by present aristocrats, patronised by dead dictators, threatened by ranting demagogues
who would come to regret their prejudice.

Egyptian wheat was the source of Roman bread. Egypt's doctors
cured Roman ills. They had the benefit of Alexandrian curiosity and a
readiness to cut up the living as well as the dead. Gynaecology was
great among their arts. They knew how the womb worked and where
its blood vessels lay. The library at Alexandria was a storehouse of medical facts observed by eye, written on papyrus and passed on to
succeeding generations and the doctors of successor powers.

Some of these things V and I knew in 1967. Most of them we did
not know. Human vivisection was a fascination only for a fellow
Brentwoodian whom Maurice called Frog. There were so many
things waiting in books. Some were facts about facts, facts from the
history of scholarship, things that could be learnt about learning.
Both for Rome and for Egypt the 'teenage years' were a momentous
time. V loved the idea that Cleopatra had a front-row seat at so extraordinary a show. She wanted to know how this Roman holiday
affected the rest of her life. With the blissful solipsism of youth, there
was no more important part of the story for my friend. This, she said
boldly, was the early sight of politics that made a politician of a queen.

V had heard terrible stories of things that went on at Brentwood,
brutality on a heroic scale that in her mind amounted almost to vivisection itself, things that among her girlfriends were mentioned only
in whispers. She disapproved of schools with a hundred football
pitches and ponds. Why were they allowed to seek out suitable boys
for miles around and have them educated into the service of a decay-
ing empire at public expense? Prime Minister Wilson would soon

put a stop to this 'direct grant' system, she said, just as Mr Nasser had done his own bit to bring Britain to reality. Almost a decade after Suez, or so her mother told me, the British were still asking what minor power meant when the Americans held all the power. It was that same Cleopatra question from Rome 58 BC.

V occasionally came to Brentwood on a Saturday afternoon. This was permitted on designated dates. I have notes of a few of them still in my 1967 diary. Each time she seemed surprised that I was still alive. Was I keeping an eye on other old Rothmans friends? How was that witty boy with thick round glasses, Maurice, the one whose insults made her laugh?

She routinely listed names and, when I could not give a positive reply, pursed her lips as though to say that they had surely disappeared into hell. Her girlfriends knew of boys who had gone there (there was a resounding stress on the word 'gone') who spent their nights in boxes, boys who had to clean lavatories with toothbrushes and play all the roles of girls since there were no girls there.

Those were boarders, I said, members of a wholly different world from that of the boys bussed in only for the days. Well, Maurice is a boarder, she said. How was he? I was not always sure. I was surprised that she cared. V was an older girl from Noakes Avenue. We were younger boys, Maurice from the big houses in the fields and I from the middle ground. We had been in the same junior school. That was all.

She was impressed, however, by Brentwood's Bean Library. This was the one reason, she thought, why a sixteen-year-old boy might reasonably spend three hours each day on a trunk road instead of going to the best school nearby like everyone else. We met there from time to time, normally on the occasion of a football match when sisterly support was approved.

The Bean, she said, was like a perfumery that she had once visited with her mother in London. It smelt of spice and leather and beneath a polished-wood barrel roof stood rectangular tables and open shelves through which we could see who was selecting books on the other side. It was this arrangement of shining surfaces that explains my peculiar picture of her in the rough-book, a drawing of black feet on tiptoes, a space and then a pale knee below a dark hem, another space and then a belt of black leather, more books and then a necklace with a single stone.

The Bean Library was home to a society where we discussed the 1964 general election and the appearance in Brentwood of Mr W's lost Tory saviour, Quintin Hogg himself, ringing his hand-bell to warn us that if we elected Mr Wilson we would soon all be wringing our hands. When voting time came, Brentwood heeded this warning and returned a Conservative to Westminster as was its wont. But the country at large did not. Sir Alec returned to his Scottish coalmines and grouse moors and the only Douglas-Home of which anyone in the Bean Library needed to take note was his brother William whose comedy, *The Chiltern Hundreds*, about a butler who campaigns to be a Tory MP when his master has defected to Labour, had been selected as our school play. V preferred the election result to the play. I did not care much for either.

One night I brought home one of Mr W's red Latin Loeb editions to set alongside my grandfather's *Aeneid*, books 7–12. My father commented that one advantage of the classics was how little of it had survived. He meant that there was so little of the ancient world to study, compared, for example, with the infinite possibilities of his shooting range over the sea and skies. Just one look at the Bean Library Loeb shelf showed how wrong that was. The classical landscape was vast. There were Latin texts in red and Greek in green, hundreds and hundreds of books. There was poetry, history and drama but also the *Elements* of Euclid, Ptolemy I's prized mathematician, my father's only good Greek.

Sometimes in the Latin books there were short passages, sometimes long passages, suddenly rendered into Greek. To read the forbidden parts of Latin poems it was essential to know Greek. To read about sodomy or cock-sucking or how Greek queens excited themselves with geese, a boy needed to know Greek well, or to know another boy who knew Greek well. Even among these school books there was an intimidating infinity of Greek and Latin as boundless as the deserts and fields of Egypt and Essex.

The Bean Library was where the rough-book was written, where Cleopatra the Second began. Without it there would not be an eighth attempt now in the theatre of Septimius Severus under the flat gaze of unfinished gods.

The tourist site is almost empty now. It is close to closing time in the rain. There are only two places in which to stay dry, a postcard hut by

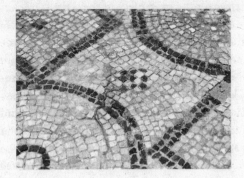

the entrance selling Tutankhamuns and, a hundred yards to the east, a glass-covered Roman house called the Villa of the Birds.

The choice of postcards is peculiar. All of them celebrate a child pharaoh from the desert south who never came to the Mediterranean, whose name not even Cleopatra knew, the heir to a father who preached the heresy that there was only one god and whose memory had already, in the first century BC, been expunged from history for more than a thousand years. There is nothing Alexandrian about Tutankhamun.

The second shelter is for vivid mosaics of peacocks, ducks and doves made by Alexandrians for Romans, portraits in coloured stone of birds that still fly and swim here. There are no postcards of the birds. The archaeological authorities – and their political masters – do not like their Greek and Roman past. They much prefer to be the heirs to pharaohs.

Now that the clouds have cleared, it is an hour till closing time on Sharia Yousef, the time that Socratis promised that Mahmoud would come, the time to discuss plans for tomorrow. The picnickers have gone. The shadows from the grey-green columns are sweeping like second hands across the sunset face of the stage.

What most amazed V was the competition at Brentwood to know things, the ancient and the modern, or to know some of them, or to seem to know some of them. There were weekly 'form-orders' for every form, league tables of individual performance in every task on every day. Competition was considered character-forming, competition in Latin and Greek especially so. There were rankings for rugby and cricket and running, but also for the collection of cold-weather data and the sale of tickets for raffles and *The Chiltern Hundreds*. There were contests in writing accounts of the death of kings for *Greenwood*, the school magazine. My *Cleopatra* was unplaced but my *Mary Queen of Scots* was a winner, the first words of mine ever put on view beyond the box room overlooking the Essex clay.

Everyone had a position in an order and, while in theory this could change with every test and examination, in practice it was noticeable how little it changed. The top seemed always to be on top. The best footballers were the best cricketers too – and the best runners once full athletics training was under way. When the lowest were raised to the highest, and the highest returned to the bottom of the pile, as happened once a year in the dining rooms on 'Saturnalia day', the result was felt more deeply than any act of religion. The sight of the headmaster carrying warm carrots and the second-formers being served by the sixth was our most self-conscious borrowing from ancient Rome. Borrowing seems too weak a word for what it was like for the orders to be briefly subverted, the lowest divisions elevated to the school heights.

Division was the daily business of life. There were boundaries between the aesthetes and the Combined Cadet Force, between the boys who mocked Mr G for mispronouncing Himalayas and those who feared his hosepipe, between those who fenced for England and those who fenced pornography, between those to whom the headmaster might read Achilles Tatius and those to whom he never would. And there was always our classical divide between the Greeks and the Germans.

When Mr W shouted 'Get out, you Huns' at the half of a class who had chosen to study German rather than Greek, it was just an ordinary day. He used this command before every lesson, sitting up on his stool behind his high desk and waving a white-chalked duster at the retreating modern linguists as though it were a talisman against their evil spirits. The regularity of the words brought equally regular results. When the master had spoken from his perch, it was as though a new queen bee had come of age within a swarm. The thirty-strong third-form class divided into two equal clouds. The Huns clattered and clanged over their bags and books to reach safety. The Hellenes, as we remainders were known, poked them on their way with pencils and rulers.

The noise of wood and flesh and metal was immense. There was more clanging than would be heard today because polio was still a potent scourge and iron leg-callipers an all too audible reminder of it. The mere clattering was the sound of boy-meets-desk at all ages and times. The peace, when the clouds had parted, was W-heaven. Once the Huns had given up their ground, we could shuffle to the front of the room, fill up the empty spaces and open our slim, brown-cloth-backed copies of Euripides' *Rhesus*, a Trojan War play about spies and horse-thieves which may not have been by Euripides at all.

This was an introduction to scepticism as well as to tragedy. The high-spending librarians of the Ptolemies attracted fakes as well as treasures. Our *Rhesus* was of dubious authenticity, we were told. But, for reasons that were never clear, availability in school stocks, perversity in the character of Mr W, simplicity in much of its language, we seemed always to be reading it. The drama was set at night outside Troy. A matching murky blackness filled our minds but at least we effete scholastics were safe for a while from the Huns.

Mr W had no genuine prejudice against those who chose German. He did have an ill-concealed contempt for the Combined Cadet Force, whose business was rerunning the last war and in whose ranks every pupil, even his own, had to march on Thursday afternoons. But a jocular anti-German approach was fine.

No one wanted trouble. Dividing one group from another was not designed to hurt. It was as natural as breathing. Then, one afternoon in the summer of 1968, the classics library, which was kept in the form room of the classical upper sixth, was ransacked by persons unknown. This, we soon learnt, was a much more serious offence to school rules than surreptitious snogging or serial buggery. It was a public crime. It was a mystery. While V and I ate ice creams at Chelmsford bus station the next day she wanted to know what I had seen, who had seen it first and who was under suspicion.

On no account, I told her, were we allowed to clear the evidence. I described to her the confetti of grey on the green floor, the occasional piece of cardboard colour, the muddy purples and blues used for binding dictionaries. I slightly exaggerated what I had seen and when I had seen it. She nodded sagely, as though humouring a child.

So who had done the deed? Who would write Homo on a book of Homer, Virgin on a book of Virgil, mix up pages, tear maps and lexica? Who, without even noticing, would have torn the rough-book with most of my Cleopatra notes? A disaffected airforce platoon of the CCF? A band of chemically enhanced physicists? Germans? The fencing team? She shrugged and broke the empty end of her cone into the waste bin. In V's view, almost anyone could have had a reason. She was surprised such assaults were not a daily occurrence like all the other assaults that her friends still reported to her.

For a week there was nothing more to report. But then a book was burned, only one book, but burning, it seemed, was more serious still. The target was a copy of *The Greek Anthology*, a collection of short poems, many from Alexandria, written over a period of a thousand years, mostly unappreciated except by zealots and at that time, in a school classroom, never opened at all. It had not even burnt well.

The culprits had used pages from tattered rough-books (one of them mine) to fuel an inadequate fire.

Mr W had the job of investigation. I could not tell him anything. No one could. Or, anyway, no one did. I had expected to be sadder at the almost total loss of Cleopatra the Second. Once I would have cared much more but, in truth, I had left it behind. Since no one apart from V knew how far it had advanced, I did not even report the damage.

Maurice suspected the boy he called Frog, a suitable candidate I agreed. Frog was not a pleasant creature. He was short, squat, obsessive, a day-boy who lived like a boarder, an undesirable hybrid. He was clever but not predictable. He fitted in nowhere. He was always keen to continue his tedious stories after catcalls and abuse, even after chalk had been pushed down his throat. He understood certain jokes perfectly and others not at all. He knew about Nazi medical experiments and once gave a lecture to the classical society, in excessive detail, on how gladiators used to slit each other's arteries. Perhaps this Frog had been both the ransacker and the burner. He seemed a very likely culprit.

In V's view to investigate the crime at all was a silliness that proved how isolated and self-obsessed we were. This was 1968, the year of revolutions from Paris to San Francisco and even changes to modest forms of socialism in Britain. Whoever was protesting, in the rooms between the Memorial Hall and the headmaster's garden, was not, she thought, protesting anywhere near enough.

Here was my friend at her most different from the rest of us. Any comparison between what was going on inside school and outside was rare and bold. At Brentwood we knew almost nothing about the wider world in which we lived. Paul Simon sang at our Folk Club and

Jimi Hendrix (whom my diary of the time spelt as Hendricks) came to Chelmsford and terrified V's most liberated friends, trying to dance with them during the interval and to lure them backstage when the show was over. That was the extent of my 'Sixties', as the word came later to be used. To understand a sacking of our bookshelves, the classical sixth did not turn to hippies or Vietnam War protesters. We could only go back in time and south in direction for our comparisons, parallels and explanations.

The headmaster himself took over the case. He conjured extraordinary visions before our eyes, the sack of Rome, the burnings of Alexandria's Library by Julius Caesar, the monasteries of Africa pillaged by Islamic hordes. It was an unforgettable performance and a perfect end to Cleopatra the Second.

Despite these efforts no culprit was ever found. There were mutterings about those few sixth-form iconoclasts who did make regular contact with outside life, who studied English, had mirrored glasses, sexual partners and pop-groups in which they sang at weekends. There were also the boy soldiers and airmen of our Combined Cadet Force to consider.

It was a restricted list. But our physical horizons were in every direction fiercely curtailed. There were areas of ignorance far closer to home than the student politics of Europe and America. Most of the school, as V pointed out, was a city as closed as Moscow. The boarding houses might have been on Baffin Island for all I knew of them. I never reached closer than the cloisters' changing rooms, crumbling red-brick catacombs where the third and fourth elevens kept their football kit in foul-smelling piles.

6.1.11

Hotel Metropole, Place Saad Zaghloul

It is 5.30 a.m. in Room 114. I meant to finish the schooldays' story last night but succumbed instead to dried vine leaves and thick Egyptian red wine. There is a message under the door from Mahmoud, delivered by the chambermaid, that he, not Socratis, will collect me for the trip to Pompey's column at 9 a.m.

CLEOPATRA THE THIRD

The screen on which V and I eventually saw Elizabeth Taylor's *Cleopatra* together was as wide as the road to London. We met no one we knew. She probably intended it that way. Even if we had been seen, nobody would have taken any notice. There was nothing to know. V and I shared only an intimacy of chance, of neighbourliness on our strange works estate, nothing more. For three hours we watched a tempestuous love story as though it were a National Geographic film about flowers in a desert.

Before the film we talked again about book-burning. Afterwards we ranged wider but not more warmly. V was still musing most of all on what was not in the film, the lost opportunity to show Cleopatra's teenage years, the triumphant return of the good daughter and her father, the murder (most satisfying, she thought) of the bad daughter and ex-queen, Berenice.

With the Roman forces that restored Ptolemy the Fluteplayer to power had come a young cavalry officer called Mark Antony, soon to be a popular figure in Alexandria for preventing many more murders that the king had hoped to commit. We had not seen a glimpse of this in the film, not even a glance across a crowd.

Nor had we seen anything of Ptolemy's death, nor of Cleopatra's consequent coronation (aged eighteen), shared with her younger brother (aged twelve), nothing of her pioneering procession up the Nile to replace a sacred bull that had conveniently died (there is a tablet to commemorate this trip, asking that the gods breathe sweet breath into the beast's nostrils), nothing of the food shortages that followed her arrival on the throne, the result of inauspicious years of low annual flooding.

So, we argued, what should be in a Cleopatra story and what should not? If it were to start again, should it include only what was certainly true, only what more than one writer had said was true, only facts that were supported by both writers and by bits of sculpture and inscription found in the ground? Should an author favour what was most likely to be true or what made the best story?

V's outrage at the lost years of Cleopatra represented, in the very tiniest of ways, the movements for youth that, in the sixties, even in not-quite-urban Essex, we were all beginning to join. She prized independence, ideas and the possibilities of change. Anyone is an Alexandrian who, like V in those days, liked to take a familiar story and look at it from some novel perspective, who wanted an old hero to be young, who saw a sideshow as the main show. That is what they did in the Ptolemies' libraries, turning old stories inside out and back to front, for novelty, to show how clever they were, for good reasons and bad. That is what they taught the Romans and two thousand years of storytellers to do.

V hated the film. She had the advantage over me of having seen it before. But that was all. The second time was much worse than the first. Elizabeth Taylor's *Cleopatra* was not Alexandrian in any sense that we had talked about – or any sense at all, bar spectacle and slush. We began a quiet bickering beside the popcorn stall about how predictable it had been.

There was that absurd first scene of smoking corpses on the battlefield of Pharsalus beneath bright-blue sky, men on horses thundering towards Caesar's tent. Who has sent them, asks a jovial Rex Harrison, fretting blithely over the deaths of the fellow Romans who had been foolish enough to follow Pompey. A dumb messenger answers. He uses the sign language for a bushy beard. A man with just such a beard arrives, thin-faced, eyes nastily close together below a commander's white plumes blowing from behind. With a booming voice, boldly hiding bad news, he tells the new master of the world that Pompey has escaped his defeat and has fled to Egypt by ship.

This Blackbeard is the Publius Canidius Crassus for whom Cleopatra would later write her magically surviving *ginestho*. Caesar bids Canidius to drink to victory and then to return with his army to Rome. This character seemed of not much significance then. All we wanted to do was to quibble at each other. When we left the cinema for a pub that served the under-aged drinker, we were still arguing about when a biography of Cleopatra should best start.

V sipped at a gin-and-tonic, smoothed black skirt over black tights, swept back her fringe and looked around nervously in case there was anyone around whom she knew. It would be bad for her to be seen with me and my half-a-pint of beer. To be seen having some sort of row would be embarrassing. It would be better, she said, if we both wrote down what we thought of the film. There was a newspaper competition to find 'Young Critics'. Her father had noticed it and broken away from his balsa model of the Marconi tower to tell her about it. We should both enter – and try our luck.

And so we did. After Cleopatra the Second had died in a burnt rough-book, Cleopatra the Third was born on Basildon Bond writing paper, a thick blue extravagance of our house, proudly typed by my mother as a film review, long now lost, for the *Daily Telegraph*.

Rue Colonne Pompée

Mahmoud arrived almost punctually at the Metropole hotel at 9.30, impatient to begin our morning walk. The streets of Alexandria, he said, were becoming 'calmer all the time'. It was as though he had been practising the phrase. The bombing was forgotten. The 'criminal suicidist' was clearly identifiable from his photo-fit picture in the newspaper. There was no mystery, no plot, no problem. Not even Socratis and 'his imbecile driver' should worry any more.

After barely a hundred yards we stopped for a coffee and water. Mahmoud's impatience had not lasted long. We should see the city today from its highest natural point, he lectured languidly, ignoring the waiter, who just as languidly failed to acknowledge him.

The Roman theatre was 'too low', he began. The library on the Corniche was 'much too low'. It was strange, he said, that they had built the new library in a place so close to where its predecessor, without the help of global warming, had already slipped into the sea. 'After a few too many waves' (he lilted the words as though lightly chiding a daughter for too many sweets), 'the shallow slope of glass, financed by so much goodwill from around the world, would be underwater, alongside Cleopatra's palaces once again.'

I smiled politely. He stopped, frowned and corrected himself, as though some senior officer in a superior department were overhearing. Yes, he had once thought that flooding was a problem for the library but had since been assured that it was not. And there were those who said that the clergy had banned books offensive to Islam. This too was not true. But it was complicated. There were many errors made by foreigners here.

What, he asked, was my own opinion of the Bibliotheca Alexandrina? 'Did you like it? Do you want to go back?'

I paused, grunted, grabbed the menu.

I wanted to give an answer that he would like. He was my guide for the day. He was not being paid, at least not by me. I was in his debt. But what would be his favoured answer? Mahmoud was proud of his city: he would want me to say how much I liked Alexandria's new library by the sea. Equally he was contemptuous of nostalgia for antiquity: he might prefer a more critical response. I said eventually that it might have been 'a missed opportunity'.

His response was sharp and, as was his way, grammatically precise. 'A missed opportunity for whom?' He looked from side to side to side, no longer friendly. For the first time since arriving, I wished I was somewhere else. I suddenly had no interest in Alexandria and its bombings. I was supposed to be in a South African vineyard. Cleopatra was a woman I should have abandoned years ago.

Or, if I had to be here, I would rather be guided by wild-haired Socratis. I had been mistaken in thinking that the two men were more or less the same. They were not.

'Why is Socratis not here?', I asked.

'He is busy,' Mahmoud snapped. 'His driver is in trouble. There are many people here in trouble.'

More coffee arrived, with no visible encouragement from Mahmoud. I wondered what the trouble was. I said feebly that I liked the President's library very much and hoped that it would last as long as its predecessor had done.

He seemed satisfied with this. Adjusting his glasses to improve his bureaucratic poise, he went on doggedly with the theme that every city had to be seen from the highest possible place. Height was essential. Height was the quality of the ancient lighthouse that mattered most. He poured salt on to the table and placed the salt cellar so as to make his point. The Pharos was a navigation aid to keep ships from the rocks and a giant advertisement to sailors with library books, slaves, jewels and other things to sell. But its height was its essence, the essence of Alexandria itself, and the tallest tower in the world before the intervention of Monsieur Eiffel.

There were visitors, he said, who ignorantly expected there still to be a lighthouse here. And there were those who luxuriated in the joy of loss, romantics revelling in nostalgia for a lighthouse that had gone. The ignorant were inevitable. Nothing could be done with them bar the taking of their money. The nostalgic were much more dangerous, sowing illusions of a city that was always lost and had never existed at all.

When we began our climb I asked for a better map. Mahmoud refused. The ancient city plan, he said, was clear without a modern copy. The rest would be incomprehensible however much I spent at the stationers. Maps, he proposed with airy wisdom, show only how little we know.

Our target was the highest natural point in Cleopatra's Alexandria, the Rakhotis hill on the western side, south of the Moon gate, the only place where people lived before Alexander came. Mahmoud was a fluent guide as long as he stayed with his script. In Rhakotis, he explained, was once the temple of Serapis. Greek and Egyptian rites there were most closely fused together. Prophets sang from holes in the ground and dreams of the future rose in smoke. There was also a machine for calculating floods and tax. When the nearby 'mother library' became full, this was the site of the 'daughter library' for new literary arrivals. Its bleached remains are now the rooms closest to the site of these first scholars' first desks.

Mahmoud's words successfully distracted me from our gentle upward march past the military bases, mosques and underwear markets. He was relaxed while we walked past rows of French furniture in various imperial styles, maybe the market which my father called Settee Street, windows and pavements filled with Louis Quatorze leopards' feet, Louis Quinze eagles' wings, Louis Seize fishing tackle, the coy female nudity known as Louis Farouk. When our path was blocked by an old man pickaxing a truck engine, Mahmoud apologised coldly. When the obstacle was a massive mound of children's underpants, each pair being individually smoothed and elastic-tested by the seller as if she were the proudest mother of their wearers, he exhaled a sad, stoic sigh.

After almost an hour of feigned shock and disappointments, at women selling Koranic texts, oil rags and black fish, he pointed to a rough brown crown in the sky above the rooftops. 'La Colonne Pompée', he cried out, unnecessarily smoothing his hair and preferring French, as he sometimes did when a scene demanded the added grandeur that the language of the Metropole might provide.

Rue Karmous

Pompey himself, known affectionately in his youth as 'the teenage butcher', can never, even in his later, lethal Greatness, have been as intimidating as the granite monster that bears his name. Some hundred feet high and ten feet thick, its plinth made from the rubble of royal tombs, it is like a massive ancient weapon threatening everything that lies below. Its polished surface, only lightly stained in deep greens, reds and greys, is missile-smooth.

Mass and simplicity must have together deterred any who imagined moving it, even from a city where so much has been exported, drowned and destroyed. Pompey's Pillar, to use its English name,  had none of the mystery of an obelisk. It lacked the hieroglyphic signs that Christian plunderers, as well as pagans, thought were the words of God. Its simpler message, hardly surpassed by later conquerors of infinitely greater resource, was of mere brute power. Louis XIV, the Sun King of France, had ambitions to move it to a Paris square and make it bear his own statue. So did lesser French kings.

If anyone had tried a removal, the column might have smashed through the tombs, bull-pens and book stores, destroying yet more of the village that was here when Alexandria was not yet a city. Alternatively, it could have rolled down the hill, wrecking the workshops, eventually joining other past glories, so many statues of so many Cleopatras, in the sands of the harbour. But, instead, Pompey's Pillar has stayed in its place. It is still empty and still here.

Its base, however, was as high as we could go. To climb the column was presently impossible. When the British ruled Alexandria there were picnics on top. There were scaffolds and ladders and the braver broad-skirted ladies of the town could take a January lunch there, spreading tablecloths on the cold granite, looking down on the guardian sphinxes, remembering Lord Nelson's victory on the Nile and comparing the site to Trafalgar Square.

Some of them probably knew the truth about their picnic site: that the pillar was not erected by Pompey, nor even by Julius Caesar as a place for Pompey's head. In Cleopatra's reign the column was a mere part of the Serapis temple buildings, maybe a support for the library or the machinery which measured the rise and fall of the Nile, that essential source for tax-collectors. Even when Septimius Severus was commissioning his theatre, this massive monument was quietly lying on its side, somewhere on its ancient destruction site. It was a much later Roman emperor, Diocletian at the end of the third century, who ordered it erected for himself.

The column has no connection to Pompey at all. Visitors today are invited to think otherwise only if they wish. But when earlier grand tourists wanted to imagine the moment when Cleopatra's time in power began, some historical flexibility was helpful. Without palace walls to climb, with no lighthouse except below the waves, much the best place to imagine Cleopatra as a 21-year-old, a queen who was fighting as well as sleeping alongside Julius Caesar, was on a picnic at Pompey's Pillar.

Colonne Pompée

Socratis's driver arrived with a packed lunch from the Cecil Hotel. Mahmoud seemed mildly surprised to see him. He said he wanted to stay here and share the olives, bread and cheese but that sadly he had to go. If I was happy to wait here for the afternoon, one of them would collect me later.

I offered to pay for the lunch. I was beginning to be worried about never paying. 'There is no need for that,' Mahmoud said, in the manner of a schoolteacher or nurse. 'You are our guest.'

In the early afternoon a band of young American women arrived beside the guarding sphinxes, the two massive half-human, half-cats that flank the pillar to east and west, looking south to Africa. The site is scattered with many sphinxes both alone and in uneven lines, lost avenues for forgotten parades. But these two are special.

At first sight they look almost identical, smug and half-smiling, two men who could make themselves into god-cats whose tails, more than two thousand years on, still stand sharp and firm, ready to flick away impertinence. The slightly fatter one on the Sun side of the pillar is Ptolemy I, Soter, the self-styled saviour, sponsor of Euclid, snatcher of Alexander's body and founder of Cleopatra's royal line. On the Moon side is his son, Ptolemy II, Philadelphos, named as the lover of his brothers and sisters, cultural despot, father of Alexandrianism, buyer of poets and critics and their books.

For seventeen hundred years these creatures gazed over the westernmost lake of the Nile delta. Today their view is blocked by a leather-treatment plant and mud-covered apartment blocks strewn with sheets, as well as by an American female sports team. The women are dressed in short red skirts and form a human pyramid. The highest of them is hugging and kissing the younger, rounder Ptolemy, somehow emphasising the difference from his father.

The group is closely chaperoned by a white-shrouded guide and two soldiers. The guide lectures them on the legacy of Tutankhamun, the heretical young pharaoh who was removed from all records until his tomb was discovered in 1922. This is the postcard child of whom neither Ptolemies nor even their librarian knew anything at all. Both the sphinx faces are of Tutankhamun, the guide says firmly.

She must know that she is lying, that these are not the faces of a boy and that, whatever the uncertainties of ancient Egyptian identification, these chubby cats of slightly varying fatness cannot be of King Tut. She has chosen his name (there can be no other reason) because it is the only name that her charges have heard before.

Ras el Teen Street

I have spent the last hour of today in the most relaxed and traditional of tourist pursuits, looking at carpets. When Socratis arrived at Pompey's Pillar to bring me here, he was not at all relaxed, scrambling through the zoo of sphinxes, unusually pleased to see me.

'Have you left the site since lunchtime?'

'No.'

'Are you sure?'

'Yes.'

His driver, it seemed, had seen me in the streets around the western harbour. He frowned. If I wanted to visit anywhere like that, I should go only with him. I was mystified, repeating that I had not gone anywhere. While wholly free to go anywhere, I pointed out, I had not. I had made a careful study of two of Cleopatra's ancestors instead.

He smiled and said he would show me the harbour as soon as we had had some tea. His friend, the carpet seller, would be bringing some tea in a moment. Ras el Teen Street, while close to a presidential retreat and a prison, was no safer because of that. Indeed, as Socratis saw matters, it was substantially less safe.

'This is our Christmas Day. There may be repeats of the bombing or reprisals for it. Who can tell?'

Alexandria, he explained as though to a child, still has its Sun side, the gardens of carefully clipped comic topiary, the herbaceous clock, the new equestrian statue of Alexander the Great whose design kept politicians occupied for years. And it has its Moon side, the port-side streets of rats and rotting cauliflower, a palace protected by its own navy on a grey metallic sea, a site of welding sheds, tombs and sphinxes famed for the disappearance of visitors and tangle of overgrown gardens along the route out to Libya, Tunisia and beyond.

Now we were on the Moon side. But this was a safe place on the Moon. This carpet shop to which he had brought me was a place for 'good men – and good carpets too'. There were piles of woven landscapes on the floor, not the usual prayer rugs but street scenes, marshlands and skies. There were holes in the white plaster walls, only some of them covered by tapestries.

I asked after his mother. It seemed polite to do that. She was, he said, 'still very unwell'. Did he know anything specific about possible suicide attacks, anything that made him especially anxious for a tourist's safety?

He laughed. 'There will be no suicide attacks. There never have been suicide attacks. New Year was something very different.' He paused. 'It was a car bomb, parked and abandoned, not a crazy man in an exploding waistcoat. Only foreigners blow themselves up. Egyptians prefer to blow up other people. The Christians are after revenge and soon they will find it. Something very different is happening.'

I had with me a copy of *The Egyptian Gazette* with a 'forensic reconstruction' of the officially condemned suicide bomber. We looked at the photofit picture, more like an ape than a man, flat fleshy nose, thinning lips, close-cropped hair and eyebrows added close together as though from a kit of disguises. Socratis snorted. Propaganda, nothing but propaganda, telling the people what they must believe.

He did not identify the propagandist. He never did mention the President. Once again he made the sign of a hyphen in the air with his hand, palm down, thumb pointing from right to left, swinging from side to side like a cricket umpire signalling four runs. For Mubarak's heir-apparent son he made a smaller move, half a hyphen. He held his breath, fattened his already ample cheek and flicked his hand like a sphinx's tale.

He then had an unexpected question.

'Can you help me please?

I smiled. I could not imagine what he might want. He explained before I could reply. 'How am I to persuade my mother that her friends from the bombed church of St Mark and St Peter are truly dead?'

Ah. Socratis's mysterious mother. He was harsh about her when we had dinner two nights ago. He was softer now.

'She did not see the aftermath of the explosion herself, as she claimed. She lied to me about that. But she knew three women whose bodies were pulped over the pavement there. That, I know, is true. She too knows it is true. Her friends are dead. But she is still talking about them as though they are alive, in the present tense.' I remembered Mahmoud's dinner-time frustration. The bombing victims too, like Jesus and Cleopatra and Colonel Nasser and everyone else she had elected to her personal pantheon, were still alive.

'Do you have any advice?' he asked. 'It is all very difficult.'

Mother and son, he said, had quarrelled. 'She is angry, quizzical now, taunting almost. She has known these friends all her life. She has always had a picture of them in her mind. She can recognise them. She knows their names. None of that has changed. She still has their images in her head. She still has their names. Thus they are as alive as they were before.'

He paused. 'She does not want revenge. That would be a catastrophic error. It would not even be based on a truth. Or so she says.'

I could not think what to say. 'What do others think? Do you expect a revenge attack?'

He shrugged. He wanted advice on helping his mother, not a request for security briefing.

I am still not sure what sort of answer would be right. Before I could say anything he rose suddenly and said that he would be back soon. I could continue my notes. Meanwhile his friend the carpet-seller would look after me – and would 'absolutely not', he promised, try to sell me a carpet.

Hotel Metropole, Place Saad Zaghloul

There was only one carpet that I might have been persuaded to buy. It was larger and wilder than any of the rest, some six feet wide and four feet high, well-trodden before it had been hung on the wall. Its makers (for it seemed the work of many hands) had selected almost precisely the perspective of the city that Mahmoud argued was the best, a picture of Greek Alexandria as seen from a high point in the harbour, from the lighthouse perhaps or the palace wall, a receding view of houses for more than a million people, a mighty city when its full extent was portrayed in tufts and knots, pile and patches, threads of silver, reds and blues.

It was an unusual piece, perhaps some kind of apprentice work, a demonstration of different manufacturing styles, a means of showing purchasers what was on sale, in weaves, carpet-felts and tapestries. Some parts were of a high quality that even I could detect; others were like rags.

The foreground was packed with brilliant detail, a long facade of columns, windows hung like stages over a wide, parade-ground promenade. Behind the walls of the closest and largest house, seen from above through an open roof, were marbled rooms for dining and drinking, rooms for preparing to dine and drink, thrones for hairdressers.

Inside were celebrants, servants and the richest ornaments of those being served. The tapestry-weaver had created glass bowls in blue and gold, white bowls with limbs of men and women in serial couplings around the rim, sharply visible as though through a microscope. The objects behind emerged more darkly as though through distant telescopic sights, different houses, broadly drawn in felt and rags, the homes not so regularly shown in Cleopatra's capital, the red and brown lanes where the ancient weavers themselves worked.

To the furthest left of the design, much closer even than the jewel boxes of the rich, so close that a watching queen on her battlements could toss a coin into their cooking cauldrons, were the tight-packed homes of the city's Jews, knotted letters in Hebrew on the walls. To the right were barred cells for criminals, black-threaded lines over pale cloth windows, barracks for soldiers, for Egyptians, Greeks and Romans, each section marked by their alphabets.

This was Cleopatra's city. Those here who spoke Latin were the remains of the army that had restored her father to the throne. They were called Gabinians after the name of their first commander and had stayed as stateless mercenaries, marrying their neighbours, negotiating for land grants and tax exemptions, and keeping whatever order they were best paid to keep. They were part of the panorama and the protection of the city that Alexander had founded and the Ptolemies ruled.

I must have been too obviously a willing customer. When the owner saw me studying this most striking of his wares, he took it down and laid it on the floor, suggesting possible sums of payment, all of them substantial, in keen defiance of Socratis's promise.

The act of removing the carpet from the wall revealed briefly the reverse side, a stranger patchwork in which the richly tapestried sections were almost exactly the gold-and-silver same, the lesser parts a muddy muddle. It also revealed a hole in the wall almost as large as the carpet itself. On the other side, stretching away till the light failed, lay a store of rusting metal, swords and scimitar blades, helmets and armour, a tunnel of khaki and rust. The owner left my carpet on the floor but delicately concealed the hole with a hideous green rug of tufted Arabic letters around a palm-tree grove.

If I had bought it, I could be looking at it now, instead of the high bare walls of Room 114 and its low-hung souvenirs of Venice. Instead, I said I would think about it.

CLEOPATRA THE FOURTH

It was a mild afternoon in the autumn of 1969, at a table on a long lawn beside the stunted remains of what the college guidebook called 'the lime tree walk'. In my second week as a student everything seemed peculiarly perfect. The lawn was dotted with other students reading and writing at tables. We are all warily watching one another, still seeing and being seen. This was surely the place for Cleopatra. I had already written eighty-five words – and counted each one. The lime trees were like a line of sphinxes, triumphal in their Oxford way, although less regular and more battered than Alexandrian remains. Doubtless there would be other inspirations in my new home.

I had not chosen Trinity College with any care. The headmaster of Brentwood had offered me, as he put it, because I had 'shewn real gifts as a classic despite being not good at ball games'. Somehow it was all the better for that. I was here by chance, the best way to be anywhere. I could do whatever I wanted to do. The school had also proposed Maurice as 'a promising actor' who was not good at ball games either. That was how things happened then. Trinity had accepted both offers. So had we.

V had preferred to go to Sussex, Essex, Bristol or elsewhere, following the fashionable view that Oxford and Cambridge were tired and old. Maurice was not disappointed. To him she was a nag and a nuisance. Neither of us was quite sure which campus she had chosen. Nor, at this time of abandoning the past as fast as it possibly could be abandoned, did we worry about it.

7.1.11

Hotel Metropole, Place Saad Zaghloul

It is 6.00 a.m. Socratis is coming in three hours' time. He has a plan that is too complicated to explain. 'You will like it,' his message says. Maybe I will. He will suggest some kind of tour, I think, maybe to meet his mother, more likely to show off his car.

These are strange days. This time in Alexandria is not what I thought it would be. I never intended to write so much here about my own life. I came with a promise to write about Cleopatra. Instead I am selecting my own memories of past promises to write about Cleopatra.

But I do select every memory by how much it connects to those promises. It seems random. But there is a reason, a pattern and, in the end maybe, a picture too.

When V made her first Oxford visit, she missed me and left only a message at the porter's lodge. On the back of a college map of the city's streets were her exclamation marks, expletives and what, to an optimist, might have been the mark of a kiss.

I had never kissed her at school. We had not been that sort of friends. Did I want to kiss her now that we had both moved on? Maybe I did. Any prospect of that, however, seemed poor. Her wording was as direct and dismissive as she had ever been: See you sometime! Who do you stars-and-dashes think you are? Does this place think it is the centre of the world?

Maybe the porters had not been polite. Maybe she had come deliberately to have her prejudices confirmed. A map which, on one side, showed Oxford at the midpoint of England and, on the other, showed Trinity as the midpoint of Oxford might have fanned the resentment she had already shown.

This is the first of my two maps on the ill-lit bedspread of Room 114. The four quadrangles of Trinity are certainly prominent at its centre. Not everyone would have thought this self-aggrandising or odd. In our Brentwood geography rooms an old pink England had always stood in the central place occupied by Jerusalem in the maps from the school Bible. For map-makers – and even more so for those commissioning maps – the centre has always been wherever one wants it to be, often where one is standing oneself.

Outwards and beyond there are the dreaming spires. There is the River Isis, the name of the Thames as it drifts past the city boundaries, and of Cleopatra's patron deity too. Traditional? Yes. Offensive? I did not think so. The map shows also what were then my most useful surroundings, Blackwell's bookshop, the Bodleian Library, the King's Arms, the roads from the station that lead to Trinity, to its ragged line of lime trees and the statues of Theology, Astronomy, Geometry and Medicine that look down from the college tower.

This map is a memoir of a kind. It is with me because it stimulates a certain sort of memory. It reminds me of the people, the sherried, the champagned and my more quietly drugged friends, the white-tied, the flower-haired, the cannabis-smokers who wanted to be hippies, the cannabis-smokers who just wanted to smoke, the tweed-jacketed and the oily-jeaned, the black-bereted and the twin-setted, the Left, the Right and the merely languid. But forty years ago it was only a map. It was never meant to mean anything more.

The second map on the hotel bed shows the southern flank of the Roman Mediterranean in the first century BC – from Mauretania, where Morocco today stares north to Spain, through Numidia and Africa, shared now by Algeria and Tunisia, to Tripolitania and Cyrenaica, the two halves of Libya, and finally Aegyptus. It is torn from a textbook. It shows abandoned towns, temples to Isis and other gods, and is designed to help the writers of history essays. Cleopatra would never have seen such a map, or a street map either, or used one to fight a war or find a city or a way through a city. That was not what maps then were for. They were political statements, claims of power and ownership, pictures to provoke, just as V had been provoked.

On the back of the Roman map is a message to me from Maurice: 'V came to see you. I told the porter to say we were out.'

At the end of our day together, after honking drives through traffic to museums – ethnological, religious or closed – Socratis became suddenly, and surprisingly, the most useful of guides. He took me back to the carpet shop, apologising for having abandoned me last night, claiming that there was much more there that I needed to see.

The street door, as before, did not invite the uninvited. Behind the barred wooden shutters the rooms of piled cloth were just as silent. A nervous boy brought us tea, his hand trembling as he set down the tiny cups. The panorama of Cleopatra's city was back on the wall. The shop-owner was nowhere to be seen.

Socratis spoke at first as though he were filling time before something more important was about to happen. He poked at different parts of the picture and then at the plaster below. His pencil left a soft, dark smudge.

'This is Alexandria,' he said gratuitously. The boy stood like a stage extra terrified of dropping his spear.

'So think of Cleopatra standing just here three years after the start of her reign, on the highest tower of her palace, looking back at the city that ancestors had built. She is twenty-one years old, a queen whom almost everyone hates.'

He stressed the last three words, leaving long spaces between them. He moved his pencil higher, off the wall and to the top of the carpet itself, to the repeated lines of background red and brown, the houses of the Egyptian poor that stretched as far as the distant marshes marked by trees.

'These people hated her because she was a Greek, a foreigner who pretended to be Egyptian. She pretended well. She learnt Egyptian. She built schools and temples but, in some ways, that made it worse.'

Next he swung his arm down to the foreground, to the largest of the houses of the rich where the tapestry-maker had expended the greatest of his efforts, on jewellery, silver bowls and ornaments for hands and hair.

'The rich Greeks of Alexandria were normally allies of the Ptolemies, their fellow city founders. But Cleopatra had abandoned them. She was now an ally of the Romans. Pompey had restored her father to power. Julius Caesar was doing the same for her. She was a superpower puppet.'

Socratis spun out those last words like a comedian waiting for a laugh. Then he stared hard again at the wall. The boy disappeared behind a curtain into the cavity of rusting iron behind.

'Cleopatra could not rely even on the Roman soldiers who lived in the houses over here.' He moved his pencil to the right, to the streets where the causeway to the lighthouse begins. 'These Gabinians, the relics of the army that Pompey had sent after her begging trip to Rome, these mercenaries had gone native long ago. Like almost everyone else here they were now on the side of another Ptolemy, the boy who was Cleopatra's brother, an ally of the Egyptian priesthood and an enemy of Rome.'

Here, he pointed, were the prison cells behind the palace walls. 'She did not have many prisoners. Most convicts were killed. It was cheaper that way. Sometimes librarians were allowed to cut up prisoners while they were still alive, for purposes of science.'

I knew about that, or about the possibility of it. Vivisection was one of the obsessions of the peculiar Frog at school.

'Library and laboratory, similar words, much the same thing in Alexandria,' I replied.

Socratis nodded. 'So a few prisoners were the least of Cleopatra's problems. They did not hate her. She was no worse than any other ruler of Egypt. Some things are always the same'.

He paused to make sure that I was listening. 'There is a lot happening in this picture that most people do not see. Or rather there is much that they do not yet see.' Almost as an afterthought, he pushed his pencil deep into the flattest brown-and-red zones of the distant poor. 'Of course, Cleopatra also had the Jews on her side. But what use were the Jews?'

We sat staring at each other. It seemed my responsibility, perhaps my best opportunity, to ask him what he meant, to find out what he was doing, what he and I were supposed to be doing together.

But, at the moment I was about to speak, the shop-owner returned and suggested that surely I must buy the carpet now. Socratis said that

it was more useful where it was. I asked if the two men were brothers. Socratis said emphatically that they were not.

Whatever his coded purpose, Socratis's description of the background to the Alexandrian War would have been perfectly respectable in Oxford. While his 'superpower puppet' message was none too subtle – and Mahmoud, or any supporter of the present regime, might easily have taken offence – his analysis of the events in 48 BC was more or less as the story is best now told.

Cleopatra was twenty-one years old when the war began. For three years she had been joint ruler of Egypt, joined in that role by the elder of her two young brothers whom, by the custom of both Pharaohs and Ptolemies she had also married. Julius Caesar was fifty-two and had been for barely more than three days the sole ruler of the Roman world. At Pharsalus, in Greece, he had at last defeated his son-in-law, Pompey, the man who had stood vainly for the cause that Rome should not have a sole ruler.

Caesar's purpose in coming to Egypt was to kill or capture Pompey who, despite his defeat, had somehow escaped the battlefield. Two pieces of news greeted him when he arrived in Alexandria, the first that the ministers of Cleopatra's brother, with help from Roman mercenaries, had already captured and killed Pompey, the second that this brother was claiming the throne of Egypt as Ptolemy XIII, as a sole ruler whose sister had disappeared. Was she dead or in exile? It was hard to be sure.

The death of Pompey was a convenient good that Caesar could greet with appropriate disapproval, sadness and reflection that there was no enemy worth fighting any more. The exit of Cleopatra, however, was an inconvenience for him, possibly worse than that, concentrating Egyptian power within a Ptolemaic court that was hostile to Rome and keen to avoid financing any more of Rome's armies.

While Caesar was taking over Ptolemy's Palace, Cleopatra proved that she was alive, smuggling herself into the harbour by boat, arriving late in the day and, as has long been portrayed in pictures, books and films, spending the night with the new head of the occupying power. Although Caesar was then married – to his third wife – marital conventions had not even a notional application to infidelities of state. Nor was moral outrage the motivation when Ptolemy discovered his sister's presence and learnt of her sleeping partner. The boy king stamped his way into the streets before a turbulent Alexandrian crowd, cried betrayal, crashed his crown to the ground and called for armed resistance against his sister and the invader.

Caesar never intended an Alexandrine war. He did not expect it. He had arrived victorious, more as a diplomatic judge and debt-collector than as a general, with only some thirty ships and three thousand men, nothing like the forces needed for a war. Suddenly, and very visibly, he was an ally of Cleopatra, the Greek queen of Egypt, besieged inside her palace by an army representing almost all her subjects, Greeks and native Egyptians as well as the Gabinian Romans who had once been her protectors. Caesar's writ ran over the whole Roman world and his protection ought to have been more than sufficient for her needs. But Caesar's immediate problem was how to exercise any authority beyond the palace itself.

He had hoped swiftly to set up Cleopatra and her brother-husband in a shared governorship over Egypt in the Roman interest. While the ultimate power would remain with him, he wanted Egyptian propriety and traditions to be upheld. The young Ptolemy and his advisers had not accepted this Roman conceit. They had been horrified to see Cleopatra out of exile and back in Alexandria at all. Fierce fighting broke out, unpredictable urban combat, unusual for the time. One of Caesar's messengers was killed. So was Ptolemy's chief minister. Julius Caesar, a man ambitious to match the international legacy of Alexander the Great, was unable even to leave the walls of Alexandria.

Caesar sent out orders by sea for food and reinforcement but neither could be expected soon. He had only Cleopatra for local help. He had to hope that he could trust her. The unkind would liken him to an unarmed boy or a woman in an occupied city; all his hopes of survival rested on keeping every door closed. He took the young Ptolemy as a hostage but even that was scant protection. The Alexandrians were not sentimental about which Ptolemy they had on their throne as long as they could pretend that he or she was a real one.

Caesar's soldiers were struggling in their street fights against Pompey's killers, helped only by the narrow spaces that prevented the full deployment of the native forces. The fleet that had brought him to Egypt was barely half the size of that controlled by his enemies, a disparity that was clearly visible – to Cleopatra, to her enemy brother

Ptolemy himself, her sister Arsinoe and to everyone else weighing the likely course of events from this peculiar family encampment.

The young queen knew much about Egyptians that Caesar did not know. From the contents of her library she could tell her lover tales from the mysterious book of the Greek historian, Manetho, the man who first described the Egypt of the Pharaohs to the creators of Alexandria. It was Manetho who first set out for foreigners the astonishing chronology of the country, the sweeping millennia between the many men who built the pyramids, the length of the reign of the first king who called himself the Sun and the rules by which women reigned in Egypt before Rome was ever imagined.

Cleopatra could talk of the pyramids that women rulers had built for themselves. She could argue with Caesar whether these edifices were idle nonsense, worth less than mines and aqueducts and other Roman things. Or were they a potent Egyptian proof that, when a ruler has everything, he or she can build anything? She could read and note, with outrage or not, that carvings of the female sexual organs denoted cowardice and those of the male meant bravery. She could argue, as we do now, about how the Egyptian histories helped or hindered the arguments of the Jews for their own ancient past.

There are also things we know about her world that she did not. She was unaware how much bigger the great pyramids had been before their lower parts were covered by sand. Nor did she know that there was once a great sphinx with them, the greatest Sphinx, as we know it now. In Cleopatra's reign it was mostly, maybe wholly, buried.

During the day Caesar fought and directed his men. At night he dined, conversed in Greek and slept with Cleopatra. Together they were fighting an inventive and resourceful enemy that knew Alexandria well, how its water systems could be polluted and which of its inhabitants could most readily be turned from one side to the other.

Socratis's quiet comparison between ancient queen and modern president was surprising but not outrageous. To the Alexandrian bureaucracy, military and priesthood, Cleopatra was a Roman stooge, the daughter of a bigger Roman stooge, and in league with a Roman tax-collector, extortionist and maybe even an occupier. To Caesar she was a necessary ally in his aim of controlling Egypt and using its treasure to pay his legions.

Cleopatra herself was only a spectator at most events. She played no part in the battle beside the Pharos lighthouse or Caesar's heroic swim through the harbour, his state papers held one-handed above the waves. She did not join in Caesar's ruthless burning of ships that he could neither man himself nor risk being manned by Ptolemy. The naval fire spread to some books of the Alexandrian library, a large or small number depending on who came to be the storyteller. But in advising on the volatile peoples of Alexandria, the rich, the poor, the Egyptians, the Greeks and the Jews, she would have been a useful agent.

She may not have warned Caesar how unpopular she was herself with the mob. To do so – or to do so too early – would have been unwise. But she could tell him much about the character and appeal of her siblings and how, when dealing with this royal family, it was wise to keep an open mind about which side each member might be on. A brother might as likely murder his sister as marry her. Often he would do both. There must have been some strange palace meetings before Arsinoe escaped to the Egyptian forces and had their commander murdered, replacing him with her own choice.

Ptolemy then left too to join his sister. Some said that Caesar deliberately allowed that escape. The result was certainly favourable to him. The Egyptian ranks, divided in loyalty between brother and sister, suddenly had also to face two armies of Egypt's neighbours, from Judaea and from Pergamon. Caesar's despatches had produced a prompt response.

Socratis was right about the Jewish support for Cleopatra's cause – but wrong to belittle its importance. Jews throughout the region had reason to join the friends of Caesar, the conqueror of Pompey, the Roman whom they hated most for his casual defilement of their temple in Jerusalem fifteen years before and the dismembering of their state. The king of Pergamon was a longer-time ally of Caesar who hoped for territorial gains from the success of his bet on the winning side.

In March 47, their two forces together marched on Alexandria. The Egyptians prepared – but failed – to counter-attack before Caesar and his allied rescuers combined. In a single battle by the Nile, this Alexandrine War, one of the stranger conflicts of Caesar's career, came to its end. Away from the twisted streets and houses, his experience in open battle was decisive.

Ptolemy was drowned and his golden armour dredged from the mud lest any worshipper of kings as gods should have a doubt about his death. His head and body would have been better proof but those were gone to the crocodiles and hippos.

Arsinoe was taken prisoner and sent to Rome so that she could march in Caesar's triumph and face whatever plans he might have for her after that. The Gabinians, once heroes for restoring the Fluteplayer, were never heard of again.

Cleopatra could safely now remarry under Egyptian rites, this time to the younger brother known as Ptolemy XIV on the rare occasions when he has been noted at all. To the surprise of the victorious Roman forces and the disbelief of the politicians at Rome, she then escorted Caesar on a short cruise down the Nile, past pyramids they could not properly see, past a Sphinx they could not see at all, partly for rest and recreation, it was said, but also to show the country who its rulers now were.

For a few days in Oxford, I made progress with my fourth Cleopatra. It was easy then. My simple idea was that I should write down what I knew, shape it into a neat narrative, improving on Elizabeth Taylor, meeting some of the ambitions of V for a more modern, feminist, sixties style – and have a great success.

Thus, by that account, in May and June of 47 BC Cleopatra could be pregnant and cruising peacefully down the Nile, or at least as peacefully as any cruise could be within an armed flotilla of river boats, between soldiers marching along the banks and priests waiting to worship their goddess queen at every stop. For Caesar this was a chance to see for the first time what, even 2000 years ago, were tourist sites, the ancient temples made of columns ten times the size of any in Rome or Greece, the towns older than Troy and the new temples and towns built by the Ptolemies in the style of the old. For Cleopatra it was an opportunity to show off the miles of cornfields that stretched out on either side, the food which, whether eaten or merely taxed, was life for foreign armies.

There was a complete break from Roman politics. There were tame crocodiles to feed and wild ones to avoid but there were no letters, nothing from Caesar's expectant friends, no reports of the surviving followers of Pompey, unchastened by the death of their leader, who were gathering in Tunisia to continue the war. Caesar had appointed his young friend Mark Antony to be his representative in Rome until he returned. There was no fixed time for that return.

In a month's slow river travel the Egyptian barges had reached the edge of their civilisation and were heading deeper into Africa. Either because of Caesar's sudden impatience for politics, or the impending birth of Cleopatra's child, or the nervousness of their accompanying troops, the great cedar-and-ivory ships turned and slowly returned to Alexandria. When they arrived, there had been pleasing progress in the construction of the massive temple that would be called the Caesareum, the columns and colonnades on what is now the site of the Metropole Hotel.

8.1.11

Pharos

Maurice was at first barely tolerant of my efforts. The project was in every way much too dull. Here we were, far from Rothmans and Brentwood, surrounded by living characters, bearded aristocrats, pallid masters of pin-ball machines, beautiful boys in dresses, glossy women who wanted us to join the Italian Society. And there was I, struggling with the identity of the dead.

A week later, just as decisively, and just as characteristically, he changed his mind. My Cleopatra was suddenly the key to his future. We sat together at the window end of our high room overlooking the dead lime trees and he set out his plan. In the yellow spotlight of a dim lamp and a sherry decanter, he told me that he had an idea. It was going to be a 'big idea'. Cleopatra and her Romans were, in every important respect, the same, the same person, the same thing, the same 'entity'. This was what I had not yet understood.

We stared at each other. We each tried to outstare the other. It was like a return to the playground, to the schoolboy who had always been there at the edges of running track and rugby field, and whose fate in the dormitories of Brentwood had so worried V. He was still smooth-faced, short-haired and mushroom-cheeked while I (as I liked to think) had moved on to a much hairier, sixties self. On that damp autumn night, he was dressed in velvet, a casual impersonation of a fop, fashionable in the way that was beginning to be possible by careful shopping at Marks & Spencer. My own style was that of suburban protest, a Fair Isle sweater, knitted by my mother from a photograph of Paul McCartney, beneath a pony-skin coat, newly purchased in Chelmsford market, which stood stiffly like an Indian tent when it was not covering my back.

We had already discovered that we barely knew each other. Maurice to me was little more than a memory of jokes and parties and my mother's aspirations that we be better friends. He was a dimly recalled comic turn on the Brentwood stage, a ghostly wing three-quarter who occasionally stood against me on a fog-shrouded field while our parents took colour slides of third-team matches.

When I had lived at the centre of the red clay estate, he had lived beyond its borders. His father was a bank manager not a plane-spotter, his sister had ridden her own ponies and their impossibly large house had parquet flooring – more like a lake than a floor, an icy lake, acres and acres of tempting polished wood. At birthday parties we could carefully slide on tasselled cushions around silver photo-frames and slender-legged cabinets of china.

On the wooden lake floor we could float, or sail, or fly, or be whatever was in our minds. There were games where all the players had labels on their backs, Robin, Hood, Maid, Marian, Miss, Leake, Bill, Ben. The losers were those last to find their partners. Maurice wanted to win. He wanted to be witty and sophisticated and, inasmuch as a child can be either, he was often both. His parents had taken me with him once to the smartest, emptiest beaches of the North Sea, to a London theatre and a restaurant, to the Planetarium and its magic dome of stars.

After we arrived together in Brentwood in the same junior school winter of 1962, his life was spent in ice-bound boarding houses while mine passed by on buses so cold that the cigarette smoke froze. He soon disappeared still further behind the barriers and distinctions of life at that time. While I was a runner, he was an actor, a specialist in drunken porters and butlers. He was a historian not a classicist, and his only connection to our classics classes had been his peculiar antipathy to Frog, whose expertise in vivisection and dying gladiators most of us were able to ignore.

Our knowledge of each other was almost wholly an illusion. Our friendship was still in the future. But at Trinity some of the larger sets of rooms had to be shared. Two newcomers from the same school seemed, to the adjudicating authorities, to be the ideal people to share them. Frog's Oxford application, we learnt with pleasure, had been rejected.

Maurice, I soon learnt, had a very specific aim in uniting the characters of Caesar, Antony and Cleopatra. He wanted to be all these characters himself, to play them all in the chief theatrical event of the first term, the inter-college competition for short plays known as Cuppers. This was the casting session for the bigger university productions in which he hoped to play a part.

On his first day in Oxford he had met a new friend, not a student but a trainee director at the New Theatre down by the station. This boy was a fanatic for the then fashionable American manipulator of Shakespeare, Charles Marowitz. The *Marowitz Hamlet*, Maurice began to argue, was 'a masterpiece of compression, comprehension, rhythmic bonding', everything that was good. Could we not produce some sort of equivalent *Cleopatra*, cutting and combining whatever scenes would make the audience's 'heart beat as one with the player's' or, if I had not quite taken his meaning, give him the biggest opportunity to make an impression? Only a single scene was necessary, in which the three characters would have an inner dialogue, revealing their essential single identity. I would write it. He would be it. Triumph would follow.

At a time when life seemed compressed as never before and when cultural shocks came every day, the request did not seem as ridiculous as it does now. Surely an ensemble could become a single being and a single being could stand for everything that the ensemble once was? Why not? Amusing? Maurice liked to amuse but not this time. He looked disdainfully at the afro-curls of my hair above the astrakhan dust of my coat. He was horribly serious as only a soft-jacketed student with ambition and a big cravat can be.

I looked at him, and out across the long lawn to the college gates that were to be reopened only when a Stuart was restored to the English throne. He looked at me, and down to the parts of the golden-stoned quadrangle that Sir Christopher Wren had built, and sideways to those that he had not. He stared hard and straight into my eyes. We would need the text in a week.

It did not seem a good idea to make him angry. We were, perforce but not reluctantly, at the beginning of another bit of life together. I was the one who knew about Cleopatra. What part of the story did he want? He stamped impatiently, already well into the sherry-hour. It was easiest to describe the possibilities through the scenes of the film. He knew of other versions too but Elizabeth Taylor and William Shakespeare were already slightly Marowitzed in his mind.

To clear our heads before dinner he said that we should climb up to the top of the clock tower, a place where I had not yet been. Nor had I seen anyone else there. It was out of bounds, he said, but he knew the hours when it was unlocked. A charming young porter had told him. We strode out past the office of the college doctor and the room where monks had once brewed Holy Trinity beer. After a tricky climb through a black door, a corridor of black gowns and a bare winding staircase, we emerged into the evening air, he exultant, I merely nervous, among stone statues of Theology, Astronomy, Geometry and Medicine, the college gods surveying circles of sickly sodium light.

Maurice stood up as though we were on school parade. He gently kicked the larger of the two bells and scanned the lawns and trees. Then he began whispering into the sky. He mouthed lists of names – butterflies, birds, underground stations, film actors. After each Cabbage White, Sparrow Hawk, Golders Green or Olivier, he clapped his hand twice, crack, crack, before moving on to the next one in his mind, Red Admiral, Robin, Leicester Square, Harvey.

The whispers quickly became shouts. I had watched Maurice play this game before, sitting round in circles in our room, chanting lists, clapping hands until someone in the ring failed to remember a fresh bird or train station and became a loser. I had also played it myself, very badly, not realising how much rehearsal took place among the winners. Maurice often won. High in the tower he looked as confident as I had ever seen him, like a fifth stone statue, Pleasure perhaps or Celebrity. He gave the mossy face of Medicine a kiss and shouted out more names towards the street.

No one looked up. One Oxford rule which we had quickly learnt was that it was fine to make outrageous displays but not fine to fuss over the displays of others. In homage to *Brideshead Revisited* it was not uncommon for inebriated aesthetes to declaim from high places, sometimes from *The Waste Land*, sometimes from symbolist masterpieces of their own. This was only a little different from that: Names of . . . Clap! Clap! Railway Stations! Clap! Clap! Waterloo! Clap! Clap!

Westerham! Clap! Clap! Warley East! Clap! Clap! These were lists paraded as a kind of art, all very Alexandrian in its own way.

After a few minutes Maurice sat down at the feet of Astronomy and grunted in half-formed sentences as though still playing one of his drunken butlers on the Brentwood stage. He was flying. He had new views. The 'dreaming spires' were an idea for outsiders, those who were stuck down on the ground and barely more than tourists. He was not on the ground any more. He was up high. Cleopatra was going to be the next step higher. Could I just remind him of the story again, the version that everyone would know?

In 48 BC, we gently recalled, Julius Caesar has just defeated Pompey's armies at the battle of Pharsalus while Pompey himself, as Canidius reports when the film begins, has escaped to Alexandria. I made the dumb messenger's beard sign to remind him of the scene. He made the same sign back. This became a code between us: it meant that Cleopatra was on our minds.

Why were they fighting? Maurice seemed genuinely to want to know the answer. The film had not been very clear.

Pride, I said. That was the main reason. He seemed to sober up. He looked surprised and pleased.

The civil war did not have to happen, I added in an effort of profundity. Two proud men made political miscalculations. Pompey made a military miscalculation too. Then Caesar made a mistake. Then Mark Antony did. Just one fuck-up after another, or history as it is sometimes called.

Maurice took a notebook from his velvet pocket and started to write what looked like a shopping list.

'So for all of them life was good as long as it lasted?'

'Yes, you could say that,' I replied cautiously.

'Then what is the main difference between Julius Caesar and Mark Antony? What will be the hardest part of bringing them together?'

'Antony enjoyed his drink,' I said. 'Caesar did not.'

I paused, and leant back heavily against Theology.

'In fact, Antony was not even ashamed of his reputation as a drunk. He revelled in it.'

'Excellent,' said Maurice. 'Let's have more Antony then.'

The clock began chiming seven o'clock. We covered our ears. Maurice would need his text in a week – a one-entity show, short, complete and comprehensive – so that rehearsals could begin.

I have been at Pharos for three hours, remembering Oxford among the fishermen, the fairground roundabouts and the market stalls. Mahmoud said he would meet me for 'a late breakfast by the crocodile'.

What crocodile? The Nile used to be famous for crocodile gods. Not now. Monotheism stopped the gods and the Aswan Dam stopped the crocs. There is no adult specimen in this dusty aquarium beside

the site of the ancient lighthouse, only a single fifteen-inch baby, with glowing slit-eyes, nose upturned and tiny toes outspread, the sole representative of the species.

The creature's modest tank is crowded, however, by admirers. This is a marine theatre where rival attractions are few. Every young visitor has a notebook. Each one is writing short words in Arabic, one above the other. Maybe these are sentences but I do not think so. They are lists of things they have seen, long lines of water creatures or things they want to buy. In the whole history of writing are there more lists than sentences? Probably.

Cleopatra, for all the scholars at her command, had no more idea of the origins of the Greek language than for two thousand years after her did we. Only in the early 1950s did an English architect called Michael Ventris decipher the language of some baked clay tablets found in the oldest towns of Greece, relics of the heroic age from the places where Homer's heroes were remembered – and where some of them may have lived.

These writings were not in the letters that we now know as Greek but they were in a language that was suddenly revealed as the most ancient of ancient Greek. Scholars hoped that we might soon possess the earliest Greek poems, or find other new clues to the birth of literature. But there was no poetry on the Linear B tablets. There were names scratched in the clay but they were random names, lists that had accidentally been burnt hard by fires, lists of food and farm equipment, livestock and taxes, animals, birds and fishes.

Mahmoud must have meant a very late breakfast. He has still not yet arrived. There is a growing lunchtime throng here now, a bazaar of wood-carvers, pebble-painters and aquarium-goers where the

Ptolemies built their lighthouse. But no one interferes with me – and my companion will be here in his own time.

Some of the greatest treasures of Alexandria's library were also lists of names. They were catalogues of characters from Hesiod and Homer, the oldest and wisest of the Greek poets, carefully managed by men such as Didymus Chalcenterus, master of the scrolls in Cleopatra's reign. Hesiod's words were the older. In his *Theogony* he had written on the origins of the Gods, from Chaos to Zeus, incantating Night, Air, Day, Sky, Mountains, Sea, Memory, Oceanus, Coeus, Crios, Theia, Rhea. Hesiod knew of the Nile – and of fifty water nymphs, Eukrante, Amphitrite and Sao, Eunice of the rosy arms, laughter-loving Glaukonome.

There was a Trinity tutor who used to make us chant these names, a man called Raven, one of those peculiarly valuable teachers who impart little knowledge. Instead he made us listen to lists – outside, on the summer lawns, when I was close to sleep but awake in ways I did not then quite understand

Homer's lists were of the ships that sailed to Troy, their captains and their countries, Boeotians, Minyans, Phoceans, Locrians, Athenians. In Alexandria's library the servants of the Ptolemies loved these ancient catalogues that they could command for their own new catalogues, explaining, expanding, putting words to things, pinning the world and words together, bickering about which came first. Priests might chant directly to the gods. Scholars had no less a role in divining the origins of sacred texts. Priests were falling behind; practical reason was rising.

Homer's *Odyssey* has a single scene set in Pharos itself. That was important. Everything in Homer had a message from the Greek past to the Greek future. In the epics of how the ships and captains of the *Iliad* came home from Troy, this piece of land existed for the first time beyond itself. It became part of history.

Mahmoud dislikes nostalgia. But I am going to ask him to think back beyond sentiment to the absolute beginning, to a city functionary in Cleopatra's Alexandria (any one will do) who is reading about Pharos in the *Odyssey*. This city, as everyone has always known, was founded by Alexander the Great and built by the Ptolemies. But in Homer there was a legitimacy much greater than that.

Pharos's first named inhabitant was a god of the sea, a shape-shifting god called Proteus who kept a flock of seals on the beach. In the fourth book of the poem Proteus meets two of the great names of Greece, Helen whose abduction sparked the Trojan War and Menelaus, who lost her and won her back. When this part of the *Odyssey* begins, Proteus has captured Helen and her husband Menelaus on their way home and has himself to be captured before he will let them leave.

This is a strange Homeric scene set in the borders between sleeping and waking, uppers and downers, sea and land, man and sea creature. Menelaus's men want to get out of Pharos. But the winds are against them and they are starving.

A nymph tells them that they have only one chance. They must hide their human bodies under sealskins, mingle with the sleeping sea mammals and seize Proteus before he wakes from his afternoon nap. Despite the sea god's wriggling transformation into lion, snake and river, they must wrestle him to the ground, grip him hard until he tells them what they need to know. He has to prophesy the fates of their friends and put the gods of the winds on their side.

This has never been an important part of Homer's work. Menelaus's journey is a sideshow in a great epic poem. It is a minor odyssey within the major one, an interrogation of an aged prophet that Odysseus himself will later repeat when, much more dramatically, he meets his dead friends from Troy in the underworld. Odysseus learns in Hades how he will die. Menelaus learns his own fate at Pharos. But for most readers this was – and is – a paler part of the *Odyssey* in every way, as Alexandria's scholars could plainly see.

Perhaps it was by a lesser writer, a younger Homer. Perhaps the story of wriggling, wrestling Proteus and the men disguised as seals was included in the larger epic to prepare the audience for the more powerful story to come. Yet a sideshow is sometimes more satisfying than the show itself. For a librarian at Alexandria this episode had to be one of the great episodes. It set Pharos island in the fixed history of the world, the history that Didymus and his fellow cataloguers here had only slowly, in the reign of Cleopatra, begun to disentangle from myth.

Mahmoud eventually does arrive, not by the baby crocodile but at a different place, the tanks of tiny-bodied blue crabs. He seems troubled and not at all threatening today. He has lost his bureaucratic poise. Today I am the calm one, he the one who looks as though he is going to be sick.

He stares at the sky. Heavy rains and storm winds are coming, he says. There might be lightning and Pharos is dangerous when there is lightning. A sealskin, he says, used to be a good protector. Pharos was once famous for its seals. The greatest emperors used to keep sealskins for good luck. Socratis's mad mother has a sealskin. But no one else has one any more.

He is not in the mood to discuss Pharos in history any further. He

pushes me out towards the causeway, leading me away past the ped-
lars, past the holidaying men keen for anything to quieten their
children and the women listening intently to the conch shells to hear
if the sound is the same as the sound of the sea.

Church of St Mark and St Peter

This is the site of the New Year bombing. The blood on the blasted
pavements has been washed away. The dead have been removed for
reconstruction and identification. Even the carcasses of the cars are
gone. It is raining lightly. There is a smell of wet paint and a quiet in
the afternoon that is rare in this city. Mahmoud was worried at first
about bringing me from Pharos to the bomb site, torn, I think,
between a simultaneous need to defend his optimism about the city's
safety and to ensure that I genuinely was safe here. It feels fine. There
is an almost empty cafe, an almost silent street, and I will be content
here until evening – probably till tomorrow too.

I said to Mahmoud that I would see him later, after I had moved
on with Cleopatra's story, past the birth of her son, past Caesar's
death and its deadly aftermath. He was not quite satisfied. Would I
have wanted to be at the Two Saints church if there had not been a
bombing? I said I would. The St Peter to whom the church is dedi-
cated was a particularly significant St Peter, not the 'rock' on whom
Christ said he would build his church but a Christian martyr from
Egypt.

Alexandria had long been a dangerous place for Christians, I added.
Mahmoud waved that I should be quiet. This was not the moment for
putting martyrdom in proportion or for joking. Was I making an

English joke? He was not sure. I should stop anyway. And was it wise that I should sit here writing about Julius Caesar? It was much better not to write about dictators who met violent ends. Socratis was right about the agitation of the police. I might easily be misunderstood.

Mahmoud looked suspiciously at the sheets of plain white paper with their smudged carbon-copied type from forty years ago. He was sorry he had been late this morning. He had had to go to the doctor. He had eaten last night in front of an open window and something had upset his stomach.

Four days after giving me his instructions, Maurice was anxious about how his play was 'coming on'. He gave the words a menacing twist. He was no easier to please than V had been. Both of my school friends knew what they wanted from a Cleopatra story that neither of them wanted to write. I did not know what I wanted from the story even though I wanted to write it. Thanks to Professor Rame, Mr G, Mr W, V and now Maurice, I was strongly committed. I was bound fast by separate links from the past that had formed a chain.

I took a sip of sherry from a glass by our window seat and described to him how, soon after the end of her cruise with Caesar, Cleopatra was in sole charge of Egypt – and a mother for the first time, of a son she called Ptolemy Caesarion. Maurice took a gulp from his own larger glass and heard how Caesar himself had not played the devoted father for long, if at all. He had immediately left to fight unfinished wars against other Eastern kings and other supporters of Pompey. Cleopatra's next decision, or his, would be whether, where and when the two might meet again.

Caesar's priority was in the furthest western territory in Mediterranean Africa, Mauretania, modern Morocco, whose king was enthusiastically welcoming the survivors of Pharsalus. Cleopatra's main concern was domestic diplomacy, revenue-raising, river-management, the survival of her child, the normal duties of a ruling Ptolemy.

'Fine', said Maurice, puffing himself somewhat haughtily in our window seat as though he were already playing all his chosen characters, all of them already combined, none of them lacking in haughtiness. So Cleopatra and Caesar are separated. That is a good start. Then they are going to come together. That will be perfect.

And then he sighed. He wanted to get back to the texts, his texts, his parts. When would we start picking lines from Shakespeare? We had been talking too much about Elizabeth Taylor. The Cuppers judges were not going to be impressed, or find anything very Marowitzian, in a one-man version of a movie. We had somehow to get beyond that. There were the two big plays, *Antony and Cleopatra* itself and *Julius Caesar*. How should we start? He had them both already. He pulled out two white paperbacks and a page of scribbled notes.

In a sense, he said portentously, these were Parts One and Two of the same play; Cleopatra is a living presence but not a character in *Julius Caesar*; Julius Caesar is a dead presence but not a character in *Antony and Cleopatra*. He slumped slightly after this. The clock in the tower struck seven. Dinner was in fifteen minutes. Could we just get ahead a bit?

I was irritated. But that was nothing new. Ours was a story of two people who had long irritated each other. I also liked the idea of writing this play, of being a playwright. I was in a hurry. We were both in a hurry. An idea of a play made from words already written by someone else appealed to me even more than to him, nothing to be proud of but true. So yes, I said. We could get ahead. But he would have to concentrate – and keep away from the decanter till we had finished.

Two years after the Nile cruise and the birth of her son, Cleopatra was back in Rome. As a child she and her father had been Pompey's guests, reliant upon him for their royalty and their lives. As an adult, she was now the royal mistress of Pompey's conqueror, installed in Caesar's garden palace in the area known as 'the other side of the Tiber'. Her new husband and one surviving brother, Ptolemy XIV, was with her too, a safer as well as more respectable option than leaving any senior family member at home.

In February of 44 BC Caesar accepted the office of dictator for the fourth time. On the first occasion, five years earlier, he had taken the honour for eleven days, the second time for a year, the third for ten years and now his one-man rule was to last the rest of his life. He had already celebrated four of the greatest triumphs that Romans had ever seen, one of them over Egypt, a parade graced by a model of the Pharos, a statue of the Nile and by Arsinoe in chains. Afterwards, because of the sympathy shown to Cleopatra's sister by the Roman crowd, she was handed to the priests of Ephesus for a decorous exile instead of being strangled.

Soon afterwards Caesar began marshalling forces for the campaign that he hoped would earn him the greatest triumph of all, a new eastern assault on the Persians that would open the way to India and finally match the achievements of Alexander the Great. Cleopatra was with him while he did so, observing the military costs that her wealth would help to bear. She may have made a brief return trip to Alexandria to ensure that all was well. She was close by, but not immediately beside him, when he went to the senate for the last time on the Ides of March.

An hour later, after Trinity dinner, Maurice stretched again for the decanter, the only object that offered any link between the minor-middle-class life we had abandoned and the decadence to which we were beginning to aspire. He was suddenly renewed, not quite shouting as he had among the stone college statues but almost as rhythmic and insistent.

He strode around the room as though it were more cage than stage. The truth would come from a random rearrangement of words, a 'mobile metaphor'. First, I should forget the facts. Secondly, I should forget the factual story. Thirdly, there was no need for any story. We needed to take elements from both the plays over the whole span of time, but we should be surprising, novel, avoiding purple-sailed barges and 'et tu Brute' and asps and all the bits that anyone might recognise.

We should reconfigure the truth from all the parts that no one usually noticed, that the audience would hardly know, beginning early in the story, yes, when she was a presence not a character (that was perfect: I should not forget that point) and then we would reconnect the hidden nerves and tissues to make a being that was instantly recognisable and wholly new. Fine, I said nervously and for the third time. I would think about what he had said.

It seemed best that we come back to the subject a few days later. Oxford study was already proving harder than I had hoped. I had a guilty secret, an ability in my last years at school to see a text when it was no longer there, not just a good memory but a photographic memory, a skill I barely recognised as unusual until I lost it. Neither the ability to memorise nor my previously remembered texts survived my eighteenth birthday – and when they faded there was the awkward task of maintaining such intellectual reputation as they had earned me.

There were also other problems. I wanted other women than Cleopatra, ideally a girlfriend, living women. There were different opportunities for writing too. Despite missing the *Daily Telegraph* prize for film criticism (or for my similarly V-inspired rock review of Jimi Hendrix), I had won in the less competitive jazz category. It had brought me an expensive lunch at the top of the newly opened Post Office Tower and as many records as I could play. There was much to be said for journalism. I was wondering whether I could do more.

The editor of the university newspaper was from Trinity and had already suggested that I join him, in the first instance, in the college rugby team and, after that, on the Cherwell 'feature' pages. Or would student politics be a better course, some potent thoughts on miners' strikes and the prospects of Edward Heath becoming Prime Minister? Possibly. Probably not.

9.I.II

Rue de Musee

Museum Street has one cafe that is open and no museum. Socratis began today by sticking keenly to his role as learned guide. I asked him if there was anything on show in Alexandria about two of the Ptolemies' finest public servants, Herophilus and Erasistratus, doctors who used to cut open living criminals in attempts to find out how the organs of the body fitted together. He said he did not know – but would find out fast.

He seemed anxious. I told him not to worry. Not much was known by anyone about the opening-up of pregnant women to discover whether girls took the same time to grow as boys – except that it is said to have happened here. Knowledge of humans, knowledge of Homer: there were so many things that nature had hidden and that librarians, without distinction between the arts and the sciences, might be encouraged to discover.

This could never be a discussion for Mahmoud, who dislikes the suggestion that anything morally uncomfortable, unpleasant, still less evil, has ever happened here. But Mahmoud did not join us today. Maybe we will see him later.

Socratis was not afraid of the awkward question but the answer, he said, would be in the museum of antiquities which was closed on a Sunday. In fact, for some time it had been closed every day. He knew a man in the next street who might help. He might even open the back door. He would return with him soon. Was I happy to wait? My second cup of coffee has just appeared – and a cake with red eyes.

A few days after Maurice had given me my instructions Geoff the Editor said I should meet him in the back bar of the King's Arms before lunch, eleven o'clock. This was an opportunity to escape from classics and Cleopatra for a while. He promised to introduce me to a great 'character'. He then wanted me to write about this character. Our university newspaper, he said, was a mass of grey type about grey institutions. Oxford was a grand hotel of the brilliant and bizarre. He wanted to bring some of the guests to life.

I was particularly happy to construct a living Oxford character if I could. Geoff did not know it but, by contrast, my theatrical Cleopatra had suddenly to be deconstructed. She (and he and they) had to be a meta-character, another of Maurice's mad theatrical requirements passed on from his mad Marowitzian friend. I did not want to admit that I had increasingly little idea what he wanted. And he was increasingly away from our rooms, for nights as well as days, and unavailable to ask.

Thus a traditional newspaper project was an attraction in itself. Writing about an Oxford character was something I might be able to do by myself. Geoff said that he would have a pint of Special and that I should 'get one in' for him to save time when he arrived. It was odd, I thought, to order a drink in advance like that: but Geoff the Editor was fashionable, blond, famous in his way and surely knew what were the right things to do.

The hour before midday seemed a little early for drinking. The front rooms of the large white pub which looked out onto Broad Street and the Bodleian Library were empty. Only in the back, a brown-painted box restricted to men, was there a fresh, flowing fug of Navy Cut and whisky. In 1969 this was a place of refuge, a room of rest for those who wished that the sixties had never happened, for dons in cream-creased jackets and for students who wanted to meet them, a place of strict rules of behaviour.

Buying two pints for one person seemed just within these back-bar rules. Talking to the large, lone man in a light brown suit beside me was probably not. I sat and waited. So did he.

Geoff the Editor's beer remained untouched. As my own glass emptied, the full glass became cloudily warmed. I felt awkward and exposed, the more so when my lone companion seemed suddenly to have company of his own. There was a sudden bubbling of words. I could not see who was speaking or hear precisely what he said.

The big man's replies were a little clearer but not much. The first distinguishable word was 'gooseberry'. After that the speaker's subject appeared to be some sort of a plague – and what had caused it. This plague, I learnt (for I had nothing else to do and nowhere else to listen or look), was passed from person to person, produced high fevers, rashes on the skin, rotting limbs and frequent fatality. Was it typhoid or smallpox or scarlet fever or bubonic plague? How could we tell?

The big man briefly paused, as though waiting for a response that he already knew. Smallpox was a possibility, he said, but Thucydides mentions no pockmarks among survivors.

Bubonic plague borne by rats? A reasonable idea if Athens during the Peloponnesian War were to have had any rats. But there was not even a word for rat in Greek, unless a rat and a mouse were judged the same.

Measles? Measles did not exist when Athens was at war with Sparta.

It needed bigger cities than any in the Greek world, bigger than any until the building of Alexandria. Perhaps the identity of the plague that so weakened Athens in its war was now unknowable, an ancient disease that had itself died. Or maybe Thucydides was not as good a witness as we think. Or diseases were defined then in totally different ways.

This was a new kind of embarrassment for me. I was in the right place at the right time with the right drinks. But nothing else was right. These were the weeks when I was relearning everything about how to behave. I was baffled, a bit red-faced. Maurice would probably be in soon. I did not want to see him. He was driving me mad. But his presence would be better than no one's – and he would have quickly disposed of the warming beer. I could wait for him maybe in the front bar where there were students, women students.

There was a pause and a noise of slurping. The speaker turned around and began to speak to me, his previous companion and to two other men who were quietly drinking through the time.

If birds eat diseased bodies, he asked, do the birds die too? Thucydides says that birds did die in Athens. But had any birds ever died from plague? If so, what sort of plague?

Any man, he said in what was now almost a shout, might go mad before he solved this problem – and that was just one problem of cause and effect in history, even in an area, that of medicine, in which we knew that effects do genuinely have causes.

The speaker took a last sip of his beer, and a shallow breath that an anxious wife might have worried was his last, and went on smoothly as though all these arguments, like all his actions, were part of a long and practised pattern. Now what were you about to say?

This was my first introduction to James Holladay, ancient history teacher extraordinary, the next figure in my history of Cleopatra, without whom it would not have lived this long. He asked what I was doing. I said I was waiting for Geoff the Editor. That was a coincidence, he said, slightly wincing at the word as though it were intellectually suspect. He too was waiting for him.

So this was my Oxford character, the one that I would soon be charged with bringing to life. That should not be hard. Even in fragments he was a very vivid thing. I relaxed. I wondered whether this might even be a good time to mention my troubled Cleopatra. But once we were silent, the back bar was as quiet as cloud and the moment passed.

Socratis's driver has arrived at the museum. He is in camouflage fatigues, concentrating hard on the written message from his boss that there is no museum in Alexandria with exhibits about experiments on criminals. The museum on this street is closed. The back door is closed as well as the front. He seems sad about this – and promises that his master will be back himself soon.

James Holladay was a useful man for me to meet. He knew about the wars of Caesar and Cleopatra. He knew as much as there is to know about how Romans reacted to the assassination of Caesar, how Cleopatra reacted, what seemed immediately most likely to happen. That was his job. He was Trinity's ancient history tutor.

His great passion, however, was not for the turmoil of 44 BC but for an earlier war four centuries before, the Peloponnesian War that had not only cost Athens its supremacy but softened all Greece for its subjugation by Alexander the Great. His particular interest was the mystery plague, described in detail by Thucydides, that had killed thousands of Athenians at the start of that conflict, destroying, inspiring, causing subsequent events. How much it destroyed, inspired and caused was one of the great questions from the war that Thucydides had made the first war of true history.

James Holladay was much less interested in Cleopatra's Alexandria. The Egyptian capital, he gestured dismissively with a swipe of his hand, had suffered briefly from mere bubonic plague. Cleopatra herself, he said, was an even lesser thing to study than her city, not an epidemic killer, merely a single human being. Her life had lacked the attention of any serious ancient historian, a significant lack since historians who had lived in the ancient world were the only real subject for an ancient historian of our own time.

This plague of Athens existed no longer, he concluded, pointing a fleshy finger. He was ever more confident of that. It no longer plagued anyone. It had gone. That in itself was a useful lesson for us all. It was not the only thing, the only cause, the only fact from the ancient world that had gone. We were all of us much too keen to connect the past to the present. We also pretended that we knew too much.

He asked some probing questions. I tried my best to look intelligent even if I could not give him answers. Why did I think that Caesar and Cleopatra had had a child called Caesarion, or indeed any child? When do we first hear about this boy? Only after Caesar is dead.

Did Strabo (had I read Strabo?) ever mention him? One of Caesar's friends wrote a whole book to deny Caesarion's Roman paternity. Was he telling the truth or protesting too much? What did I think of 'the Continuators'? I must have looked inescapably blank.

How did I evaluate the 'Continuators' of Caesar's own books once Caesar had been killed? There is no mention of Caesarion by them either. The four years before Caesar's death are some of the best

reported in all ancient history. But had Cleopatra even had an affair with Caesar? No one says so at the time.

I badly wanted Geoff the Editor to arrive now – or Maurice to arrive, or almost anyone. This conversation was not going well. The idea of turning this man into a newspaper article seemed impossible. The flow of scepticism became a flood. Cleopatra was once again a dream. Mark Antony's was the story I should write, the only story that a historian could write about at all.

He pointed a finger past the frosted glass screen towards the front bar which was now beginning to fill.

'Just think about that young man there. You know nothing about Cleopatra. You know nothing about him either. Many people think that they know him but they do not. The present and the past are often not so very different in that respect.'

I nodded glumly without seeing precisely whom he meant.

There was a boy on the other side, in front of the window with the view of the library, dressed in velvet like a vole. 'Homosexual. No harm in that. There it is. Lots of people seem fascinated by him. Maybe you all are. He works at the theatre and likes to chop up

Shakespeare.' The old don took another sip of beer and a longer breath.

There was a stir by the door to the street. Two new arrivals brought champagne which they had purchased elsewhere, most certainly a breach of King's Arms' rules. The velvet hero of this hour – precisely midday on 20 October 1969 I can say, since I have the note here in my pocket now – said nothing as the wine was poured. Everyone else was already saying more than enough.

Maurice came in last. The theatre boy ignored him in the way that only those do who are lovers, who have recently quarrelled, or are still quarrelling. Words of shouted abuse came in waves – most of them against the failures of imagination showed by others, by fellow actors, company managements, stupid students. His admiring audience seemed gradually to have heard enough. Soon Maurice too joined the bored majority and the boy was alone.

James Holladay also lost interest in the scene. 'I've got a friend who thinks that Caesar and Cleopatra were essentially the same person,' I said, thinking that something more original might now be risked and that the next donnish rebuttal could hardly be more deflating than the ones that had come before.

'Hang onto him. He might be onto something. They were both great bureaucrats. That is sure. Bureaucratic power was always essential. Never forget that. Look at the men in the middle ranks. Remember their names: Hirtius, Plancus, Dellius, Canidius. Study them closely. Don't give up when the going gets tough. *Nil desperandum*, as Horace says. Read the poem in which he says it.

'If you have to choose one man, choose Lucius Munatius Plancus. You will soon find out why. Forget the biggest names. Leave them to those who write for money or for children. Ignore the nameless masses. Leave those to Marxists. Just watch the office men, the trimmers, the men who were always watching the events most carefully themselves. Watch Plancus most of all.

'Remember how Caesar himself was a bit of an office-man, dictating two letters at once to different secretaries while all three of them were on horseback. Cleopatra had the world's first great bureaucracy at her command – and one of the few things that we do know about her is that she knew how to use it. So imagine them both at each end of a partner's desk, passing memos.'

It would have been churlish of me to say that this bureaucratic blend of anonymity was not what Maurice had in mind for his Cuppers performance. In any case, the historian had already 'talked shop' quite enough. He began to speak and drink more quickly, on subjects that were wholly different – not all of them easily understood – the loss of corkage fees for his friend the King's Arms' landlord, Vietnam, the Normandy landings, gooseberries again and whether the food at Trinity could any longer be held superior to that at neighbouring colleges.

In a minute he had skipped out, with a surprising and sprightly skip, and was on the other side of the bar, a journey of five yards and as many decades, in a place of light and other sexes, buying a half-of-bitter for a round woman, about half his size in every dimension, who through their sharing of smiles and small movements could only be his wife.

Next to them was a curtain of posters that hung from drawing pins, so many posters, so few pins, and in front of that, beside his pint of Special, stood Geoff the Editor with a copy of Cherwell in his hand, speaking inaudibly to the Holladays and waving that I should come out to meet them.

*

Late that night, after a dinner in college and a double emptying of the sherry decanter we talked again about our play. Maurice's mood was subdued. It seemed that, without even showing him any words, I had already failed several tests. First, my attitude: my heart had not been in the project from the start. Secondly, my subject: I was a classicist and that meant that my subject, any ancient subject, was a barrier between me and my emotions. I read Latin and Greek because English was too much for me. Thirdly, my past: I had always been the one who wept when the teachers read Dickens at school. I had adopted Cleopatra because I could keep her at a distance. I could control. I could edit, I could desiccate. That was what classicists did.

Marowitz, by contrast, was only for the most intimate of lovers or the bitterest of enemies. I would not possibly be able to match the master. Our project would be a disaster. Did I know that the New Theatre, Oxford, had just fired a major interpreter of Marowitzian Shakespeare in favour of some jerk who did pantomime? There had been a miserable few drinks to say goodbye in the King's Arms. Perhaps he had seen me there. Perhaps he had not. Everything was wrong. Everything had to change. He had other options. A Cuppers actor could play many parts and he was going out to find them. The Trinity Players would have to find something else too.

One week later, that is what we did, choosing some scenes from a Greek comedy, *The Frogs*, about a trip into the afterlife to wake up the dead and bring the best playwright back to earth. Maurice had particularly liked the name because it reminded him of our Frog from school, the sinister obsessive who was somewhere in the suburbs retaking his A levels.

There was an ideal leading part for Maurice himself, the young playwright Euripides, a vain, radical writer keen to deconstruct the assumptions of the past. Suddenly it seemed much easier to 'play' an artist than to try to 'be' one. Maurice, we agreed, would be perfect for Euripides.

Sadly, there would have to be rival actors too. Maurice could not now play all the parts. He would need to compete for attention from the judges. But then nothing was perfect. There was even a line in *The Frogs* that showed Euripides as the genuine author of Mr W's *Rhesus*. My tutors might approve. That was beginning to be important.

Two weeks later, on the splintering wooden stage in the Cuppers hall, we produced our thirty-minute production of *The Frogs*. There was a clinging white gown for Maurice, less attractive costumes for the other main actors, diaphanous dresses for the non-speaking women and less praise from the judges than Maurice had hoped for.

10.1.11

St Mark's Cathedral

St Mark's is protected by armed police as though it were the top target for future bombs. There is a machine gun for every black iron railing. This grey-grassed garden of Alexandria's Coptic cathedral, its entrance concealed between a confectioner and a chemist, is even more silent than the street in front of the Two Saints. The calm is like the inside of an automaton, mechanical, purposeful, enclosed.

There are men inside in small groups, noiseless like chess pieces on their own fixed squares. There is a seriousness without sound in these footpaths of parliament. The only trouble comes from the resident mendicant, with three dogs and no legs, who rejects my Egyptian currency with a scream of 'No good! Dollars! Dollars!'

Mahmoud says she is an actress. All the beggars are actors. She has legs we cannot see. Her dogs deter the curious and her crutches are like wings. They are all her props. Alexandria has always been a great theatre city. Perhaps I should like to visit the Opera House. It is very peaceful there too. Or he could find me a restaurant. He had no time to join me but it was unhealthy for anyone to write so much and eat so little. Was I happy to be left to continue my Cleopatra story with the actress of St Mark's? He would come back later and take me to lunch.

Even after the loss of his Marowitzian muse Maurice was prepared to give Cleopatra one last theatrical chance. He discovered that Trinity

College owned a unique account of her court, the bequest of a wealthy military family from the Lake District called the Dansons. In various parts of the college three generations of the Danson clan had left their name on benefactors' plaques and in one room they had left an inventive collection of classical pornography.

This was a secret library in which Virgil, Homer and the Alexandrian anthologies were much enhanced by colourful phallic shepherds and captured nymphs. In amongst the shelves there were also greyer guides on how best to punish female servants and other material made almost respectable (but not quite) by bindings in gold and contiguity to classical language.

The book which attracted Maurice's attention was called *Crissie* and it described a London staging of Cleopatra in Queen Victoria's last years. In our sober Danson Library, alongside red-leather translations of Horace, sat the green-leather story of Signor Frigaballerina, a theatre director who began every afternoon with an innocent new recruit to his casting couch. The story of *Crissie* set out at some length the doings of this lustful Signor and the undoings of the would-be dancers whose 'litheness of limb' and 'subtlety of buttock' fell into his hands.

The rarity of the Trinity copy lay, it seemed, not in the English text itself, distributed to many a discriminating purchaser by the Al Hambra Press in 1899. Nor, Maurice had learnt, were the sea-coloured case and marvellously marbled endpapers a necessity for collectors. The glory of the Danson *Crissie* (and possibly only the Danson copy) lay in its enhancements, the exotic pink-and-blue depictions of those sensual arts for which Cleopatra and her friends were famed.

Crissie begins with scenes of casting for the roles as silent Greek statues and the costume fittings of gauzy enhanced undergarments. There is dialogue of protesting squeals and diagrams, formulaic but freshly painted, of every sexual act. Each stage of selection is addressed by the anonymous artist whose works, of varying page sizes and precision, fully illustrate the journey from stage door to stage.

Within 154 printed pages, between the gilt phallic decorations of the cover and the phallic cannon of the final full stop, there are parts for many minor players, suitable for such ingénues as Miss Daisy De Nuderham Blockington whose 'bloodstained drawers' hold up the narrative for an unreasonably long while. A Monsieur Zama takes the role of Mark Antony and fights violent back-office disputes about why he is required to 'fock' the heroine as well as dance with her around Signor Frigaballerina's living statues.

Maurice wondered whether it might be daringly modern to transfer this wordless tragedy from the college library to the college lawn, perhaps as part of a future Commemoration Ball. A series of silent tableaux, enhanced by appropriate readings from the Danson *Crissie*? Perfect. I did not quickly enough disagree.

We would, of course, still need a Cleopatra. Crissie Cazarotti, according to the text, had to stand out distinctly from the reluctantly undressed ladies of the chorus. The leading lady of the play was a creature of 'stark and carnal lust', only five foot high in her ballet shoes but of massive and hideous libido. As the author describes her, 'Crissie is all the better for being a bit of a drab: she is just the little bitch to make the part of Cleopatra look as hot and whorish as it should be.'

There was one ambitious undergraduate of a faraway woman's college whom Maurice thought might fit the part. He sent me out to discuss the possibility with her. He thought I would be the more gently persuasive of us, the less threatening. I was to talk only in the broadest terms, stressing the artistic integrity and limited learning required. But sadly, I had to report, this Crissie was anxious about her Politics and Philosophy prelim exams and offered only to think about it for another year.

Mahmoud and Socratis have each warned me, quietly and separately, to be careful what I write, and to be careful even about what I remember. There are 'mind police' among the security forces of Alexandria. If it might be unwise to sit in a cafe and recount the assassination of an ancient dictator, the telling of Crissie's story, I realise as I write it, might be even worse.

There must be material just as amusing behind these garden walls. Even a Coptic cathedral has its secret cabinets, locked and lightly guarded shelves where the bookish can broaden their understanding away from the public gaze. Rain is starting to fall. The drops are just enough to sit like oil on the beggar-polished slabs, not yet enough to make mud from dust. The custodian beckons me inside and motions me to a pew with its own wooden desk.

Despite the rebuff from one potential Cleopatra, Maurice had still not given up on his staging of *Crissie*. He also complained of wanting a woman off stage. I agreed with him. He began to talk openly about 'normal sex' and the lack of it. Yes, I said. When Maurice wanted something he always wanted it very much more than I did. He thought briefly that his theatrical and sexual ambitions might be combined.

In the Cuppers audience for our *Frogs*, clapping politely while others were being less attentive, had been a group from a local college for would-be women teachers. Among them he had met a dark, commanding Nigerian who had asked for our advice about Greek plays for primary schools.

He did not know her name but she had muscled shoulders, fierce eyes and a mannered, mildly mannish walk, a combination that somehow convinced Maurice she might be an ideal Cleopatra for his casting-couch. This Nubian in her fire-red dress, as he quickly redefined her, would surely 'come across' if the rehearsal conditions were propitious.

He saw no immediate competition. He chose a Friday evening when I would normally be in the library. He had to have our rooms to himself. He was insistent that I should follow my book work with a late night in the King's Arms. All would be perfect. I agreed – with every aspect.

'Wait', he said. There was a second problem: how to impress his target with appropriate subjects of shared interest, some knowledge of Africa perhaps. He could hardly last long discussing Greek comedy for eight-year-olds. Could I bear to return briefly to Cleopatra? Had I said something about her being black, or a bit black? Or had he been too sherried or Marowitzed at the time? Had I not said something about women in ancient Alexandria being more free, more sexually liberated than they had been in either Greece or Egypt before? Was everyone bisexual then? Or was he confused about the truth of that that too?

Forty years on, it is hard to remember whether I said anything useful. Today there are biographies that claim Cleopatra as a lost black icon, a Mrs Martin Luther King in the white-dominated past. There are books about how the ancients had sex, with whom, in what position and why. There are claims that all Greek philosophy and science came out of Africa, research projects on Alexandrian body-piercing, contraception, homosexuality and clitoridectomies. There was none of that when Maurice was looking for conversation points to turn his African queen into a Cleopatra, any Cleopatra, from a bewitcher of Roman generals to a star of late Victorian burlesque. The seventies were a simpler age.

Masged El Attarin Street

I feel faintly embarrassed by that last episode. It seems a little sleazy, something to forget rather than remember. But, in the months before he died Maurice did remember it. And I am remembering it again now because it is part of the Cleopatra story. Good taste cannot always be my guide. If there is sleaze, there is not very much sleaze.

I am now in what is probably a restaurant. Socratis eventually

arrived at St Mark's to bring me here. There is no menu outside or inside and not even a name. Like the carpet shop it may be sometimes just a house. But it does have marble tables and iron chairs, a bar as thin as a plank and a staff of at least one. There is lunch on the table though I have ordered nothing yet – tiny fishes upon a plate patterned with tiny fishes, pastes like damp fish food.

On the way to Masged El Attarin Street he asked if I needed anything first from the hotel. We stopped outside the Metropole and I walked in quickly, pushing past the security guards, electric gates and potted palms. Without being asked, he followed me, abandoning the car in the road beside a pair of horses. I did not ask him to come up to Room 114. He came anyway.

Once inside, his heavy body filled the cramped space around the bed. He threw open the shutters, shuffling my papers off the counterpane, riffling through the piles for the different decades, looking for anything, it seemed, in letters large and clear enough for him to read. He seized the few pages that were typed, fanned them in front of his chest and stepped out onto the balcony as though he were about to make a speech.

He posed. He strutted. If there were cameras to record this act they were invisible to me. And then he laughed, turned his back to the sea and, within seconds, was back inside, squinting at the two maps of Oxford and Roman Africa, dropping the first back on to the bed, carefully studying the second.

In Cleopatra's time, he asked quietly, who was properly in charge here? He then snapped a second question without waiting for an answer to the first. What difference did any dictator make to anything? What difference had Julius Caesar made, to Africa, to anywhere?

Socratis has never alarmed me before. Mahmoud has been the

sterner of the two, Socratis sometimes the more dissident but, even in the carpet shop, the more relaxed. Perhaps I have misread them all along. I am nervous of Socratis now, almost for the first time fearful. Maurice once said that I was unduly trusting of men with uncontrollable curly hair like my own. The thin trust the thin and the fat trust the fat, he liked to sing. What would he have thought now?

There was nothing wrong with Socratis's question. What exactly had Caesar achieved? It was a reasonable thing to ask. It was not clear what sort of answer he wanted. I wondered what was the safest answer.

Only one thought came instantly to mind, an old thought. At Brentwood Mr W said that Julius Caesar's greatest gift to mankind had been to save Gaul from the Germans. On his way to his dictatorship, Caesar had made his name and fortune in Gaul. He had killed and enslaved hundreds of thousands of Gauls. He had written his own story of those wars, the book which began: 'All Gaul was divided into three parts.' But Caesar had left Gaul a Latin country. The Germans had been left outside. Caesar was the father of France. That was a legacy that lasted ever afterwards. It was not always easy to find such legacies, even for the greatest of men. So that was what I told Socratis as he stared out to sea.

Socratis forced a thin smile in return. In Egypt, he said, there was no reason to dislike the Germans. They had done much less damage here than the French and the English. And anyway history was just a code. It did not tell us anything. It merely helped to disguise what we already wanted to say.

Had I collected everything I needed for lunch and for the rest of the day? Yes, I had. When we arrived at this restaurant without a name, he stayed only for a glass of lurid juice, a thick layer of orange beneath an alcohol haze. I did not join him in that or any other drink, intending a sober afternoon at a solid table in a warm, anonymous space.

Maurice did not enjoy his Nubian night. When I returned from the King's Arms, I found the would-be seducer sitting on our two-seat settee almost exactly where I had left him. The trainee drama teacher, in her plain red dress, most assertively still in her dress and looking not at all as imagined in our Cleopatra lesson, was also on the settee. The distance between them would not have troubled a chaperone. He said that V had called. Maurice said her name sourly. She had been wholly unexpected and unwelcome. She had not stayed long. She had said that she was looking for me.

More trays of food have now arrived, red leaves, green pastes, yellow grains, a fifties sweetshop of artificial colours. Service for me, the only diner in this restaurant, is inattentive. But there is no harm in that. I have the whole day ahead.

CLEOPATRA THE FIFTH

In the new year of 1970, I began to follow James Holladay's advice. If I wanted to understand the aftermath of Julius Caesar's death, I needed to look at the lesser people left behind. What did they think would happen? What did they fear would happen? What did they want to happen?

The assassination on the Ides of March left a huge hole in the politics of Rome. Cleopatra was just one of those uncertain which way to turn. Aulus Hirtius, one of the names first mentioned to me in the King's Arms forty years ago, was another. Cleopatra was famous even then. Hirtius was not. But that did not make her view more significant than his – then or now.

How do we rescue the forgotten people? The general, Aulus Hirtius, is one of them. He was not the dullest man in Rome. He was one of the so-called Continuators, not just an ally of Julius Caesar but one who had committed himself to finishing his master's literary works, keeping the Caesar legend alive. He was not just a general. He was a pleasure-seeker, an aesthete and a gourmet too.

More food has arrived, dancing dishes, delights that even Maurice might have liked. I can imagine my old friend here now, selecting among pavone, tartufi, ostrice, cervelli, strozzi and ricci di mare, translating for me the truffles, oysters, brains and sea urchins. I can imagine Hirtius here too, a good soldier, a loyal aide, a moderate general, an indifferent politician and an epicure of renown. None of that has saved him from being forgotten.

Maurice was a wonderful cook himself. Perhaps if Hirtius had been a cook he would be better regarded in our culinary times. But any job aimed at pleasure for others was a disgrace to a Roman grandee. One might as well be a Greek prostitute or a flautist like Cleopatra's father. Hirtius knew about enjoyment and style. He knew that if a dish had a Greek name and Alexandrian ingredients it was likely to be smarter (and much more expensive) than anything in Latin. No *farcimen* please, I'll have an *isicium*. Keep your country sausage, a sophisticated rissole for me.

His wine list? I can look here even if, for the sake of continuing to remember, I cannot drink. At Hirtius's table there would have been Egyptian wine and wine from Cos, Canidius's domestic competition as well as his personal monopoly brand of imports. There would have been Falernian wine too, full of sediment unless one took care. The skilled pourer could separate the liquid from the solids with a dove's egg. The albumen could drag the dirt to the bottom of the flask. Throw nothing away.

The Romans often liked to mock a gourmet. There were attempts in Caesar's day to impose the vegetable diet of the Greeks as a Roman virtue. But vegetarianism was a cultural import that the Roman rich preferred to avoid. Fine food was becoming fashionable. Imported poultry was as much desired as imported poetry. The state was in chaos after Caesar's death. What better time for the expensive and the new?

Even vegetables could be attractive if they were rare and imported, like silphium, a giant fennel from the coast of Cyrene not far from Alexandria, growing then in no other place, a heart-shaped seed which cured fevers, prevented pregnancy and tasted delicious. Caesar had a friend, Gaius Matius, who was a famed cook (or perhaps his son was the cook; it is often hard to say). Matius wrote books on fish and pickles and helped to organise Caesar's funeral.

Yes, there was the famous funeral, the pyre in the Forum, the 'friends, Romans, countrymen' speech (or something like it) and the fear of so many unknown futures. Cleopatra herself did not attend. She did not hear Mark Antony rouse the crowd against the killers. Nor did she immediately leave town. She was on no one's side now. She had no wish to please Brutus, the pompous son of Caesar's mistress, or Cassius, Pompey's useless naval commander, or any of the rest of Caesar's assassins. She wanted only time to consider what might happen next.

There were many men – and women too – who without the protective shade of the Dictator were not quite what they had been before but who still had hopes. Lucius Munatius Plancus, the dead Caesar's governor in Gaul, was one of them. Publius Canidius Crassus, was already on the side of Mark Antony. Hirtius himself was cautiously optimistic of exceeding them both. Rome seemed grey after Caesar's brightness, cloudy after clarity, but there was still much at stake.

Hirtius was not grand enough to be in any way Caesar's successor or even a successor to part of his domain. He was a reliable trusty who wanted now to be more widely trusted. He had his ambitions and his dreams. It is easy to forget the dreams of those who fail.

He was a writer. As a good servant, he hated the idea of a job unfinished, a duty undone. Caesar's own political story was there to be completed. Hirtius could continue that literary part of their shared mission to the end, or to some sort of end.

It was Hirtius and the Continuators who wrote the account of how Caesar finished his Gallic War and his wars with the implacable supporters of Pompey. He had to do the best job he could, admitting to a friend that, while he knew Gaul at first hand, he had not himself been present in either Africa or Spain. He had borrowed the description of the harbour battle against Ptolemy from a sea battle that Caesar had fought during his Gallic wars near Marseilles. He had added some bits from the Athenians' harbour battle at Syracuse 400 years before. That was how history was written then.

Hirtius had not always been personally at Caesar's side. But while he had not been an eyewitness of Caesar's last civil war battles, he had talked to Caesar about them and about restoring Cleopatra to her throne. Like many devoted followers of Caesar he thought that defence of a continued dictatorship was wholly justified. If only Pompey's vicious sons had seen the inevitability of their failure. With good sense, good Roman common sense and acceptance of might's rights, everything would have been fine.

Instead, Caesar was dead too. Hirtius thought that his master had been too generous, too willing to forgive, too ready to treat his enemies as kindly as his friends. He had failed to placate his opponents and failed to give those who loved him the rewards of that love. He had been a living lesson for students of politics and history. But now he was on his way to join the gods. Aulus Hirtius saw himself as one of those left standing, often having to struggle to remain on his feet while Mark Antony drank and the whole world went mad. Writing, even not very good writing, was a relief.

Caesar had been a great artist. The longer that he had been a writer of history, the more of an historian and the less of a mere reporter he had become. Hirtius had watched that change happen – and could keep it happening. At first Caesar had seen himself, his leadership and courage, as the cause of his success. But at the end of his life of war he was beginning to believe in causes beyond himself, the power of Chance, the real power of the goddess Fortune.

Hirtius had listened carefully to everything that he had heard in the master's presence. He had written first drafts of history before. Caesar often asked his legates to provide accounts of their actions. This was both to help him plan the next moves and to select which moves should be remembered by others. A victory could be conjured from very little. A defeat could be buried beneath distraction from another theatre. The charge that Caesar had burnt Alexandria's library was countered (rather too defensively in the view of later historians) by the claim that the city of the Ptolemies was of solid stone and absolutely fireproof. When the completed book, *The Alexandrine War*, appeared, this builder's detail was on its very first page. Hirtius was a master of such art.

Whether the words were to be literary in ambition, as Caesar increasingly preferred, or merely military, Hirtius knew what was required. A higher style was appropriate when the enemy was a foreigner like little, golden-armoured Ptolemy. A lower note was better for Roman foes. It was Caesar's genius, Hirtius wrote, that his words stood in the way of future writers telling different truths. It was hard to contradict such a man. Once Caesar had breathed his magic on the prose it was fixed for ever, proof against interpreters. While he, Hirtius, lacked such powers (he made no pretence of being Caesar's equal in any respect), there was value in his being a Continuator nonetheless.

There is much still to admire in Hirtius. He knew the importance of modesty (mostly insincere, however much justified), the desirability of access to the highest authority and closest eyewitnesses (the first being often more useful than the second), the ability to write fast or to seem to be writing fast, the superiority of unfinished copy over not filing copy at all, and the essential need to note the contribution of bureaucrats.

Hirtius was more than merely a writer after Caesar's death. He was the designated consul for the following year, designated by Caesar himself. When he led an army to stop Antony himself becoming a dictator, he was briefly a hero. When he looked as though he might have defeated Antony in battle, his star rose still higher. But when the first war reports, as so often, were proved wrong, Hirtius was defeated and dead. He had outlived his master by hardly a year.

Neither Hirtius nor any other of the Continuators who contributed to *The Alexandrine War* mentions Caesar's sexual relationship with Cleopatra or Caesarion, their alleged son. Cleopatra, it is said, was made queen at the end of the war merely because she had been loyal and had stayed at home in the palace. Did these ghost-writers dutifully follow the party line of silence that Caesar himself had set? Or were their minds so restricted within the sealed world of Caesar's court that they knew of no other reality?

Would V have been any more impressed with the Continuators than with the film-makers? I doubt it. She had her own views. I was sorry to miss her when she visited on Maurice's Nubian night. I would have been angry with him for sending her away if he had not been already so deflated. It would have been unfair of me to be angry. He had no idea that I wanted to see V that night. Neither did I until he told me I had missed her.

II.I.II

Place Saad Zaghloul

Lunch yesterday was wonderful. Breakfast today at the Metropole is not. The waiters are few. The bomber is dead, says the man making the omelettes. His accomplices are also dead. Normality needs to come soon. In the restaurant I am alone.

In October, 1970, V asked politely how my book was coming along. For a year after her interruption of the Nubian night we had not heard from her. That did not seem to matter. She looked little changed, still stubby and pugnacious, still restless, still apt to identify a person of possible privilege (not hard in Trinity gardens) and, as we sat together beside the battered lime trees, still asking and answering almost exactly the same questions as we had in Essex, 1968. How was Maurice and how was Cleopatra?

The condition of the queen of Egypt was the easier to describe. She was back in Alexandria after Caesar's assassination. It would have been good to know what she was doing there but more is guessed than known. The Roman mayhem was relevant to all Alexandrians but mostly it was hidden from them – by misinformation, mischief and hundreds of miles.

The odds were first on Mark Antony succeeding Caesar. He had support from many of Caesar's generals, including Canidius, Plancus and others of those lesser men that James Holladay had said should be watched. It seemed possible that all good men, Caesar's killers, Brutus and Cassius, as well as Antony and Octavian, Caesar's competing heirs, might come together. But that possibility was brief. It is doubtful that Cleopatra could have made much sense of the ensuing thefts and murders even had she known of them. Few in Rome could. Meanwhile the Queen of Egypt's job was to maintain power in Alexandria and collect the news as best she could. We paused and poured some tea.

'So how is the "queen" of Trinity?' V gave a triumphant smile.

I must have looked surprised. Maurice was still careful when he talked about sex. He liked to show openness in his preferences, a boy like a velvet mole, a Nigerian primary school teacher, whatever or whoever might be next. It was just a matter of mood and modernity. To hear him called a 'queen', not the most negative word then but not a kind word either, was a surprise. I tried not to show it.

'Don't worry,' she continued firmly. 'Maurice is not different. He has had difference thrust upon him.' She laughed. I tried to look sophisticated and severe.

This was not a success. Pretence with V was never a success. In some way, it seemed, his enthusiasm for men was all my fault. Or, at least, I was an accomplice to the fault, if only by attending the same school, the place where we listened to Rider Haggard and inscribed A THING OF on his thigh under the teacher's desk.

I protested that this abuse had been nothing to do with me. Again, she mocked. I was embarrassed. She was once again a superior, prim fifteen. I was trying and failing to be something different from what I had been. I tried to tell her about the end of the Nubian evening. But she already knew what had happened (and not happened) after she had interrupted the scene. She knew everything. There was nothing she needed to ask me about Maurice except as a check on what she already knew.

V and he had been talking already that morning. She had arrived the previous night, with nowhere to stay, had found Maurice and stayed with him in his bed. She said this apologetically. She had tried my room first.

'He is not really different,' she said, reproducing the same 'Queen of Trinity' smile. 'But he is easily led.'

Socratis was back in the doorway of Room 114, breathing aniseed and olives towards the dressing-table mirror. It was midday. He had been to 'a small party' at the shop of his friend the carpet-seller. Everyone had been talking about a much bigger party. It was going to be wonderful.

I had no idea what he was talking about and took a step back onto the balcony. He followed, pressing his face too close. It seemed as though he were about to repeat his interrupted address to supporters below.

There would be tents in the square right under the scolding scowl of Mr Zaghloul himself, he continued unsteadily. Who cared now about the old man – or any of the old men? All of them were forever looking out to sea, 'the other way, the wrong way for where the trouble was coming, the wrong way for the Cleopatra Ball'.

Next January, a whole year from now, would be the perfect time. Either the bombing would be forgotten and he would be helping the tourist trade again; or Egypt would be free (he made his sign of the long and short dash) and all of us could celebrate the assassination of Julius Caesar or anything else we liked.

There were other possibilities, he said. Maybe Egypt would be on the brink of its own civil war, hosting one of those eve-of-battle

balls that no one ever forgets, the season of 1914, the ball before
Waterloo. In every eventuality there had to be a big Cleopatra party.
His mother said so. Yes, she was much better now. If we were fortunate she should be there herself. Your mother or Cleopatra? Both. It
would be wonderful.

He stepped back into the bedroom, misting the mirror with his
breath. Not all his words were easy to hear.

'A few difficulties', he said, would have to be overcome. In the
Metropole Hotel there was no room to cook. The regular food was
proof enough of that. But oxen could be roasted on spits outside in the
road, down where the horses waited for the caleche customers and the
Polish drug addict darted among the honking cars in the hope of pol-
ishing a windscreen for cash.

Each ox would be ready to eat at different times, perfectly ready for
every guest's whim, just as Mark Antony once demanded. If we ran out
of oxen, we could roast the tourist horses though probably not the
wild pigs that Cleopatra cooked nor the Polish boy. The Ptolemies
loved vivisection but, as Socratis conceded with a burp, they drew the
line at cannibalism.

Mahmoud's religion would not accept the pigs, the favourite meat
of the meat-loving Romans. Horses were off the menu too: the nags
would be worth more alive than dead. The Metropole's street boy
could be gainfully employed for the first time in his drug-driven life,
gathering dirty glasses and half-smoked cigarettes. It would be a
smoking ball. How far would you English come for that? Cleopatra
didn't smoke? Well, she would have certainly smoked, if she had
known about smoking.

Socratis took an untipped Cleopatra from the packet that
Mahmoud had given him and lit it theatrically against the grey sky

over the harbour. There was a knock on the door. Mahmoud was suddenly here himself, with a briefcase and a clipboard. He brought the smell of sweat instead of Pernod. We were packed against each other like fish in a tin.

They both began to speak as though in a duet. On either side of the entrance on the Rue Zaghloul there would be wooden needles, Cleopatra's needles, like the ones now in London and New York. We would need to find out exactly where they had been before they were taken away, where they had once announced the Caesareum. The precise site was probably somewhere now under the Metropole reception desk. That was unimportant. The needles had to be outside. They had to be seen. They would certainly be seen.

Inside the ballroom there were five giant chandeliers. Each would have different-coloured bulbs, powered by thundering generators since the electricity was a little sluggish at the Metropole. Even at the best of times, the lamps responded to the flick of switch with a reluctant and only slowly growing glow. A sunrise every time you click, said Mahmoud, putting his characteristic best possible gloss upon a problem.

And from the 'Versailles window' on the stairs a many-coloured light would shine, not just on the guests climbing the red-carpeted staircase but, by means of wheels and mirrors, on those dancing in the ballroom too. Normally it was a tawdry dining-room where a waiter conducted a laptop computer, sometimes singing, mostly pretending to sing, while a few Americans argued about the price of water. It need not be like that. It had once been a ballroom.

The red-panelled walls and gilded frames of flowers need not be as they were now. They could be something else. The flowers on the red carpet could be something else. In the side room, the green one with the frieze of river vegetation and cabbage, there could be the bar.

This was not an ideal green. It was not even an Islamic green like that of the posters of the President's sphinx-like son. Nor was it the shiny green of olive leaves. It was a fainting green, a green to swoon and be revived to. But if we used pink lights the cabbages could become roses, said Mahmoud: 'the scent of roses has always stopped drinkers getting drunk'.

If this was a rebuke, Socratis did not hear it. Both men continued. There would be rooms within rooms, a maze, magnificent marquees. There would be water in all the fountains, even in the Dead Sea fountain by the cafe. All the hotel furniture would have to be cleared – out into the road if there was no rain or back to Settee Street where it all came from fifty years ago.

The singer with his musical laptop would have to get back to waiting on tables. There would be mezzos and sopranos, Socratis boasted, pushing out his chest. Maybe his mother would sing – or maybe better not. There was nothing wrong with the fake singer. If a man could not be a fake singer in Alexandria where else could he ply his trade?

All the guests would have disguises, goddesses and housemaids, mermaids, mermen and other monsters. Who would be Cleopatra? Everyone could be Cleopatra. At her own parties long ago she had sometimes dressed herself as a street-girl or a flower-seller, Egyptian Isis or Greek Athene. Her generals had been giant sea creatures. Even a consul of Rome, a governor of Gaul, had been a merman, slithering across the floor between the tables. The mermaids could be anyone or anyone's. Who could be Cleopatra? Who knew who was Cleopatra? Anyone. No one.

The ball-planners left two hours ago. The square is unusually empty. The miserable view from the balcony is of almost no one near the

Zaghloul monument. Police with guns patrol every entrance. A few pink food wrappers have blown around its mock-pharaonic panels, wind-blown paper patches, the only colour in the place. Inside this room where visitors are urged to feel the joy of the queen and her Antonio the yellow wallpaper is pale in the evening sun. Only the tiny pictures of Venice are reminders of how Europeans once wanted to see Alexandria, a city of romantic waters, royal barges and secret sexual excess.

Socratis wants to change much more in Egypt than the decor of a hotel. He does not like to be cautious. It offends his masculinity and his Coptic pride. Mahmoud is happier with his bureaucrat's role. But at heart they are not, I think, so different. If the bombing of the church is the beginning of the end for President Mubarak and his son, they will both be pleased. Whatever their jobs or employers now, Socratis will be pleased first. Mahmoud will quickly place whoever or whatever comes next in his pantheon of Egyptian 'good men'.

On my bed the scraps of past Cleopatras seem increasingly aggressive in their claims for attention. Top of the pile now is the reminder of the night when Maurice first revealed his own passion for party-planning.

It was well after midnight in a low-ceilinged Trinity attic, by an open window with almost the same view down the lawn as from the grander rooms which Maurice and I had shared the year before. The only sound was the whish and whirr of a suitcase-sized tape recorder whose music-to-write-by had ceased many minutes before. My oldest friend, not now a very regular visitor, stamped a slippered foot against the rhythmic flapping of tape-end against spool. He was excited. He had a speech. He wanted me to listen.

There was a red tent within a red tent within a red tent. That was what Frog said. The walls behind were grey-green and damp but in front of the canvas slit that led to the sanctuaries were dry roses. Inside the first encircling corridor the floor was warm leather. Through a second slit into a second circle there was a different carpet, silk or satin, light enough to show the outlines of the limbs that lay bodiless beneath.

Maurice paused as though this were a very suitable place to pause, not because he was nervous or had lost his place. He did not want to continue until he had assessed my response.

These limbs were lower legs, both right legs, the soles of their covered feet fixed upwards, the faint shape of the sweating toes visible beneath the cloth. The higher parts of the thighs were out of sight inside the final red tent on the floor of the innermost chamber. There was no opening by which to pass through and see why two women, probably women, were lying face down in the hidden heart of this strange construction; or why one of each of their legs was stretched outside into the corridor as though for some reason surplus to requirements.

The only instruction was on a pink card secured by a jewelled brooch, carrying words in Greek, 'veiled in the obscurity of a learned language' as Edward Gibbon once noted on a similar occasion: 'Menete! Nereidais Kleopatras Palaistra' ('Wait Here To Wrestle with Cleopatra's Mermaids').

I said nothing. Maurice took a drink and a rasping breath and went on. I turned a page and continued to take notes. He seemed pleased.

Maurice had met Frog. That was the start. Maurice had met Frog in the King's Arms, and Frog had taken Maurice to the Red Tents, at an address he had been given before finally he had left the protective embrace of Brentwood School. Frog was a late arrival in Oxford but he already knew a city that neither of us yet knew.

Maurice admitted to me that he had not seen everything for himself. He had not been allowed inside the innermost tent in the grounds of the great house. But Frog had been in. There were both men and women playing the parts of mermaids there, each with one leg pinned outside under the red silk drapes and another dressed in green gauze as though it were a tail.

There was the scent of dried roses. There was a secret code. Each sea creature asked its visitor whether Alexander the Great was still alive. The right answer was 'yes, he is alive and in power over the world'. Gibbon's injunction to use 'the obscurity of a learned language' was in his account of the Roman empress Theodora, whose sexual pleasure was to place corn grains among her pubic hair for gentle consumption by geese. The historian deemed this more decorously described in Greek. The creators of the Red Tents agreed.

How strange that Maurice had discovered all this with a boy whom he had so recently seen as so lacking in the lightest touch of grace, who had had the nickname and the sexual appeal of a small frog, a spotted frog, not even a frog naturally spotted in a *National Geographic* way but spotted as a laboratory frog might become through fright.

Frog, it seemed, was rather different now. He had never been a quitter, said Maurice, with a suddenly more admiring view of the boy he had once so despised. He had also, it seemed, acquired or reacquired friends who would have fitted into the most febrile Roman imaginings of life in Cleopatra's court, into an ancient exotica which the words of my failing biography had not approached, not closely, not at all.

Frog had 'gold on his tongue'. Maurice paused again, this time for nothing other than a dreamy dramatic effect. He was lightly drunk but less so than on many a quieter sherried night.

What did he mean? I had no idea. In Brentwood days Frog had often looked shifty to me, a bit oily, as though he had sluiced his lips in a tin of peaches. Had he now moved up in life? Did Frog wear jewellery in his mouth?

The Greek Egyptians, I ventured, used to put gold in the mouths of their dead so that they might charm the inhabitants of the next world. The password to the Red Tents, 'Yes, he is alive and in power', came from the legend of Alexander the Great's sister, Thessalonike, who swam the seas looking for sailors to trick into the wrong answer. Maurice did not even pretend interest in this.

The flow of news babbled on. Frog had found himself a base as bar manager in his college, a useful post, Maurice mused. Our former unloved school creature had also, Maurice added softly, delivered a full confession for the great Brentwood book-burning of 1968. He claimed 'diminished responsibility'. The new Frog was really very amusing.

At this point we fell silent. Maurice cleared his nose and throat into a pale-blue cotton handkerchief, one of the dozens that his mother sent him. He had nothing more to do or say. There was no more about Frog's Oxford that night. He left the room like a cat.

After a few minutes he was briefly visible again through the window, out on the long path through the college lawn towards the gate with empty plinths awaiting the Stuart Restoration, then clearer

against the night lights through the gaps in the lime trees (long awaiting their own different restoration) before vanishing, flouncing,
towards his own room beside the Library – where the late studiers
were smoking their cigars.

12.I.11

TELEPHONE 41891

TRINITY COLLEGE
OXFORD
OX1 3BH

Dear Peter, Your part
in life is indeed devious and
fascinating. I shall be glad
to give any help I can on
Alcibiades. I shall be in Oxford
until 5 Sep. when we go
to Greece. The college is shut
now but the K.A. sees us
most evenings at about 7 pm.
Yours
James.

Place Saad Zaghloul

Maurice began to go often to the Red Tents. I was not sure quite how often. In that second Trinity year I knew less and less of what he was doing. Our paths remained parallel but less close. There was no more sherry. He admitted that the tented mermaids were more often men. The bodies under the red cloth were not the same men all the time. Indeed the right to be pinned down on the satin floor was highly prized; a senior merman could choose his time for the most active hours of the night.

What sort of action? He was never very precise. Sometimes there were girls, he said, as though to reassure me. The only requirement was that all should appear to have a tail instead of legs, an illusion most easily achieved by the spare limb being pinned outside the canvas walls. Frog had once seen a boy with a polio-shrunken leg of the kind we knew so well from school. But this had not been as much of a success as the organisers had hoped. Maurice's homosexuality then still seemed theoretical, experimental, like cannabis, cocaine, cross-dressing and the Marowitzing of Shakespeare. It was secret. But everything was more secret then.

He spoke sometimes vividly, or vividly as it seemed to me, of doors beyond doors beyond doors, dark rooms behind the light, lines of basins with alphas and epsilons in lipstick on the mirrors, nobody about, then suddenly a crowd, planks to trip over, drains to piss down, coloured clothes in cardboard boxes, white colonial wear, sailor suits, cheese-paper blouses on meat-rails, feathers, wax fruit, dried flowers in profusion and curly heads against a drinking fountain.

For the first time the telephone rings in Room 114. There is a silence that ends with the news that Mr Socratis has his car waiting down-stairs. I triple-lock the door, pass the red panels, the green cabbages and the Versailles window, and leave through the security shield. Socratis is tapping his foot on the pavement. Mahmoud is in the back seat behind the driver. He is pleased because the police have found another of the conspirators. There is a new video on YouTube of a man with blacked eyes, bloodied mouth and no sign of life.

Socratis is not so pleased. A different security force, one of many serving the President's purposes, is clearing the streets of derelict cars, reluctantly for the most part because an ill-paid policeman can make good money hiring out back-seats to prostitutes and addicts. The cars are now judged terrorist havens.

Socratis has several threatened vehicles, not only on the Moon side of Alexandria but in Cairo by the airport. Their night-time users would be needed for the Cleopatra ball. He hoped that the clean-up campaign, like past efforts of its kind, would falter on economic grounds before it reached his retired Toyotas. Meanwhile he wanted me to accompany him back to the library. There seemed no good reason not to agree.

Bibliotheca Alexandrina

Maurice called the place of the Red Tents '*my* Mermaid Club'. The phrase was a form of protest since there was another Mermaid Club in

Oxford that he would like to have joined. The invitation to me to join this older Mermaid Club came from Geoff the Editor who described it, in the fake antiquarian way then fashionable, as 'a brotherhood committed to Restoration Comedy and the restorative powers of claret'. We had a venerable membership book with violet signatures, menus and arguments about the appropriateness of plays. Each meeting began with lines of John Keats on the subject of the Mermaid Tavern, a city hostelry that had once been the haunt of Milton and Ben Jonson, maybe Shakespeare too:

> Souls of Poets dead and gone,
> What Elysium have ye known,
> Happy field or mossy cavern,
> Choicer than the Mermaid Tavern?

How the meetings ended I can no better recall here in Alexandria forty years on than I could in Oxford on the following morning. We were a self-perpetuating cabal of authorities on the first halves of Restoration comedies, from Sir Fopling Flutter to Sir Courtly Nice, the obscure to the very obscure.

The membership included many of the kind of men not much seen in Essex, men whose names already stood for something in the world outside, from castles to accountancy firms or for family connections of their own to poets dead and gone. For most of us it was a club which provided a light experience of Oxford tradition and a heavy taste of hangovers.

What was the Latin for hangover? One of the thinner-faced, blonder-haired Mermaids gave me a little lecture on Mark Antony's notorious *crapulae*. He also knew much more than I did about

Cleopatra and the dead poets. He began each bottle with the opening lines of *Nunc est bibendum*, 'Now is the time for drinking', Horace's Cleopatran ode. Sometimes he even recited in English to the end.

> Now we can have a drink. And a dance. And dress the room for
>   the divinest party.
> While that queen and her drunken crew were still at loose, the
>   time was not quite right.
> Sozzled with hope she was. They all were. Their fleet on fire
>   soon sobered them up.
> Caesar was on to her like a hawk at a pigeon, a hunter at a hare.
>   Next stop the chains of Rome except
> That she was never going to die like that, nor slink out quietly
>   and hide herself away.
> Staring straight at her ruined palaces she took her last drink, the
>   venom of the snakes,
> 'Free, the mistress of herself, winning a triumph of her own.'

Occasionally Cleopatra's name appeared in games when modern politicians had to be cast as characters in old plays. How Hamlet-like was hesitant Edward Heath? Incidentally, why had he never married the beautiful Kay Raven whose picture was by his bedside, it was said, and who occasionally came to Trinity to see her brother, the tutor who read aloud to us in verse?

How Cassiusesque were Harold Wilson and James Callaghan? Would Reginald Maudling, then considered one of the cleverest ministers of his time, better suit the parts of the harmless drunkard Falstaff or the more dangerous drunkard Antony?

There were still the popular 'names of' clapping competitions.

There were games in which members had to find their pair, Robin and Marian, Cleopatra and Antony, barely an advance on the Essex polished floors of 1956. And then there were always the lost Act Fives in which the stage directions ran into the dialogue and the drink ran into the ceilings of the rooms below.

'Do you still write about politics?

Socratis had been away only an hour but seemed now to know rather more about me – that before my authorship of *Trente Jours* I had been an editor of *The Times*, a political journalist in America as well as Britain, that I had survived a cancer that was supposed to kill me and had written about it in another diary called *On the Spartacus Road*.

'What is Tony Blair like?'

Socratis knew too that I had spent time with Tony Blair and George Bush during the Iraq War and had now subsided deeply, though he did not know just how very gratefully, into Greek and Roman history and a nine-year editorship of *The Times Literary Supplement*. This knowledge was no more than he could have found in a few minutes at a computer but it was beyond the interest that he had shown before.

'No,' I told him, 'I no longer write about politics. Or, at least, only very rarely, and not about any of the countries on my Roman map, not about Morocco, Tunis or Libya, not at all about Egypt.'

'What do you understand of being an Alexandrian?'

I paused, wondering if he was asking about the first centuries BC and AD (answer: riotous but politically ineffective, disrespectful of authority but dictatorially governed, innovative, artful, always out for a good time if one could be found) or about the city of today. He did not wait for either answer.

'There is someone I want you to meet.'

This man, he said, would tell me everything about Alexandria. He would come to the library and find me there.

'If you have to wait a little while, that will not matter, will it? You can always entertain yourself in a library.'

'You could read your own book and practise your French,' added Mahmoud who had been silent till then.

The driver began laughing until his employer poked him hard in his plastic-covered paunch, harder than would be necessary for a driver more normally dressed.

I have now been in the library for almost another two hours. I am expert on how the window-cleaners conduct their spidery dance on the roof above. The glass is tipped at an angle chosen to represent some ancient observation of the skies, not steep enough to require the swinging harnesses worn by those who ply their trade on office blocks, too steep to move as easily as on a roof that were flat.

Various visitors have come and waved a ticket in my face. None has been Socratis's Alexandrian. Each time he or she has been keen only to claim a pre-booked desk. Each time I have moved further down the steps, past the sculptures representing literature, past the exhibitions of linotype machinery, past plaintive paintings on the theme of the Rosetta Stone (lost to the British Museum) and the great lighthouse (lost to the sea).

So, before the age of institutionalised regret, what did it mean to be an Alexandrian? Confidence was important. So was making the best of weakness, finding calm where one could and fun when one wanted it. Alexandrians captivated the Romans with techniques of twisting, reshaping not merely possessing. This city conquered Rome long before Rome conquered this city. Alexandrians might later be seen as dull and dry, products of court life without political freedoms, not properly Greek. But they made magic for export.

The librarians here were both scholars and entertainers. There was Callimachus, who liked short poems, and Apollonius, who liked long ones. Both squabbled their way to reputations. For centuries poems poured in and out of Alexandria, piling gaiety upon the grim lessons of the past. Ink from everywhere came in on the tides past the Pharos. This was the import that the Ptolemies most prized, red ink from the ochre of earth, black from the burning of insects and wood, waves of words on papyrus rolls which artists could study and make different. The harbour waters were the way into an unprecedented place where the curious and the state-sponsored could pick and prod for pleasure.

The study of these pickers and prodders was our Oxford study too. Our textbooks were guides to how the greatest poets in Latin had continued and adopted what the Alexandrians had begun. We read closely in those Roman writers, Catullus, Virgil, Horace, whose works have lasted through the centuries – and speculatively in those whose efforts, much lauded in their day, have been lost.

Virgil had a friend called Cornelius Gallus, an Alexandrian in art who was born in the same year as Cleopatra. He also shared a mistress with Mark Antony. He had many claims to be in Cleopatra the Fifth. But from all his once-famed poems we had just one elegantly balanced pentameter line, rescued from an unreliable book of 'rivers mentioned by Roman poets', the kind of list that cataloguers and games-players have always loved.

Its subject was the Hyspanis, known today as the Southern Bug, a river once deemed to separate Europe from Asia. *Uno tellures dividit amne duas*: With one stream it divides two lands. There was the 'one' at the beginning, the 'two' at the end and the word for division dividing the line: it seemed then a magical thing. In the seventies we were told that Gallus, if only we possessed more of his work, would be the link between two ages of art, the learned entertainers and the deepest, most personally passionate poets, between Alexandria and Rome. Hellenistic literature was the hinge on which literature hung. Our teachers always hoped for more of it.

In Alexandria's Greek anthologies there was never any direct challenge to the old masters, no equal to Aeschylus, Sophocles, Euripides or to the comedian who mocked them in *The Frogs* or to the Homeric poets from whom the idea of Greece began. There were instead the men who made Greece for Rome and for everywhere. Alexander's menacing mermaid sister was right: her brother was still alive and in power over the world.

Consider, as Mr W used to say, even one of Alexandria's most mocked of scholars, Didymus Chalcenterus, Cleopatra's librarian, commentator on Homer, long seen as a figure of fun if seen at all, sometimes called Forget-me-book because he wrote more books than even he could remember. This Didymus explained the choruses of Sophocles and uncertain attributions in Euripides. He listed thousands of Greek words whose meanings, he argued, were not quite what they seemed.

Didymus made enjoyment happen. Short poems or long ones? Callimachus from Cyrene or Apollonius from Rhodes? Let the readers choose what or whom they liked best. Green marble or red for a bathroom, white or brown for a dining table, polished wood or plain for stairs? He wrote the handbooks and guidebooks. He was at the heart of the project for Alexandria to conquer Rome and beyond.

This was important, the promotion of Greek not just its existence. No one in the past sixty years who has ever claimed to be a classicist has escaped the jeering charge: why, with so much else from which to choose, do you want to do that? Completing Cleopatra's lives, in a way that not even I expected, close to where she once lived, is now my own small, best answer.

There is still no sign of Socratis's friend at the library. There is a cold rain outside where the seekers of cigarettes and fresh air meet. Each new arrival at the desks has a wetter coat and a better need for her headscarf. Mud streaks the carpets.

Among Cleopatra's contemporaries was a man named Crinagoras. His name appears in several of the anthologies of tiny poems that were first made here and are back now on Alexandria's shelves. He came from Lesbos, the same island as the politician-poet Alcaeus. But Crinagoras did not hymn the death of tyrants. He wrote poetry that pleased his present more than the distant future. He had a ready line for the death of a slave boy, a slave girl or for a lover who bestowed the name 'Love's Island' on the place where he died. When Crinagoras wrote of eagles it was not to praise their soaring flight like a tragedian but to note how their wing feathers, when neatly cut and purpled with lacquer, made quill pens and toothpicks. He had the perfect inscription for a caged parrot whose call echoed the name of Caesar to the woods and hills.

Alexandrians pioneered the art of wrapping art within art, poems on one subject in the packaging of another, stories of the present inside stories of the past. Crinagoras was good with gifts of all kinds, happy to send roses in winter and copies of lovesick, drunken verses as long as they were from library books dignified by antiquity. He told stories of faraway places, how Alpine bandits fooled watchdogs with kidney fat, how the sheep of Armenia made cries like cattle and bore their young three times a year, how a washerwoman might drown on shores whose waves were monstrous surges of death.

He hymned obsequiousness and obscurity. He liked words that no one had used before and never would again, the *hapax* as we call them now. He adopted and adapted Homer. His profession was to be diplomatic, to represent Lesbos to its Roman masters, praising Julius Caesar's victory over Pompey at the same time as Cleopatra did much the same and more.

Pharos

The light is fading over the sea. If I were still a newspaper correspondent or editor, today would not have been a success. If the bombing of the Two Saints church were ever to be seen as 'the beginning of the end' for the Mubarak regime (or some other journalistic commonplace), I would have been in the wrong place with the wrong people. Socratis's friend, when he finally arrived, was cold, polite, keen only to ask questions not to answer them, all of them about what I was doing and why I was here, none of them about the nature of the Alexandrian character. He wore an elegant, dark, four-buttoned suit and dark glasses that lightened as he spoke. He would not give me his name.

He was mildly disturbing. He hardly registered the name of Socratis or Mahmoud. Maybe he was from some deeper part of the Egyptian state. After he had gone, I felt nauseous again, petulant, perplexed, an unattractive mixture of emotions, a kind of angry embarrassment.

I did not 'see red', the phrase my mother used to use for my childhood anger. I was not sick again. I saw the coloured sky I had seen here before, suddenly full of glass, glowing clouds of blue, a shattered sundial shooting towards the sun. Needles spun through the air. Bright alphabets formed and reformed over the waves. Pages of print fluttered soundlessly like butterflies.

The dark man did nothing wrong. He said nothing wrong. He was polite, a bit firm at times but calm. I was the one in the wrong. I wondered whether I should go back to the Metropole in order to write about something else, or more likely sleep. Instead I have walked back here to Pharos, quickly, almost running, far along the modern Corniche, fast down to the end of the Ptolemies' causeway.

After an hour I am almost alone by the site of Cleopatra's lighthouse, Alexandria's lightning conductor, this place with the fort now that changes its marzipan shades in the setting sun. There are no tourists, no shell-sellers, no crocodile-watchers, three taxis and five policemen. The wind has eased, the rain has gone. The Oxford part of this story can end here too.

There are still some remaining relics of Cleopatra the Fifth, a book that died slowly, somewhere between my leaving Trinity and beginning to earn a living, between the end of life as a classicist and its recommencement as something else. It might have died at an advertising agency dinner, a trade into which Maurice had briefly introduced me. Its last night might have been when the IRA bombed the teenage drinkers of Birmingham, the first time I saw mass death for myself, when I was working for the BBC and for the first time had a proper job. There was the night that a literary agent suggested that another classical subject, Spartacus, Alicibiades or someone else, anyone else, might produce better progress. I cannot remember.

Frog died too. There seems no other way of putting it, of rounding off his peculiarly distant part in these memories. He has no lines of his own in this book. There is nothing from him that I can place within quotation marks as a journalist should. I have merely my own school-boy ill will and Maurice's reports of some of the things that he later said and did. He is a minor character, and like many minor characters in many histories, barely a character at all but not necessarily less influential for being so.

I did eventually learn a little more, how much of what Frog said was true, how much Maurice did and did not do in and out of the Red Tents. It was not a simple story. But here by the missing lighthouse both men exist only in the flatness of now, the level present of their existence here in this tense and troubled place.

Frog died long before Maurice, very soon after the events in this chapter, some forty years ago. He took a train to Amsterdam, found the tallest, most luxurious hotel with the brightest roof-top bar, spent money that he did not have and on the sixth or seventh day (there was some dispute about how long at the time) he threw himself briefly in to the air, spreading his arms as though playing at swans or giving his Classical Society speech on the glory of Roman gladiators, escaping as though by drinking or writing, by being somewhere and someone else, before finding the traffic of the street below. The last of us to see him, on the same Amsterdam train by chance, was one of the older actors who had judged our Cuppers play particularly kindly and who now works in television in Wales.

The policemen have taken the taxis. There are only gulls and geese now, in and out from behind the walls like thoughts, here and departed like pictures of the past, elegant in the air, gangling on the ground. These are the birds that have always been at Pharos, here when the stones soared into the greying blue, permanent ghosts, their lives surviving in the way they wheel and wail, shrieking and rising. Their circling around a lost wonder of the world is a summons to remember so much that is lost. They trace figures in the air, figures of speech, metaphors moving in and out of sight. A letter in the air is a letter in a line, an O a C or an S, a line from the library, a line in the sky.

13.1.11

Hotel Metropole, Place Saad Zaghloul

In the thirteen days of this year Cleopatra has thus far been a name, a
space-traveller's hostess, a feminist's missed opportunity, a reason for
learning about a city and a subject for Oxford scepticism and fantasy.
This is now the middle of the story. The single reason for staying in
anxious Alexandria is that I have to finish Cleopatra the Eighth. I
have only a few small reminders of what I have done before. There
can be no Ninth, a matter of no importance to anyone else but of
some importance for me.

This is the point at which most other books about Cleopatra also
divide. Julius Caesar is dead. Mark Antony stands ahead. Behind her
is a life that none would have much remembered had it ended after
the Ides of March in the terror that followed Caesar's assassination.
Ahead of her is the barge, the pearl and the asp.

Two years after Caesar's death Cleopatra received the good news from
Philippi in northern Greece that Caesar's assassins had been defeated
by Caesar's heirs. Brutus and Cassius were dead. Antony and Octavian
were triumphant. Of these two victors, Antony was much the more
triumphant: Octavian had been hiding in thick marshland, too ill to
lead his legions himself and had been mocked for his absence. Antony
was the coming man.

This certainty from Greece contrasted with uncertainty from

Rome. It was hard for Cleopatra's informers to know precisely who was up and who was down. She knew personally at least one of the consuls for 42 BC, Lucius Munatius Plancus. He had been one of Caesar's army commanders and a visitor to their house. A consul's power was not what it once had been but Plancus was at least Antony's consul – on the more promising side.

There were reports that rich Roman women, by a new decree, were, for the first time, to be taxed. This was both mildly amusing in its immediate effect and disturbing in its novelty. What else new might happen?

More serious news came from the Greeks of Asia. In Ephesus Cleopatra's sister, Arsinoe, spared by Caesar after his Alexandrian triumph and transferred to benign imprisonment amongst the priests of Artemis, had suddenly declared herself Queen of Egypt. There were accompanying rumours that their one surviving brother, and her own official husband, Ptolemy XIV, was Arsinoe's accomplice. There was even the rumour of a pretender claiming to be her dead brother, Ptolemy XIII, the one whose golden armour had been dredged from the bloodied waters of the Nile.

Nothing on the home front, however, was yet beyond her control. Her brother-husband could be killed without risk. Arsinoe was still far away. The fake Ptolemy could be found and drowned. Meanwhile, Cleopatra was waiting nervously for Quintus Dellius, a Roman whom she did not know, to arrive by ship at her eastern harbour.

Dellius was the ambassador to Cleopatra from Antony. Even by the pragmatic standards of the time he was a man of flexible allegiance. In the past few years he had supported most sides, Caesar himself, a dissident critic of Caesar and Caesar's leading killers. He had also taken a variety of intermediate positions from which he hoped to profit, or at least to stay alive. He was now not only the emissary of Antony but his procurer, bringing him girls and boys, keen, it was said, in any way to atone for his previous errors.

Cleopatra had not been Antony's enemy. She had kept all of her options open. She had offered only the most cautious support to Brutus and Cassius. Her Egyptian reinforcments never reached the assassins' side even though Cassius had come close to invading Egypt to claim them. She had sent out ships for Antony and Octavian too, and welcomed them back when the weather turned sour.

How much these manoeuvres were by design, misinformation, or mere good luck, would be hard for anyone to know. Unfortunately, if anyone were likely to have such damaging knowledge, it would be Quintus Dellius. Antony's new man was a very knowing pimp with pretensions himself to be a Continuator of a kind, a gatherer and twister of stories, a historian of the campaigns that Caesar had intended to fight against the Persians and which Antony, in his bid to be Caesar's undisputed successor, was planning to undertake in his place.

Dellius was not her ideal choice as an escort to the new Roman ruler of the East. But Cleopatra was not in a position to choose. Dellius's orders were to bring her to Tarsus, a small town on the River Cydnus in what is now southern Turkey. She had little choice but to go. To disregard the call would leave her without a Roman ally and as open to invasion, coups and plots as her father had been. And if she wanted to go to Antony, to explain herself, to offer soothing financial help for his Persian campaign, there was no alternative but to travel with Dellius the pimp.

Antony seemed a man with whom she could do business. He had proved himself by holding Rome for Caesar during the Alexandrine

War. He had rallied the Roman mob after Caesar's death as soon as it was clear that the assassins intended to kill no one else. Philippi was his solo triumph. For Caesar's party – and she was herself a famous member of it – he was the senior figure.

Antony also understood the Greeks and their ways of being ruled. He had been popular in Alexandria even when, as a junior cavalry officer, he had helped to put Cleopatra's father back on his throne. He was Alexandrian in mind. While not the first Roman to dream of equalling the feats of Alexander the Great, Antony was the first to share his spirit.

He was in every way more malleable than Caesar, notoriously relaxed, a successful general even if not a hardened one by the hardest Roman standards. A conflict was coming. Antony was a man of Caesar's own generation while Octavian was six years younger than Cleopatra. As well as the dog-like Dellius, there were Plancus, Canidius and many more who wished to continue Caesar's grander causes – and all of them had decided that Antony's was the cause they should best be backing now.

So she would go to Tarsus even though this place of meeting was no more ideal than was her escort. Tarsus would give Cleopatra little of the theatrical advantage that she had used on Caesar at home. Its unpaved streets were nothing like her Canopic Way between the Sun's gates and the Moon's. The River Cydnus at Tarsus was cold and narrow, as nothing compared to the Nile.

But the best of Alexandrian artifice was at her command. The Greeks of Egypt had been long adept at turning any water into theatre. They never lived in the heart of their country. They always processed through it by barge, past riverbanks that were the best seats for their shows. She could not choose her Roman escort. But she could keep him waiting while she dressed her stage. She could use the time to prepare a ship that would be a home away from home. She had artists who worked in thick marble, gold and ebony. She had others who created lighter illusions. Impressing war-blasted Tarsus ought not to be hard.

14.1.11

Alexandria Courthouse, Route du 26 Juillet

The meeting between Antony and Cleopatra on the Cydnus became one of the most famous of all meetings. Shakespeare made sure of that. 'The barge she sat in, like a burnish'd throne, Burn'd on the water. The poop was beaten gold; Purple the sails, and so perfumed that The winds were love-sick with them.'

It was probably Dellius himself, Continuator and pimp, who first described that breathless scene. Cleopatra's unwanted guide may have both planned the competitive banquets and gifts and then, to make sure his work was not wasted, put them into words, describing first the seduction, then the twins that arrived in the following year, the boy and the girl, the Sun and the Moon.

Plutarch repeated the picture in his *Life of Antony* two centuries later. Shakespeare made the scene indestructible. It is almost irrelevant to wonder how much of it Cleopatra had ever made happen.

CLEOPATRA THE SIXTH

A job in one of the world's biggest business bureaucracies was not what in 1977 I either wanted or expected. But a job was a job. A job in the oil industry, after failed experiments with advertising and the BBC, seemed at least a different kind of job. Maurice approved, but from a distance. V had disappeared from our lives. Cleopatra was fading with them.

In Big Oil House the grey was the greatest shock, not the greyness itself but the kind of grey. It was like neither the light polished slate on the walls where I had worked briefly to sell chocolates, nor the heavy steel of newsrooms where I had for an equally short time reported pub bombings and cricket. The grey in the office where I was due to meet Miss R meant neither fashionable frivolity nor public seriousness. It resembled rubber erasers last seen in winter classrooms.

At the end of a long carpet was an empty chair whose green leather had long lost its lustre and beside it, rather than behind, a peculiarly ill-balanced desk, the left of the surface piled with pale files, the right supporting a cinder volcano in a rolled-glass ashtray.

The closest to life, as well as whiteness, came from the birds whose droppings dripped and dried down the outsides of the windows. There was an equally stark black briefcase with a matt metallic combination lock. Everything else in view was from the median tones of smoke. I waited as long as I dared until the prospect of causing offence seemed greater than the potential benefits of being where I ought not to be. Miss R, I had been told, was the woman who could help me most with my problem but, after five minutes and without achieving any part of my aims, I turned around and left.

Back in my own, smaller office, filled with many desks, I and my new 'Employee Communications' colleagues had other problems. The latest instructions from above were both studiedly imprecise and perfectly clear. Those of us on the Big Oil House fifth floor in the summer of 1977 were not to know when 'A. Brown' would arrive. But when he did arrive we knew what we had to do. We had to avoid looking at him or disturbing him in his work. We had to be helpful, if we were asked to help, but otherwise we had to continue with our own work. We should not conceal any items relevant to Mr Brown's investigation.

Neither should we point out anything on the walls that he might have missed. We were not authorities on the paintings, prints and drawings owned by the Big Oil Company and somehow now misplaced. We were not authorities at all. If there were any difficulty of any kind we were to direct Mr Brown to someone who had been appropriately briefed.

There was only modest debate among us all about what this might mean. Our desks were scattered. The raising of voices was discouraged. To be standing suggested one was not working. So that too was discouraged. These were ancient days before computers and there were no electronic means of ruminating upon which artwork might have gone astray, whether there had ever been any art in any room where we had ever been, and when Mr Brown would come. A brief meeting around a drawing board produced the consensus that the chaos in the mysterious upper levels of management was no greater than usual. Then we all went back to our places.

The board belonged to RJ, the designer of *Big Oil Times*, a magazine for employees made in the then fashionable manner of the *Sunday Times Magazine*. RJ's desk was the centre of my working world. He was a leather-vested, thin-lipped man in his early thirties whose over-the-collar black hair was shiny at his forehead and dull at the back, like the metalwork of a not-quite-new machine. His pride was in the ownership of a red Ferrari which no one had ever seen and was always a few parts and 'a few grand' short of what he needed to put it on the road. For regular use – although he came to work from Deptford by train – he had a white Lamborghini.

The Editor of *Big Oil Times* was RT. RJ helped RT to make the ordinary look exciting. While *The Sunday Times* in those days would show the inner tubing of a Big-Oil-powered aero engine only when its failure had spread a hundred bodies over the Atlantic Ocean, *Big Oil Times* would show the same engine when it was working as it was supposed to do, powering the economy, empowering civilisation, making every employee proud to come to work, even those in Big Oil House whose closest experience of engineering was a well-turned paperclip.

RT needed RJ because RJ knew about airbrushes and other modern means to make a printed page appear aluminium. RJ needed RT because no one else would pay him handsomely enough to satisfy the Ferrari repair-man. Together they satisfied the Big Oil management view that, in the best spirit of John Betjeman, John Piper and other calendar-artists commissioned by Big Oil in the past, it was worth spending substantial sums on making customers and employees feel the soothing power of paint. It was only unfortunate that some of these past masterpieces, their prime purpose of distinguishing July from August long ago fulfilled, had gone missing and that this Mr Brown had to be given the job of finding them.

RT himself, a square-faced, blue-blazered man from Clacton-on-Sea, had no interest in oil or engines or any kind of machinery. His passion was for fiction with original unclipped dust jackets. He had a shiny briefcase divided into two internal compartments, each tightly sealed against the other, one filled in the morning with egg sandwiches and apples so that he did not need to waste his lunchtimes sitting down for lunch, the other filled in the afternoon from his midday book trafficking through Covent Garden to the Charing Cross Road.

A modest antiquarianism did not make RT an unsuitable man for Employee Communications, the department in which we all, in different ways, were paid to work. *Big Oil Times* was created to encourage outside interests amongst employees, some sense of what lay beyond, but not too far beyond, their daily workplace. RT knew a good deal about Guides and Calendars, the Art Deco architecture of Big Oil House itself, its clock with the coffin-shaped hour hand and the cricket-bat minute hand, one of the biggest in London, known to older wits as Big Benzine. He knew why the colour yellow was used for safety helmets.

He did not know much about how a refinery worked but that hardly mattered. Most office workers, the readers at whom his magazine was aimed, had no knowledge of refineries either. RT's job was to employ writers who could explain catalytic cracking and associated mysteries, to choose photographers and artists who could remove the grime and make the crackers glow, and then, much his most important responsibility, to make sure that anyone in the company with a right to complain about his magazine had the chance to complain and correct the pages before they went to press. In Big Oil UK this was a large number of people.

RT always preferred the articles about the bees and water voles, some of the many creatures whose lives, we wrote, were studied and enhanced wherever oil was discovered, sold or used. In 1977 there was the added excitement of North Sea exploration, offering him the chance to show not only floating rigs and storage buoys the size of Nelson's Column but monstrous fish from depths that fishermen had never reached before. The illustrations of these were, in RT's view, the equal of any lost thing that Mr Brown might be seeking.

These men had the job of introducing me to bureaucratic life. Both James Holladay and Mr W had stressed the role of the office-worker in understanding Alexandria. This was the year in which Cleopatra the Sixth lived only between nine and five. The story quietly recommenced – beyond the perfumed barges on the River Cydnus – in between reporting on inter-refinery football matches and the social responsibility demanded of pipeline-layers. It was always better to be seen doing something than nothing.

Everyone in Big Oil had an assistant. Many had an 'opposite number' too, sometimes a person whom they had never met, who did a similar job, often the same job, in the other part of the company whose offices were in Holland. This was part of a political accord in which neither the British nor the Dutch should dominate the other. It was a system whose balancing intricacies would have fascinated the courtiers of any time and place, one which mere communications assistants like me (though not ourselves possessing doppelgängers in The Hague) had also to understand. There was never just one executive with whom we could 'clear' copy or pictures for publication, whom we could ask whether the screw-top of a million-gallon oil barrel was an industrial secret, an environmental hazard or a technical triumph to be paraded for employees. There were always at least two 'clearers', normally many multiples of two, not always in the places where it seemed logical that they would be.

Miss Q was RT's assistant, tall, tightly strung in the muscles around her eyes, elegantly tailored in red, as financially extravagant as a Ferrari. She spent much of her mornings on telephoned arrangements for nights out with men who sounded much older than her when she spoke to them and much, much older still when she spoke about them to her girlfriends the next day. Some, we gathered, were powerful and famous, some not. She seemed masterful in balancing their interests against her own interests, successfully for herself for the most part. She knew a great deal about the oil industry through her mother, who was close to a senior man of Whitehall. She also knew where one would most likely find a missing John Piper. Chelsea galleries were like childhood homes for her. But none of this expertise seemed to serve her professionally as well as she hoped.

Big Oil information had to flow, like the oil itself, through the proper channels. RT had not appointed Miss Q himself and they did not speak very much. It was RT who had told me about the 'chain-smoking depressive' of immense seniority whose office at the end of the Public Affairs corridor was labelled Political Relations. This Miss R, it seemed, was the controller of everything. But she would no more have consulted someone from our own office about petroleum revenues than keep her mouth free of a Marlboro. The mysterious Mr Brown might possibly have more sense. But more likely he would not. Miss Q did not do much at all. But then none of us did much at all. Doing much was not a virtue in our part of the oil industry. Those who did too much faced all the usual dangers of the active, as well as some that were unique to this strange time and place.

RT's boss – and mine – was a long-distance swimmer. Lew D had been a successful provincial journalist, tempted into Big Oil first because his journalist wife, whose job was better than his, had wanted to work in London, secondly because he could not get a job on Fleet Street himself, and thirdly because nowhere else could a man make the equivalent of a cross-Channel swim each week in the office pool. He was a gentle superior who enjoyed gentle domination by women – by Miss R in the office and by his wife at home. Each one trained him for the other. He looked like a kindly weasel, lean, sharp, short, quick-moving, with darting eyes. He modelled himself on the then best-known editor in England, Harold Evans, whose ability to be everywhere at once, in the newsroom, on the squash court, on war fronts and in swimming pools was already a thing of legend.

Lew supervised four publications, each with their own editor, for which he had the 'higher responsibility like that of a regional editor in chief'. Or that was how he put it when we first met. As well as *Big Oil Times*, there was *Big Oil UK News*, a tabloid for refinery workers and tanker drivers, and *Explore News*, a paper stapled like a school exercise book containing inspirational prose for our North Sea pioneers, only a few of whom spoke English. Last and least there were the Newsletters, an occasional series aimed at communicating certain specific corporate virtues, such as how carefully the company restored the countryside after it had built a liquefied natural gas pipeline.

Lew affected disdain for those who stood above him in the towering ladders of seniority. His own editors felt the same way about him, not just the superior creators of *Big Oil Times* but the polyestered man who promoted Transport Cafe of the Year for *Big Oil News* and the Nordic-faced thriller-writer who printed safety warnings and helicopter timetables for riggers from Korea. If an idea came from above, it had to be considered, managed, minuted with care but, ideally and if at all possible, not commissioned for publication. Therefore suggesting a story to Lew D was something that only a newcomer would do, a 25-year-old graduate with brief experience in chocolate advertising, some very nominal training in journalism at the BBC and an ambition to write a book of ancient biography.

The most defined of my responsibilities was for the Newsletter series. But there was not, it seemed, a consistent need for picture books of arable tranquillity over pipes of refrigerated high explosive. RT had tried me out on a trip to Heathrow Airport to describe how smoothly Big Oil fuelled the planes; RJ had allowed me to write captions for a colour spread of Scottish wasps; Miss Q had shown me how to help her clear copy through some peculiarly impenetrable thicket of the company organogram. A few months after I arrived some even more senior figures decided that we should aim to make the area around Big Oil House 'come alive' for our fellow workers. This was the first time I had heard that phrase since Geoff the Editor introduced me to James Holladay.

The summer atmosphere was torpid. Not even the imminent arrival of Mr Brown seemed quite as surprising or urgent as it had before. When Lew asked to see me, I was quite unreasonably surprised. Had I thought any more, he asked, about the things-to-see-around-the-office instructions? What could we say about the statues that stood between Big Oil House and the Thames? Would one of them make a little feature for the *News* or *Times*? I was ready for this. I had taken a look while on a walk to the other side of the river, home of Big Oil's bigger international brother, the place of fabled free office lunches and Olympian facilities for swimmers.

The Victoria Embankment Gardens were full of bronze figures, mostly social reformers and fortunate soldiers, all well past their date for inspiring anyone. Also suitably nearby was a war memorial given by the people of Belgium in thanks for their liberation by Britain in the First World War, a curved white stone wall encompassing three figures in a blob of bronze. But our Dutch friends were, it seemed, unpredictable on the subject of Belgians, Germans too, especially recent Germans – indeed on all modern history, since a good oil company had so often to be a good friend to all sides.

My suggestion instead was that we cross the Embankment and describe Cleopatra's Needle, the thin granite column, watched by two bronze sphinxes, where the pleasure boats picked up tourists for river trips. This was something, possibly the only useful thing, that I

already knew about. Its pink sides and pigeon-spattered tip could be seen from any window on the Thames side of our building. If there were to be a direct line drawn between us and our international centre, Cleopatra's Needle was the pencil that would draw it. Any office messenger on his way to the pedestrian bridge might briefly stop and ask himself where it came from, why it was there and what the signs on the side (notably better preserved than those of the Belgian War Memorial) might possibly mean.

And he might also ask 'Who the fuck was Cleopatra?', said Lew, interested enough to push his pencil jar away but worried perhaps that his feature story could become a tutorial in hieroglyphics. 'Yes, we can explain that too,' I replied, 'though I should say now that Cleopatra probably didn't do much more with her needle than move it from one part of Egypt to another. She may not have even done that. It was already more than a thousand years old when she was born. We gave it her name because she was the most famous Egyptian we knew when it arrived. We hadn't discovered Tutankhamun in 1877.' I was stumbling. Lew looked up as though he was just about to call a halt. A blue pencil, spun between forefinger and table-top, was rolling towards him. He wrote down the date on his pad. One form of impatience turned instantly into another. Pulling his shoulders back, he said: 'So it's been here a hundred years, it's a centenary, let's do it.'

I was not quite quick enough to grasp the point. This stimulated a diatribe on how an anniversary was the perfect approach to any story like this one. Not to see that immediately was a failure. Then quickly we were back to Cleopatra. This was going to be a test. He had to go to a meeting across the river and while he was away I was going to write down a list of points about her that would interest Big Oil readers. 'Put the most important first. Then build out from there. Remember what I said before. A news story is like a pyramid, the main point at the top, then gradually expanding and falling away until the bottom points only survive if there is nothing else to print. Yes, a pyramid, rather appropriate for this story, don't you think?'

He rummaged in his centre desk drawer for his swimming trunks. Did Cleopatra build her own pyramid? He mused with a smile as though it would simply be nice to know. Anything to do with oil? He asked this second question with more seriousness. His first trunks, blue, damp and smelling of dust and ammonia, were found, sniffed and discarded into his holdall to take home. He took a second red and dry pair from his briefcase, wrapped them inside a yellow towel from another drawer, wrapped the whole seaside roll in a bag marked 'Documents' and said we would talk further when he was back.

I have spent a whole day at this cafe table by the courthouse, the first day of seeing neither Socratis nor Mahmoud. Perhaps their lives have returned to normality and they are working. Mahmoud has a job in an office that is part of the court system, not here in the old city centre where the prison vans ply back and forth, but somewhere out to the east nearer the empty palace of King Farouk. Socratis said he was going west to collect up his cars before the police did – and to make sure that his mother was getting the due attention of her son.

Soon it was lunchtime, a hallowed hour in Big Oil world. How to leave the office was a recognised business skill, requiring the skills of a silent waiter sliding a kipper onto a breakfast plate. If the fewest questions were to be asked, a conjuror's arts could be useful too. On the desk of the fifth member of our little team, Miss P, secretary, assistant, knower of all things, 'lifer', as those near retirement called themselves, was a list of where everyone was and how long they might be. RT and RJ were seeing the printers and had a meeting at 2.30. Miss Q was with her mother and had a dental appointment at 3.00. There was a question mark beside both of these entries.

Beside the name Peter was a blank space followed by the words 'dry cleaning in wardrobe'. This meant that in our largest grey steel cabinet was my grey suit from Walters of the Turl, purchased in Oxford for interviews four years before and perfect now for Big Oil; also a pink button-collared shirt, one of three bought from a sale in Jermyn Street for my first job, advertising trainee and strategist for Curly Wurly chocolate bars, enthusiastic participant in meetings where the names of chocolate boxes were dreamed and tested. A narrow horizontally striped tie in petrol shades was also from Jermyn Street, bought singly, very sensibly too, despite the advice from my ad-man adviser that clothes should always be bought in volume to show consistent style.

RJ's desk was the only one by the window. Such pale light as came through the grimy gauze and glass was reserved exclusively for our resident artist. The note about how to behave when Mr Brown arrived was the most visible part of a small wedge of paper keeping apart the frame and sill and allowing a very slight breeze to rustle the motoring pages of *Exchange and Mart*. It was impossible to look out and see Cleopatra's Needle. But I knew it was standing outside with a pigeon on its tip. There was always a pigeon on the tip of what had to be the oldest work of art in London. Part of Lew's advice during the blue-pencil session had been to note carefully the first thing thought or said about a story, the first words about it delivered at the time. Often this first thing was the story itself, the peak of the pyramid. So often in his news-editing days he had heard the real story from a reporter's lips and then found it nowhere mentioned in the copy. That was a lesson worth learning. Back at my own desk, this was the first of my points, not necessarily yet in the right order, but a start.

1) Oldest thing in London; carved from Aswan granite about 1500 BC. Correction: oldest work of art in London outside a museum; oldest man-made object open to rain and pigeons every day. Not a great fate for an obelisk sacred to the Sun god and designed to bring old friends back every day from the dead.

2) First erected near what is now Cairo in the reign of Thothmes III to celebrate his third celebration of the festival of Set. Interesting? No.

3) Cleopatra did not build pyramids. This was one of the questions that Lew had asked. A lesson of the blue-pencil session had been the need that a reporter should answer his editor's questions. Ideally, he should give a positive reply. It was not possible to pretend that Cleopatra had ever built a pyramid. Cleopatra cared more for theatre and politics. A good show was cheaper than rocky reality – and better

for posterity too, since who remembers any Egyptian Pharaoh's death better than hers? As for the main point: no pyramids.

4) The energy industries of ancient Egypt were the slave trade and what we know now as 'alternatives'. The annual flooding of the Nile was the greatest alternative energy source in history. Its source was a secret like the Philosopher's Stone. It too turned earth into gold. Cleopatra had less land and fewer slaves than the great Pharaohs of the past, including the one who had her needle made. But she still had a unique source of water power (a fashionable 'alternative energy' subject for Big Oil in the seventies and one on which a Newsletter was already planned) as well a level of slavery which only her most ambitious competitors could match. As for oil, in her Arab territories a black ooze sometimes rose to the surface and could be sold at a good price for making primitive forms of cement. We might say that she had a modest bitumen business.

Almost two hours had gone by. There was still a stuffy silence in all our offices and in the corridor outside. Not even Miss P was back, which was odd since she had the most limited of excuses why she should not be at her desk. Twenty yards away Miss R, oblivious of my failure to see her, was holding important conference calls about profits from the North Sea fields. I read again my Cleopatra points and wondered which to choose next.

Where was Lew now? Probably on his hundredth Olympic length, recognisable only by grey curls and a clear plastic goggle strap on the back of his neck, halfway to France in his mind and in a hot-metal print room in his dreams. No. Suddenly he was back, without his document bag, without his jacket, with a memo in his hand, red-eyed and ready for a hard afternoon.

He wanted a meeting immediately. There was 'a flap on'. 'Is it to do with Mr Brown?' asked Miss P who had arrived like a rabbit in a half-successful conjuring trick, just a few seconds after her boss and carrying two plastic bags. 'Never mind that,' said Lew. 'Where is everyone?' Miss P consulted her list and read it aloud from printers to dentist, omitting any words like lunch or mother that might not be helpful. 'Well, we'll just have to wait,' he moaned. 'You come on in now,' he barked at me, 'and at least we can get on with fucking Cleopatra.'

His office was much as it had been before, the scent of chlorine a little sharper, the limbs of its occupant less taut, almost languid. 'So what have we got?' he said. 'Anything yet for me to see?' I had hoped that this conversation could have been postponed, even forgotten. I pushed the pages of Cleopatra points across the cratered surface of the table, more to show effort than usefulness. They were not even typed since Miss P had not been there to type them.

He read slowly and in starts, like a man reading a railway timetable. 'A good start and some good appreciation of the problems', he finally announced. 'So how does the story go?'

'Do you mean our Big Oil story? I hadn't quite got the angle on that.'

'No, not yet,' he replied. 'I was thinking about this during my conference across the river, a lot of interminable nonsense that you wouldn't believe, and I was just wondering what went on at all those parties. You've seen the film, the one with Elizabeth Taylor?'

'Yes,' I said, 'but do you really want to know?'

He leaned back, half-closing his eyes: 'I'll tell you when I'm bored, and when I am you can go back to the Alternative Energy Newsletter.'

'Right, this is the potted version,' I began breezily.

'Never patronise your readers,' he snapped, subsiding further into his deep executive chair as I meandered through marble colonnades, libraries and lighthouses. After the third course of wine, women and jewellery, he seemed to be fading into sleep. I asked if that were enough for now. Lew hardly moved. 'Enough for ever?' Then the mood changed. 'We have to get you doing something. Get RJ to sort out some pictures. We'll want Taylor, of course. Were there other versions? And then, of course, there's the bloody needle. He can get one of his extortionate photographers to take that. It's amazing how much they charge for taking pictures of something that doesn't even move, that hasn't moved for a hundred years. What did Cleopatra eat? Did she watch her weight? Don't forget the centenary angle. But we can come back to that.'

He crossed the corridor to find Miss P still in solitary charge of five desks. 'RJ and RT will like this idea, nothing to do with oil, or not much, and great for photography.' This was not the time to say – or even to think – that, however attractive an idea this might be for *Big Oil Times*, it was not one which RT and RJ would like if it came from Lew D. If Lew were enthusiastic – and it seemed strangely as though he was – it might be better if this initial keenness were first allowed to cool. Fortunately neither of them were yet back in the office. Miss Q, according to a note on my desk, had called to say she would be away till late tomorrow morning. I left the same message: I was going to be 'in the library'. If Mr Brown had come then for his picture check, he would have been guaranteed all the lack of disturbance that he was alleged to crave.

On the way out in the corridor I saw Miss R herself. Miss R was never normally seen out of her office. There were rumours that she sometimes slept there. To my amazement she invited me in, almost pulled me in. She ignored the toppling ashtray.

My plan had been to ask whether there might be a better job for me somewhere, maybe in her own department. But before I could speak she placed her square face within inches of mine, pushed two tweed-covered elbows towards me across her desk and asked what I was doing in Big Oil at all. After a few minutes of feigned interest in North Sea oilfields, I told her about both Cleopatra projects, the long-standing and the latest.

'Then why are you wasting your time here?' she replied, tapping hard on the table and turning the ash-mountain into a long grey river. She reminded me of V. 'The only thing worth anything here is what the engineers do and what I do. They get the oil out of the ground. I make sure we pay as little tax as possible on it. The rest is rubbish. Get out while you can. Stick to Cleopatra but get her right. Remember: raising money, spending money, taxing, avoiding being taxed: that is most of what there is.'

What about Mr Brown and these lost pictures? 'Please, please,' she grimaced. 'Don't tempt me. There was once an Antony Brown here, somewhere in security. Now it is just a house name. Antony Brown is whoever gets the pointless job. You can't imagine the non-sense that keeps men, mostly men, employed in a place like this. But then if you can imagine it you will never escape it.'

In the library the following day there were only three readers at 9 a.m., a teenager with a *Morning Star* under his arm studying *The Guardian* on a wooden rack, a stooped woman whose size, shape and mackintosh colour matched precisely the revolving bookcase into which she peered, and a man with a briefcase and a knife who was neatly transferring dust-wrappers and the occasional illustration from public ownership to his own.

Half a shelf of Roman history survived here, like the obscurest part of a forgotten empire. Its books had not been knifed, deprived of their jackets or touched much at all except to push them tight together to make more room for the twentieth century. They always seemed to squeal with relief when taken down and spread upon a desk.

Lew wanted to know what Cleopatra ate. Chicken was the new dish of the time, more fashionable than pigeon, quail and ostrich. She had caraway, flax, lettuce, sunflower and sesame seeds and the now-extinct silphium of Cyrene. There were olives, cabbage, courgettes, raw onions; coriander, scattered in tombs, was popular for taking to the next life. Was this what he wanted to know?

I had to imagine what the readers of *Big Oil Times* wanted. I would not be the first – or last – to write a book like that. A very short summary for Cleopatra the Sixth took only an hour and a half. The thin man had not even opened his *Morning Star* yet. The woman and the revolving bookshelf were still entwined in indecision. The book thief had just begun to read *The Rachel Papers*, after removing its black-and-yellow wrapper, and had not reached much beyond the conflict between the young Martin Amis and his shaving mirror. At this rate Cleopatra could care for three children by two world leaders, make a bad call in one of the world's most important battles and die in mysterious circumstances, possibly involving snakes, and all before Lew had begun his daily assault on the Continent.

All that I have done in the unusual absence of both Socratis and Mahmoud is to remember events that I barely ever think about at all, a patch of colourless Big Oil past that is a part of this Cleopatra story because it would be incomplete without it. James Holladay had said that bureaucrats and trimmers were the key to historical understanding. The people who made things happen might be grey. The prisoners going in and out their buses today are particularly grey.

15.I.II

Hotel Metropole, Place Saad Zaghloul

In the early morning darkness, beside the check-in desk at the Metropole Hotel, no one is as calm as yesterday. A pale waiter in a white robe delivers coffee as though it were the alcohol of his reluctant evening work, each cup like a liquid explosive cursed personally by his imam. The guards are not only awake beside their electronic gate but alert. The woman who two weeks ago greeted me reluctantly to the home of 'Cleopatra and her Antonio' is now not even pretending a welcome. There is a line of supplicants in front of her desk. The stained light from the Versailles Garden staircase falls on foreigners seeking rooms.

From my armchair by the window, I can see both the empty side-street and the queue inside. There is the guide I last saw at Pompey's Pillar, the one who was lecturing about Tutankhamun. The same young women are behind her, maybe a table-tennis team, and behind them a man, dressed for winter, with a Canadian passport in his hand.

Closest to me, in the space where guests sit to check their messages and their bills, and wait for taxis, is the picnicking family from the Roman Theatre, the ones who had hoped for better weather but were making the best of the cold. Wherever all these people have been staying before, this morning they want to move here.

Journalists learn a sense of when there is news. 'Has something happened?' I ask the guide. 'Not here', she snaps as though I were about to molest one of her team or seize one of her rooms. The Canadian stamps his feet. The picnickers punch their phones.

I wish that they were not here. I have worked long and hard in these quiet armchairs, longer and harder than at any time I can recall, perhaps since my attempts to restore some academic reputation for myself in Oxford forty years ago. Honour Moderations was the name of the exam. This too is like an examination. I have no books, only a few scraps of paper in Room 114 upstairs, final revision notes as it were. It is remarkable what remains catalogued under Cleopatra in my mind when I have forgotten so much else.

CLEOPATRA THE SEVENTH

A year after leaving Lew D in Big Oil House, after he had wished me good luck and made a joke about 'fucking Cleopatra', I was with him again. We were on a tour of pubs that he had especially requested. I was showing him the places that had 'once been favoured' by my fellow journalists at *The Times* and *The Sunday Times*. Lew wanted to see where his hero Harold Evans worked. He wanted to drink in the Blue Lion, the Calthorpe Arms, the Pakenham Arms and the Apple Tree.

We were in bars likely to be favoured no more. For only three of the past nine months had any copies of *The Times* newspapers been published. In one of the angriest industrial disputes even of those disputatious days, all of us were 'shut down' or 'locked out' (the language depending on one's political position towards the unions, the management and the government) and it was far from clear to the journalists that we would ever again open up or be allowed back in.

I was now the newest recruit to the Business News section of *The*

Sunday Times. Lew was touchingly pleased to see me out of Big Oil and into journalism, the opposite direction to the route he had taken himself. But he was sad to find that I was so soon describing the legendary haunts of his newspaper heroes as though I were a tour guide here in Alexandria, offering disappointment, decline and neglect.

He was wearing a leather jacket that I had never seen before. Maybe it was what he had worn for work at the *Daily Mirror*. But he had the same gaze, the same reddened eyes and watery smile that got him each day from one meeting to another and from Dover to distant yachts at lunchtime. We had barely sat down in the Calthorpe Arms, a quiet hovel where even in better times it was possible often to find a table and read or write, before he declared himself equally determined that I should give up Cleopatra.

That was the main message he had come to bring me. I had a proper job now, he said. I had been lucky enough to leave Big Oil. I had been even luckier to get a job on *The Sunday Times*. I was a newspaper man. If I had to write about someone else's life, surely I should at least take on Margaret Thatcher instead. I tried gently to change the subject. I would be wrong to make quick decisions. Surely he understood that. No, he did not.

I said I had just returned from Syria on a Lufthansa flight for journalists. Any free trip that kept us out of trouble was an approved assignment when there was no real work. I had visited Palmyra, an ancient site that Lew had reluctantly visited in his youth. We had talked about it before in Big Oil House, the ruined palaces of Queen Zenobia who, two centuries after Cleopatra's death, had idolised her memory, dined on her dinner plates and even briefly conquered Alexandria. This time Lew remembered only how ill he had been in Palmyra.

He took a sip of Calthorpe ale. Margaret Thatcher was what he most wanted to talk about. She was new. She was a big story, whether or not she crashed and burned or came out on top. I had already met her. He was respectfully impressed by that. Yes, there were journalists who thought and hoped she would be here today and gone tomorrow. That was all the more opportunity for a young man with a future in newspapers. And yes, there would always be newspapers. The shut-down would be short. We journalists were still being paid.

Was he suggesting, I asked, that Mrs Thatcher was somehow like Cleopatra? Was she somehow a modern substitute? No, the beauty of her was that she was not. She was nothing like her. Why did she have to be like anyone that was old and gone? I needed to 'get real'. That was the beauty of journalism. Its characters had to be real. He did not mean the people writing the stories: some of them were fantastical and always had been. He meant those they were writing about. If I did not understand that, I would never succeed.

My Big Oil writing tutor was rambling a little and suddenly he seemed about to fade. For someone who talked much about drink he did not drink well. His *Big Oil Times* staff had often joked about that. Then just as suddenly, with a fresh burst of nostalgic enthusiasm, he abandoned his lecture on newspaper skills and asked, as though he were a tourist, where all the 'back-stabbers' now came, reeling off the names of pubs around Fleet Street where it seemed that many backs had been stabbed, the King & Keys and Coach & Horses, places where I had never been.

They came here to the Calthorpe, I replied, entering into the spirit of his memories. But only, I added, those back-stabbers who were the most determined and secretive. He settled back as though I were about to narrate a home movie of his life.

It was best, I said, to sit outside on the benches if you did not care who saw you. That was always supposing you could focus your eyes away from the swirling-seabed, green-and-yellow tiles around the walls. Most of us used to go inside. You could squat down in the back bar with the chloroform clowns from the Eastman Dental Hospital along the road. This was privacy – at only a small price that most were always happy to pay.

Lew's eyes were bright in the sickly gloom. Normally the clearest words at the Calthorpe were about the cost of gin. The dentists would shout out as they mixed it with the beer, laughing as though they were still sniffing their anaesthetics. If a newsroom reporter wanted a conversation that he would later want to forget, one that never happened, this was the nearest place to come. That was what I told him.

My old boss listened carefully. He stared up at the pub sign of two loin-clothed bodyguards between a red-tongued, red-eyed beast. There was one of those meaningless mottos for which Latin was long judged so useful: *gradu diverso via una*: one way by different steps. I had an immediate desire to ask about the Cleopatra project I had left behind. Had *Big Oil Times* ever finished what we had begun? He cut off the question, talking again about old newspaper days, the great figures he had seen, worked with, worked for, seen at the same bar. There were characters, professional characters of the trade, who had no personality at all; and there were personalities whom it was hard to characterise. Character-building was the hardest art.

He sat back deeper in an unsteady chair. He pulled from his pocket a swimming hat, which he pushed to one side, and a damp envelope which he pushed towards me. Inside the envelope there were some identically sized photographs, clinging together like a pack of cards rescued from a drowned man. Lew looked around but no one else was looking. At the bar there were only two dazed dentists and a plasterer speaking to himself in Welsh.

The pictures were a peculiar mixture. If they were for a card game, it was not clear what the game might be. The first showed the body of a defiant young woman seated on a table beside a matronly marble head, a juxtaposition of two types of nakedness, the living and the dead, stockings and grey stone, both classical in their different ways, one with black lines of eyebrow and pubic hair, the other with pale curls and lips. The second and third were shots of Elizabeth Taylor on a horse and with a dog.

The fourth card of the pack showed a sultry, broad-shouldered matron with her hand to her ear. On the fifth was a poster of Miss Taylor on the wall of a Big Oil filling station. The sixth portrayed an ecstatic angel with a snake. From the seventh a gauzily clothed girl stared out, while being herself inspected by a balding carpet-seller. In the eighth and last a sharp-faced man with a wreath on his head looked anxiously sideways at a woman who was scratching her ear. Lew looked them over like a gambler who could not believe there was so much bad luck in the world.

I was confused. I mumbled. Had the lost Big Oil collection finally been found? Was this it? Had there really been an Antony Brown? Did he know that my school had been founded by a man with the same name? Lew scowled. We looked at the pictures together again.

None of them looked much like corporate art, like lost John Pipers or illustrations suitable for motoring guides or calendars. The woman in the black stockings was magnificent. There was something memorable about the chancer in the laurel wreath. But there seemed no reason for them to be lying on a Calthorpe table, smelling of chlorine, absorbing yet more moisture in spilt beer.

Lew's mood was in steep decline. He took each picture in turn, dealing it face down. Then he tore the whole sodden pack into small pieces, the model with the classical prop, the velvety titillations, the bizarre souvenir from the Morocco souks and the old woman snatching a pearl earring while her husband ate oysters.

He snorted. He had the dry nasal irritation of the long-distance swimmer. Of course, these were not the lost masterpieces of Big Oil. They were the 'fucking Cleopatras' that his staff had given him. RT and RJ had been taking him for a ride. They had found Elizabeth Taylor with Lassie. They had not even got a decent Needle.

The queue of new Metropole arrivals has disappeared. The table-tennis team went elsewhere. I watched them leave. The others must be somewhere on this site of Cleopatra's temple for Caesar, maybe with views like mine. It would be odd to stay here and not want a room overlooking Old Zaghloul and the Mediterranean Sea. Now that the street outside is awake and honking, the guards inside are calmer. As long as I am on the first floor for breakfast by 10 a.m., I can stay all morning. My room may even be cleaned while I am away.

Back at the Calthorpe in 1979, Lew wanted to continue his tour. He was tired of the ghosts of journalists and wanted to meet some real ones. Instead I could describe only where the reporters used to sit. I could describe them because I could almost see them still there, plotting, gossiping, boasting, the big men of the business who had written thousands of words that year about miners' unions, coal stocks, strike strategies, flying pickets, secondary action and peak power. That is just one of the oddities of journalism: we acquire the most detailed knowledge when we need it. When the story changes, the facts disappear. They have all gone now.

I took Lew next to the Blue Lion on the other side of the road. There were two newspapers then on the Gray's Inn Road, both with *Times* in their title but not much else in common. *The Times* was the older and grander. It was *The Sunday Times* that made the money, paid the bigger salaries and noisily prided itself on everything.

The Times was very much 'the other occupant' of the street, a 200-year-old institution, the most famous paper in the world, proud but more quietly so. The spirit of *The Times* was a resentful modesty, one well befitting an indigent who had been moved from his City home to where he might more easily live off his richer younger brother. For those who worked on the two papers there was not much shared drinking time. The two offices were connected by a bridge, but only in the least meaningful manner.

The *Sunday Times* office held the printing presses for both papers, the massive metal monuments that ought decades ago to have been melted for scrap or exiled to a museum. There was not much encouragement for any journalist ever to visit them. The printers jealously guarded their exclusive rights; they rightly feared that computers and keyboards would end their hereditary grip on their jobs. On the rare occasion when a reporter visited 'the machine room' he risked abuse as well as raging heat. On the rarer occasion when a reporter from one paper joined the staff of the other it was like a man sleeping with his wife's sister. It was a family affair – but not in a good way.

The Blue Lion had no pub sign. It kept its armorial enamel under its eaves, altogether smarter than the Calthorpe. It was a place where the top *Sunday Times* reporters went to be seen, where their 'space barons' held court, where bylines were won or lost over pints of

Greene King, where the black marks on the ceiling came from some-one's detonator souvenir from the Lebanon.

These 'space barons' were the men of power. In 1979 newspapers were small in pages and large in staff. Most of what was written never appeared in print. For a century *Times* correspondents had grown used to writing despatches read by no one other than the editor and his so-called 'leader writers'. That was one reason that the paper's opinion was so respected: it was based on original research, facts that the readers never knew.

In the expansive sixties more stories had appeared each day, some even with the byline of the writer attached. But even in 1979, if any story were published at the length it had been written, it was a mira-cle, and almost certainly a mistake. 'Space' was the prime asset of the paper. The 'space barons' were the men who dispensed it, who decided what was published and what was not. On *The Sunday Times*, with only one publication a week and dozens of teams and hundreds of individuals wanting to fill it, the barons were like kings. The Blue Lion had been their court.

Lew also wanted to visit the Pakenham Arms, a place on a corner of two empty streets at the back of the offices. The Pakenham was an 'anywhere pub' that might have been in Brentwood or Chelmsford, a place of satisfyingly small distinction. He had been told that this was where 'the Business News boys' met most nights, the reporters whom he might sometimes need (or pretend to need) for his own Big Oil work. This was partly true. I was a Business News reporter myself. My new colleagues did meet there some nights, but not, I said, most nights.

Unpredictability was a useful tool. Business writers then were not as open to businessmen as they later became. They were often hard for businessmen even to find. The best qualification to be a business writer was to hate business. Theatre critics loved actors; the Labour staff loved trades unions; cricket writers batted and bowled every Sunday. The correspondents in Washington and Cairo and everywhere else were men who loved their temporary homes. But business writers deeply distrusted businessmen, and much preferred talking to each other. When they wrote biographies, they were like the historians of ancient Greece and Rome; they wrote in bold colours, for purposes of occasional praise and frequent damnation, about people who would never meet them and whom they never met.

By the time we left the Pakenham that evening it was almost nine o'clock. A large black car stopped beside us and a large limping man stepped onto the pavement. This was a rare sighting of the boss of bosses at Times Newspapers, a man whose destination was the office back entrance and who could not at that time have safely had a drink in any of the bars where Lew and I had been. Marmaduke Hussey, or Duke as he was known, was the man charged with modernising the machinery, making the unions as museum-worthy as the presses. He had much on his mind. His campaign was not going well. He was not producing any newspapers at all. Each week their readers were fleeing to rival titles still in print.

He noticed me only because, unusually, I was wearing a blue Trinity tie embroidered with the black griffins of the college crest. He was wearing the same. He asked my name and I introduced him to Lew who knew much more than I did about the Chairman, an industrial hero of the Thatcher age, and was delighted to meet him in person.

V signalled her imminent arrival at *The Sunday Times*, just as she had done at Oxford, with short, mocking, mildly abusive messages, each

signed with her initial. The notes did not arrive with quite the regularity of the Trinity post. On one visit I found three. Our post came in sacks that stayed unopened for weeks. Our strike-struck offices were on a form of bureaucratic life support. We were alive but not functioning, anaesthetised, ready to be brought round at a moment's notice, a moment that was perpetually postponed. No one knew whether the unions or the management would be the first to crack.

Every few weeks we came to Gray's Inn Road to hear the news of the dispute. We held trade union chapel meetings and news conferences on 'long-term projects'. Lew was surprised that I had joined the journalists' union but as a newcomer, and a latecomer to newspapers too, it had seemed a good idea. There was no other way to hear of management tactics or the printers' response. Lew thought that 'Duke', whose hand he had proudly shaken, would defeat the printers, become a Thatcherland hero and need never again skulk into his office by the Pakenham Arms' back door. V, as was clear from her notes, hoped for a very different outcome.

My old friend scrawled that journalists were 'scabs' who should 'back your brothers'. My old boss thought that every trade unionist was a threat to the national order. My own view was somewhere in between. The dispute was yet another chance to continue with Cleopatra while, for the first time, being able to claim that that I was being paid to do so.

Most journalists took other jobs – and thus were being paid twice. At every meeting we listened to fraternal delegates from faraway places and prided ourselves that, without our appropriately paid inactivity, there would be no newspapers to reopen when the dispute was over, whichever side claimed the victory.

None of V's notes prepared me for the shock of first seeing her in the newsroom, swinging her legs on a grey metal desk during an explanation to us of what expenses could and should be claimed for work which, while not producing stories for next week's paper, was necessary for maintaining contacts, conducting long-term investigations and generally ensuring our permanent readiness to return to life.

I recognised her immediately. I did not expect her to be there, not in person, but she was dressed more or less as she always had been, in black, in a short skirt and shaggy sweater (my mother, and probably hers too, would have called it 'old dishcloth') but hardly different at all from my rough-book drawing of a dozen years before. The only addition was a badge in support of NATSOPA clerical, one of the many warring union branches.

She looked superior and smug. She refused to meet my eye. My only aim was to work my way to the side of the room and get her out as fast as possible.

Out on the broad grey pavement she laughed and pointed across the road. I wondered which of the pubs was the least unsuitable to take her. The Blue Lion was too public in every way. The Apple Tree was always packed with printers. Journalists there were generally discouraged. The Pakenham maybe? She would have felt at home among the anti-capitalist reporters of our Business News. But I was not sure I wanted my prickly new colleagues to meet my prickly old friend.

It had to be the Calthorpe. A few minutes later V became the first woman that I had ever seen there amid the medicinal gas, the sea-coloured tiles, the club-wielding bodyguards and the Welsh. I bought us two beers in bottles, the safest choice. After some brief words about teachers' union solidarity committees, threats to craft skills from foreign capitalists and other cries from the chapels, we continued almost as we had done in 1971, as though we were continuing the same conversation, first reprising the main points lest there was something we had forgotten.

'How are Maurice and Cleopatra?'

I had not seen Maurice for a while.

'He is still advertising,' I said.

'Himself?'

'No. Dog food. He met a very nice boy a few months ago at Crufts, while persuading the champion chihuahua's owner that he owed it all to the chunky goodness of Maurice's client.'

She smiled but not for long.

'And Cleopatra?'

'Well, it's not easy,' I said, 'what with all the uncertainty of the dispute.' I had just written a peculiarly dull passage about the Perusine War, a string of battles in which Antony and Octavian, still nominally allies, had fought through proxies over the fate of unfortunate Italian towns. I was not feeling very confident.

As before, my floundering did not go unremarked.

'I don't think you are going to get Cleopatra round here.' She looked around the Calthorpe as it slowly filled with middle-aged anxiety.

'What about the useless males Cleopatra had to deal with? Remind me again of those.'

'Canidius, the general, the one you thought was stupid at the beginning of the film?'

'I don't think he would get you very far.' In 1979 no one yet knew about Cleopatra's handwritten assent to his tax-breaks for wine, the exemption certificate that had lasted two thousand years in a coffin.

'There is Hirtius. We talked about him once. Greedy, pompous, a writer.'

'Better.'

'Or Dellius, the pimp, Cleopatra's escort to Tarsus. Also a writer.'

'Too easy.'

'Plancus. What about him?'

'Try me.'

'He changed sides. He was famous for changing sides. He was the closest man to Antony and then abandoned him. He thought Cleopatra was a bad influence.'

'Promising.'

'A big man at Oxford once told me he was the most important of them all. He was not in the film, or in Shakespeare, but he did at least two other things that once made him famous, well infamous really.'

'You mean the pearls?'

'Yes.'

'And the slithering about in a mermaid costume?'

'Yes. How do you know about that?'

She ignored the question.

'You should write about what you know. You don't know Cleopatra.'

'I don't know Plancus – except that he judged the contest between Antony and Cleopatra over who could put on the most expensive dinner.'

'Yes, and she dissolved a huge pearl earring in her wine to win the prize.'

'Plancus did stop her dissolving her second earring too.'

'Maybe.' She nodded and pulled a piece of cardboard from her beer. We were undeniably raising the tone at the Calthorpe Arms. 'There was also the time that he slopped around Cleopatra's throne as a sea god with a mermaid's tail, full blue body make-up too. Unusual for a Roman Consul.'

'Well, it was a probably a fancy-dress party. All Alexandrians liked dressing up. But anyway, why do you know so much about Plancus?'

V paused. She knew she had a good line ahead. 'Plancus was always in the Red Tents. He had an axe and a cane. He was the man in charge.'

'What Red Tents do you mean?'

'Maurice's Red Tents. Plancus was the MC, the ringmaster, the man who kept us in order.'

I tried to hide my surprise, unsuccessfully as ever. She paused.

'Don't worry. I wasn't one of his mermaids under the carpet with their legs stuck out into the corridor. Those were nearly always boys.'

'I was one of the statues around the sides. We wore veils and not much else. Sometimes I was the one who played Alexander the Great's sister and asked for the password. And once I was Cleopatra when the usual one was away. Our Cleopatra was never available to customers either. She liked to watch. She had finished her exams by then.'

'So, Maurice did put on his play, the one from the college erotica library, but not in the college gardens.'

'You could say that. Someone else started it, someone else from Brentwood. Quite a school. Didn't I always say so? But he died, threw himself from the Amsterdam Hilton, or so they said. Maurice took it on, made it more fun.'

'But why you? Wasn't it rather unpleasant?'

'Only sometimes. It was more show than anything else. Not much happened, at least not where I could see. The tent within a tent within a tent was always a bit impractical. It looked good. It was a job. I got paid. And I got to spend time with Maurice.'

The Calthorpe was by now almost full. There was an intensifying whiff of gas and a louder bubbling of Welsh vowels. V continued for some while to speak to me as though she were still the older girl, still embarrassed to be seen with a young boy outside a cinema.

At lunchtime there was a message and a map from Mahmoud, showing the coast road to the east. At 4 p.m. he was waiting, as promised, where the Montaza beach meets the road, by the pink-and-white holiday resort whose last regular occupant was Egypt's last ruling king. It was safer at the edge of town, he said, which was not the reason he had given when he had first mentioned my coming here. He had insisted then that no one writing about Cleopatra should come to Alexandria without visiting these fantasy turrets.

King Farouk had lost his throne in 1952: 'when you were only one years old', said Mahmoud.

The king, he said, was 'not a bad man'. He had shown 'youthful promise', even if his biographies show him only as a harmless collector of red cars and razor blades. He had been harassed by foreign powers and ungrateful Egyptians like old Mr Zaghloul.

Yes, his life had ended in ignominy and exile, famed for his pornography collection and dying, eventually, from one too many Lobster Thermidors. But he was 'not to be derided for that'. In fact, said Mahmoud, 'his memory was increasingly revered'.

We could not go inside the Montaza Palace. Only the President, the fourth in line of the non-royal pharaohs of Egypt, was allowed to use it and he never did. But we could admire the generous use of the letter F in the decoration, a recognition of the immortality of not merely the king himself but of his sisters, Fawzia, Faiza, Faika and Fathia – and of his children, Ferial, Fawzia, Fadia and Fuad.

Mahmoud's tone was rather different from before, mildly mocking, not quite as deferential to the 'good men' who had always ruled his country. 'F for Fascist too,' he added. Farouk liked Hitler because Egypt's British 'protectors' behaved as the Roman protectors once had done – and the Germans had done less harm here than the French. But that was less an issue now. It had faded from memory along with the king's collection of sexually explicit snuff boxes and green alabaster baths.

Poor Farouk had hormonal problems. He was seen almost as a 'good man' again now, much better than the man who was ordering new cameras and microphones into Saad Zaghloul Square. The police were searching for terrorists but listening to everyone. They said that Jihadists were Egypt's enemy, when almost everyone was Mubarak's enemy. They planted bombs to make the British and Americans afraid of the Jihadists and supportive of the regime.

This was a surprise. So Mahmoud, too, was suggesting that the New Year bomb was Mubarak's very own work, a sharp change of view from the quiet apologist who had adopted me only two weeks ago at the Metropole Hotel. On January 1st both Socratis and Mahmoud had seemed to be on the same side – with different degrees of enthusiasm. Then Socratis had given his carpet lecture, his story of how Cleopatra ruled, how she was propped up by a foreign power and hated by almost everyone. The ancient Alexandrians had a name for that sort of message, an *ekphrasis*, a picture described with a purpose. And now Mahmoud, rather more directly, was back in line with his friend, a very different line from the one before.

Why then, I asked, had we come to a presidential palace, even one not used by the president? Was this really his 'safer place'? What was going on?

This place was controlled by 'the old security', he said, the part that barely functioned. There were 250 acres here and as many different kinds of palm tree. He smiled, as though newly unburdened. And anyway, was this not the closest to the queen of the Cleopatra Ball that I was ever going to get?

Perhaps it was. If I wanted to conjure scenes of Antony, god of intoxication, Cleopatra, the ruthless and insatiable, Dellius, procurer of boys and girls, and Plancus, master of all ceremonies, this would be the place. We could forget the Metropole ballroom.

There was a brief scuffle when two young English women, trying optimistically to soak up some pale sun, sought a piece of sand for their towels that two Egyptian businessmen, with black suits and sandwiches, thought was rightfully theirs. An argument between the almost naked and the over-dressed will normally favour the latter; and so it did. But after this there was almost no movement, no distraction at all.

Mahmoud said he had to go back to work but would meet me at 7 p.m. at the Palestine Hotel in the palace grounds. Meanwhile I could select a writing place beside a bank of reeds, an indigenous variety among a wide choice of more exotic shrubs.

This is a place and a chance to think ahead. The rest of this book is going to star the Queen of England as well as Egypt, a hero of Anzio, a cancer-stricken editor, a Hollywood actor, strange men on stilts, Margaret Thatcher at the height of her powers in the Miners' Strike (even though I never wrote that first biography), a lost escapologist (£350 for the evening), a thousand bottles of free Bollinger champagne and a Dutch master's painting. There will definitely now be a bigger part for Lucius Munatius Plancus. V has made sure of that.

So who was Plancus? Aside from the good stories, where does he fit in? Like most of the Romans whose names we put in history books, he was a soldier, a diplomat and a politician. There was nothing unusual in his lines of work. He was an aristocrat, but from one of the newer families, the kind then most likely to see their future with Julius Caesar. Like Antony, but lower down the ranks, he helped the conquest of Gaul. He earned a reputation for hunting druids. He might have been with Caesar for the invasion of Britain. He knew Hirtius. He disappears from the record at the time of Pharsalus and the Alexandrine War but was probably there at both. His is the second name mentioned in Caesar's *African War*, the bloody mopping-up of Pompey's defiant supporters. He might himself have been one of its Continuators.

In V's view the middle-aged character of Plancus was as necessary in 1987 as the teenage years of Cleopatra had been twenty years before. She saw him as a forgotten character, and no less important for that. He was a trimmer, a chancer, a boaster, a Roman who played for almost every side in Rome's long civil wars and whose sole thought, at all times, was of who would win, how would their battles be won, when should he join the winner and how he could help himself from the victor's spoils.

In V's view, he needed rescuing. He was important. He was relevant. He was missing in too many versions of the story. He was the man most like the men she saw about her. This unreliable ally of Mark Antony was the consul who dressed in weeds and wode and slithered among mermaids at the Queen's command. He was the judge who decided whether Cleopatra's priceless pearl in acid wine should win the wager. The shaking of this cocktail was the act, in some ways the single most essential act of Alexandrian extravagance, science, theatre and technical invention. Plancus was the ringmaster, the producer. He had gained only small credit from historians for stopping the show before the second earring too was reduced to sour wine and scum.

The English women on the Palestine beach have given up their struggle with the men in black suits. They have dressed and joined their sometime disputants at the bar. Closer encounters seem almost certain. The larger of the two men is dancing and one of the women is trying to pull him back down to the table. I may be able to follow their progress more closely when Mahmoud comes back for dinner.

A few weeks after our encounter outside the Pakenham Arms Duke Hussey asked me for a drink – out of Trinity Oxford solidarity, I assumed, rather than for any other reason. What other reason could there be? I was nervous. Might it be some kind of interview? Surely not. Duke was the boss of bosses. I was the newest recruit. Duke was 'management', a word used derisively in the Blue Lion and Calthorpe. Management did not talk to journalists any more than trade unionists talked to journalists. No one talked to anyone – except in formal talks – or talks about talks.

We met at Brooks's Club in St James, an unlikely pair, he acknowledging fellow members, staff and even the portraits on the walls, I looking downwards onto a grime-ground carpet. We both had a dry sherry, the first sherry I had drunk since the days of Maurice's decanter. I ordered what he ordered. It seemed the safest course.

He began by being complimentary about articles I had written for *The Sunday Times*. Before we had been forced to stop work I had been 'coming along well'. He thought that I was picking up the style. But he said the words in such a way as to suggest that the newspaper's style was not his own, nor one of which he much approved.

I had already made my first mistake – in telling the Business News men of the Pakenham Arms that I was having the lunch at all. So I would have to bring back some news, some gossip or insight. What was I supposed to say? Duke seemed to be one of those men who could say nothing for hours on end, mixing pleasantries with mouthfuls of plaice and peas.

Duke was a military hero. That much Lew had told me. The industrial campaign to defeat the trades unions of Gray's Inn Road was nothing much, it seemed, in comparison to what this modest, bluff, flat-faced man had known in his youth. He was confident of victory. We had only to be patient.

We talked easily enough, about Trinity, James Holladay, the King's Arms, the gardens. He asked about my hobbies as though he were interviewing me for a senior position in domestic service. I mentioned Cleopatra, but carefully. From his flickering eyes came the message that an ambitious reporter, a Trinity man too, should have more immediate matters on his mind.

Duke knew, however, about one character in the Cleopatra story, the same one, strangely, that V had identified. Duke and V had nothing else in common. It would have been hard to imagine her in Brooks's. He was her enemy, her class enemy, in the seventies the most potent kind. But they both knew bits of what little there is to be known about Lucius Munatius Plancus.

That was mere coincidence then, a discovery made over two dishes of sponge pudding and custard. But it is also the only reason that I am writing about Plancus now, with my back against the soft bark of a tree once owned by King Farouk. The consul with the mermaid's tail, as Duke explained, was a Roman of more than mere historical interest, not just a part of Cleopatra's life but part of his own. He spoke for what seemed an hour or more. I had not yet learnt that the coffee stage of a club-land lunch might last twice as long as the soup, fish and cake.

There are many reasons for knowing about a character from the past. I already knew about Plancus because any biographer of Cleopatra has to know him: he was the man who organised her fancy-dress parties and the financing of Antony's armies. James Holladay knew even more about Plancus because it was his job to know more – and because he considered unreliable allies to be some of the most consistently important chracters in history.

V had played alongside a Plancus in the Red Tents of Oxford, looking down at the mermaids and the wrestlers. Any admirer of the poet Horace will know about Plancus, the recipient of a beautiful and mysterious poem beginning *Laudabunt alii, Others will praise* and followed by a list of seaside towns. But Duke knew about him because, in January 1944, he had passed by Plancus's tomb. It was like a giant pillbox, he said, like a great brick drum built by Hitler's finest engineers. He had been on his way to losing his leg at Anzio at the time.

The long last phase of the Second World War in Italy had given the young Marmaduke Hussey a fresh perspective on ancient history. His fellow officers, he said, included much better scholars and teachers than he. Many knew of the Continuators. They had read the second half of the *Aeneid*, the battle for Rome itself. Quarrelling commanders, disagreements about battle sites and cavalry tactics, and whether Rome was even worth fighting for: all these questions filled the Latin pages of their schoolboy memories.

In 1944, Duke reminded me, the Allies were advancing painfully through Italy, arguing among themselves about the speed and direction of the drive against the enemy. Neither the landscape nor the questions were so very different from how they had been 2000 and 3000 years before. So many of his companions were steeped in the classics, the easiest way for them to talk about the present was to place the roads, rivers and mountains in the past. Not much had changed. The British, American and German armies were the latest and bloodiest heirs to Aeneas and Antony fighting up and down the peninsula known as Italy.

Lucius Munatius Plancus's 2000-year-old tomb, once topped by cypress trees, dominated the allied invasion routes of 1944 at Gaeta by the Bay of Naples. So, when Duke's transport ships passed by, several of his friends knew exactly what it was. They talked of how it was the most spectacular spot, close to the place of Plancus's birth. The old Roman had made his tomb, 500 feet above the sea, to mark the achievements by which he most wanted to be remembered: his good deeds, his consulships and priesthoods, his triumphs over Swiss tribesmen and the foundation of Lyons. Had he perhaps persuaded Virgil to begin Book Seven of his *Aeneid* there, with the burial of Caieta, the hero's nurse, those lines about whether life was worth remembering, the first in Latin that I ever read? Maybe he had.

What did I think? Were his friends right? I was able to add a few thoughts, the first of the lunch that Duke seemed to listen to. In his old age, I suggested, Plancus was rightly worried that his bad deeds would outlast the good. More shocking to some than the pearl dissolved in wine was his rumoured part in his brother's murder and his exploitation of Antony's money-making raids on the aristocracy after the Ides of March. Plancus, it was said, had wanted his brother's house at Tibur, the most fashionable riverside suburb of Rome. Antony could ensure that this theft was legal. But it was still a stain on his character.

Plancus knew that he would be attacked after his death. He had enemies who were already writing the bad obituaries. 'Only ghosts fight with corpses,' he jibed at them, *'cum mortuis non nisi larvas luctari'*. But Plancus was a vain man. He wanted the best possible credit for the best that he had done.

Duke nodded. By February 1944, he said, the British army had fought its way from Sicily and reached a line just south of Gaeta. The Germans were as divided as the Allies about whether or where they should fight in Italy and they too had the tomb of Plancus on their maps. Duke's masters took a fateful decision (absolutely fateful for him) that rather than fight their way on land past Gaeta they would sail past it, to Anzio, the beaches of ancient Antium.

A schoolboy's idea of Anzio was a place of warmth, wine and art, the sculptures that Plancus and his kind had stolen, bought and sold, the grapes they had grown and the sun that had shone on them while they did so. The Anzio beaches in 1944 were a classical landscape of a different, darker kind.

Duke clenched his fist over the table as he recalled the scene. He was now a wholly different man from the one who had arrived at Brooks's, cold as he recalled the sodden sands, the rain like corrugated-iron sheets, the clinging mud like the mess on an abattoir floor. This was classical only as an amphitheatre for gladiators is classical, sand where there was nowhere to hide, overlooked by high boxes, booths, protected places with perfect lines of sight.

When it came to his own part, Duke paused. He arrived after the first wave of the assault, among the reinforcements required to fill the gaps left by the dead. He did not want to talk about what happened next. In his memoir, *Chance Governs All*, published much later, he described his encounter on a bramble-covered hillside with 'the worst shot' in the German army, the machine-gunner who at a range of three yards took his leg when by any likelihood of reason he should have taken his life.

It was a matter of chance. Chance governed everything, he said. Confidence and luck were the keys to any life.

We returned to talking about Trinity. This was easier, though increasingly disjointed. He told me what I had never known, that James Holladay, the heavy-bodied hero of the King's Arms, had been a gunner in the D-Day landings, going over on a Gooseberry. A Gooseberry? Yes, part of a Mulberry, one of the artificial harbours. Did I not know about them?

Incidentally, did I ever go to the Calthorpe Arms? He preferred it to the Pakenham. I said I was surprised he knew either. He said he knew the Calthorpes quite well. The one who gave his name to the pub was our naval commander in the Mediterranean in the First World War. Arthur Calthorpe accepted the Turkish surrender. *Gradu diverso via una*. That was his motto.

In his London club, forty years on from the event that had redirected his life, Duke seemed surprised to be taking an hour or two away from his industrial wars, musing about ships and scholarship and about Plancus, the man in the Gaeta tomb. Was he an evil traitor and a trimmer, a betrayer of his brother, a stealer of his brother's house, an unreliable ally, debauchee and drunk? Or was he just what so many of us would have been, if we were lucky, a man of all wars who waits to see who is going to win and enjoys himself as best he can while waiting?

Duke did not encourage long answers – or any answer that strayed too far from his centre of concern. He did not seek the bigger picture. He did not care about Cleopatra or Antony. He was a minimalist, happy to define his knowledge in his own way, a lover of order, an artist of organisation, an Alexandrian in many ways. When he argued for Plancus, he did so doggedly, as though the Roman were a wartime companion fallen upon hard times. On a troop ship from one theatre of foggy fighting to another, Plancus had been a relaxation of a kind. The tomb itself, he said, had suffered from both allied and German bullets but it was well restored now. There was a prison nearby where for a long time they kept some of the nastier operatives of the SS.

These days of returning to childhood passions and student studies have been peculiar in many ways. I am both a better and worse classicist than I once was. Like so many others who have learnt Latin and Greek, I read as a child what I barely understood and have understood as an adult what I barely now can read. I had only a few answers for Duke back then. I have a few more now.

Lucius Munatius Plancus was, as James Holladay said and V could see, one of those men who live and strive just below the surface of politics. Although he does not appear in Shakespeare's plays or on screen alongside Elizabeth Taylor, he is a serious figure in Rome's history books. For example, while Antony was at Tarsus waiting for Cleopatra's barges, Plancus was in Italy arranging the land that Antony had promised to his veterans. This was much the more difficult of the two challenges. Not everyone can be part of the love story. Some do not even like the love story. Duke certainly did not.

In the summer of 41 BC there was a brief, brutal war between Antony and Octavian, Caesar's two heirs still nominally in alliance. No commander knew what to do, whether and where to win or how much to win by. Plancus played a typical part, as victor in an unintended battle, advancing, retreating, halting, waiting and then retreating again – before Octavian took decisive action and the most devastating revenge on those nearest to him at the time.

A full civil war was looming – with one side backed by the wealth of Egypt. Timing was critical for both sides. Antony had a chance to

deploy his bigger navy against Octavian but, with Plancus as his coun-
sellor, chose instead uneasy peace. Both men had a mass of unfinished
business. Antony promoted Plancus to command the rear of his
coming eastern campaign against the Persians.

In Italy the civil war was by propaganda. Octavian branded Antony
as the plaything of a royal whore, a debauchee and a drunk. Antony
claimed Julius Caesar's military mantle and argued that there was
honour in being a drunk. Octavian's brutality began to outweigh the
popularity of his land grants. Antóny's eastern ambitions fell close to
collapse. Both sides struggled to match words with reality.

Occasionally there was better news for Antony from the East. After
one small success, Antony began some boundary reorganisation of the
empire in favour of Egypt, moving new peoples and countries under
Alexandrian control. When I told the Big Oil men about Cleopatra's
modest bitumen business on the fringes of Arabia, that was one of her
gains at this time, territory given to her as a down payment in antici-
pation of much bigger things to come.

Antony soon found that he had no choice but to fight Octavian
directly for the right to rule Rome. The great Antonians, Plancus
and Canidius to the fore, headed fast for Alexandria where Cleopatra
generously rewarded her Roman allies. The Ptolemies had always
known the power of bribes. Some of Antony's officers hated everything about her but her money. Some were not bribed enough – or
smelt arrogance and the possibility of defeat. But most could be paid
and swayed – by cash and by parties, routs and revels.

Cleopatra and Antony were lovers, sexual partners, partners in politics. No one can know which partnership was the most important.
Some have been honest enough not to ask or answer that question. At
massive coronation ceremonies, they promoted their children, and the

boy they called Caesar's child too. Lands and titles flowed to Ptolemy Caesarion, and to their young twins, Alexander the Sun and Cleopatra the Moon. These were rewards which, like the bitumen business, would be followed after victory by much more.

Both sides were readying rapidly. Octavian's admiral, Agrippa, captured bases along the western coast of Greece. The sea belonged to Octavian. Suddenly, characteristically and critically, Plancus changed sides and divorced himself from Antony. He sensed that he was on the wrong side.

Canidius Crassus had his *ginestho*, his promise of eternal financial security from the Ptolemies. Confident in Antony's army too, he stayed loyal. Antony and Cleopatra began a tour of Greece and Asia to raise further funds and forces. More would be needed than even the wealth of Egypt could supply.

Over the twelve months of our occasional conversations in 1979 Duke lost his battle. He wanted the right to run the printing plants on behalf of the owners, to use modern computers instead of machinery of the medieval guilds, to decide who worked and what they were paid, to ensure that the papers were printed each night without stoppages, strikes and sudden demands for more pay. The unions were determined not to lose what they saw as ancestral rights to their own money and mercenary power.

The conflict seems like ancient history now – with causes barely recognisable to journalists today, whose worries are elsewhere. At the time it was like an ancient siege, a contest over which side could best endure the hardships of not working. Both sides bluffed and counterbluffed. Both sides threatened and blustered. But the unions in the end could endure the longer. All newspaper owners had bribed their printers for decades – and had no strength to manage without them.

There was the business question of whether any *Times* or *Sunday Times* readers would be left if the fight lasted too long. But there was a battle of political will too. The owners were the ones who lost heart. We returned to work in conditions hardly different from those we had left. We were still using typewriters rather than computers although, for me, any keyboard was a technological advance.

The Cleopatra project progressed well during the war but failed with the demands of a phoney peace. I moved with Harold Evans, from *The Sunday Times* to *The Times*. The present became more consuming than the past. Margaret Thatcher squeezed out Cleopatra, as Lew had hoped she would. *The Times* itself was turbulent. Duke's hopes and the unions' fears were merely postponed. Coming very soon was the last year in which newspapers would be made with molten lead on museum-grade machinery. Rising soon, on the other side of the City, past Tower Bridge towards what were still then the old Docklands, a new print works was being built, one which would be revolutionary until the next revolution – that of Web and wireless – overtook us in turn.

In the Calthorpe, the Blue Lion, the Pakenham and the Apple Tree no one knew how soon the change would come. But beside the Thames, barely more than a mile away, it was already beginning to happen. Every news editor, sub-editor and reporter already had a desk planned for him or for her, in 'work-stations' linked by computers, in an office that no one had seen and most did not know even existed.

Duke was by then not controlling the company any longer. As soon as his campaign had failed, his authority became more honorary than real. Among his gentler responsibilities was a party to boost morale, a bicentenary ball for *The Times*, a celebration which he called a Rout, a name from the Georgian royal court that seemed to him to strike the right tone. Not everyone agreed with him – either about the name or about whether we should have a ball of any name or kind.

'A Rout', said the Literary Editor to the Labour Editor, reading from a dictionary: 'a large evening party or fashionable gathering much in vogue in the eighteenth century; a company of rioters; an assembly of persons leading to an unlawful act; a disorderly retreat of defeated troops.' There was consensus in favour of the fourth definition, or possibly the third.

This was a year when no one could manage anyone except by force, when printers, miners and politicians combined to cry havoc, when there were Irish assassinations, a freezing winter when sterling stood at all-time lows as though in sympathy with the thermometer. And this was the year when Duke brought in acrobats, tumblers, royal processions, fancy dress, commemorative champagne, escapologists of every variety, all for the great Rout of Hampton Court, all in the great Alexandrian tradition of partying problems away.

Mahmoud came back an hour later than he had promised. He sat down with his back to the sea insisting that I should enjoy what remained of the view. He seemed in good spirits. He was going away for a few days, to Athens, the only city to which Alexandria was connected by direct flights. Did I want to go with him? Had Cleopatra ever visited Athens? Would it be pleasant to continue the story somewhere else?

Yes, I said. Cleopatra had visited Athens. She was a minor goddess there. He smiled. The Ptolemies had their own temple in Athena's city. Four hundred years after its prime it was still wealthy, still look-ing to become powerful again. As the last battle loomed of Rome's civil wars, the Athenians, like everyone else, were keen to identify the winner. I could hear myself sounding like a bore and he looked suddenly very bored.

But, no. I did not want to leave Alexandria. I had promised myself that I would not leave till my book was finished or, at least, certain to be finished. I knew Athens well and I could readily imagine Cleopatra there if that was what I wanted to do. I was not sure that it was.

He began objecting. Surely it would be easier to write in Athens about Cleopatra in Athens? Was not that just what I liked to do? He frowned. He looked down to where I had been sitting in the gardens. A wind was rippling though King Farouk's collection of trees. By the shore there were reeds swaying and there was a line of men in brown suits, standing straight and gently swaying too.

Mahmoud turned sullen. He pressed me again. He looked out at the men in brown. I asked what he was anxious about. Nothing at all, he snapped. Oddly shocked, I thought, that I would not join him on his Athenian trip, he ordered little and ate less.

After half an hour a car arrived, with two men inside, one in the front passenger seat the other in the back. The first left the car and stood with his face towards the palace gardens, waiting for Mahmoud to join him, to take the spare place in the back and be driven away.

16.I.11

Place Saad Zaghloul

I have slept for most of today in Room 114. Mahmoud was right. I do need to see the world of 32 BC as Cleopatra saw it. I do want to think what she was thinking. It takes concentration and quiet to come close to another's mind. There is never complete quiet in the Place Saad Zaghloul but tonight I do not need to sleep.

So, yes, I will try to see Cleopatra in Athens, the city where once upon a time (precise dates do not help) she came down Singrou Street (let me choose that street, any street) looking for men and money. This was a route that has always been there, the way to and from the sea, the straight line to the open port. I have often stayed there. It is one of the most easily imagined lines in the city, easy to imagine Cleopatra surveying her prospects there.

Nine years have passed since Tarsus, the seduction of Antony on her barge (not so hard) and their political alliance (always a little harder). Much is well. At home her throne is secure. There have been no more pretenders. Antony has given her Cyprus, Armenia, Parthia, Syria, Cilicia and Libya. Her children have new crowns. The Egyptian crowds had new achievements to cheer. Antony is a popular ally. The Alexandrians like his boyish fondness for fishing trips, fancy food, masqued balls and pranks. Her lover wears the two theatrical masks of the Greeks, the Comic in Alexandria and the Tragic in Rome. Long may that continue.

Her sister, Arsinoe, is long dead, almost forgotten now. Antony ordered her to be strangled. After Tarsus it was almost the first order that he gave. In Ephesus no one seemed to have missed Arsinoe. Or no one said so while Cleopatra and Antony could hear. They were both royally welcomed in that great Greek city of Amazon heroines carved in stone, of lion-hunting children, of massive eyeless masks above the theatrical arches.

In Italy there have been a few troubles. Antony's official Roman wife – 'the cunt' as the soldiers jovially used to call her – waged her own war on Octavian, courageous in its way but irritating rather than even wounding him. And then this would-be Amazon died, mourned by her soldiers but leaving an empty place at Rome, an opportunity for Antony to marry Octavian's sister. This was a common enough form of peace-pact, a very temporary pact in this case. Antony did not want Octavia for any other reason. To Cleopatra the marriage was inconvenient, socially awkward among Athenians who for some reason rather liked Octavia, even upsetting on some nights, but not important.

Only the Queen of Egypt has Antony's twins, Sun and Moon, new arrivals soon after Tarsus, child monarchs now in their own right. They are both her retort to Rome and her recompense for entering the Roman world. Antony was generous to Octavia (he is a practical man) but he left her as soon as leaving her was necessary. He came home to Alexandria and married Cleopatra under Egyptian rites, the only rites that mattered.

Celebrations after that were incessant – also essential. The people needed a distraction. Further east Antony was neither so decisive nor successful. His war against the Persians failed badly. Great propaganda skills were needed to ensure that his failure was not total. He was defeated by heat, cold and traitors. But, according to Roman oracles, only a king could ever defeat the Persians. Antony might yet be a king in Rome as Julius Caesar might have been. There would be time for many foreign victories once Octavian was dead. Meanwhile there were enough prisoners of war for the theatre directors of Alexandria to confect a magnificent triumph.

Plancus is no longer her friend. Antony's sometime second-in-command is not even her ally. He has defected to the other side. She should not be upset. He could not change his character, only his mind. His faithlessness proved as fixed as the stars. Plancus is in Rome as Octavian's man now, spreading malice about the madness of Alexandria to anyone who cares to hear. The drunken parties that he so enjoyed are suddenly the poison that he had to drink, the debauches he was forced to endure.

Plancus left her because he thought that the young Octavian, backed by impressionable allies, would defeat Antony, backed by Cleopatra and the treasure of Egypt. Worse, Plancus thought that Cleopatra's backing was not an advantage for Antony at all, that instead she was a personal distraction, a barbarian temptress, a prime target for Roman propagandists. The war that Octavian has just declared is against Egypt, against Cleopatra, not against Antony, his fellow citizen, former brother-in-law and friend. Officially, she is the sole enemy now.

Yet is it not a gain for her to be without Plancus? For a decade he read almost every letter that Antony ever sent. He was closer to both of them than any man. Better by far the enemy without than the enemy within. Plancus always wanted to be better than he was. There were so many men like that. In leaving her he was at least, for the first time in his life, a leader not a follower. He jumped without being pushed. The Roman who slithered among the mermaids of her court, who played judge when she melted pearls into wine, changed sides without even waiting to join a crowd. At last he was what he wanted to be.

How many others might follow? How many towns and cities too? It is hard to say. Cleopatra knows her Romans better than she knows her realms. The boundaries of the Ptolemies encompass places where no Ptolemy has ever been. There is that pretty, pear-shaped port on the western end of Crete, closest to Italy, whose people used to send her ancestors bulls made of clay, their horns gilded as though by apprentice butchers or master-makers of toys.

Every year the Kydonians sacrifice these replicas of the real animals that the grander gods of Egypt demand. In Kydonia there are deep tombs where mourners stare year after year at the sealed dead of their kings, where magicians are wreathed in golden snakes, where women twist their hair with dazzling blue stones and combs from the bones of river monsters, ornaments as old as the oldest Egyptians, or so the magicians say.

Kydonia is not quite her domain. She is realist enough to know when she can freely enter a town and when she cannot, even a town that she has never seen. Have the Kydonians of Crete truly turned their back on their Ptolemaic past? Have they really chosen Octavian as their Roman ruler? It is hard to know. Cretans are easily overexcited. From the bottom of their cups stare big eyes warning the drinker not to take too much. Like some at her own banquets, sometimes even the perfect Antony himself, they do not take proper heed.

And anyway, all Cretans are liars. So one of their philosophers once said, presumably excluding himself since otherwise there would be all sorts of logical problems, the kind with which librarians tired her mind. Is there any sure answer to anything? Maybe merely most Cretans are liars. Plancus too is a liar. Both Plancus and the Kydonians will pay appropriately when the coming war is over.

Canidius is still her ally, a privileged Egyptian landowner now, the type of man on whom a monarch can rely. When Antony's officers were arguing about tactics, Canidius said that Plancus was wrong about her impact on the war. To Canidius she was not just a financial necessity; she was a political necessity too. The coming war would be fought in Greece. The Romans regularly fought their civil wars in Greece. Antony's Greek legions and eastern allies cared more that she, Cleopatra, someone like them, should win, much more than that one member of Julius Caesar's party should triumph over another. That was surely true.

Canidius is a wise man. She readily signed her *ginestho* on the document that promised him an eternity of profits from wine and grain. Tax-exemptions are so much more effective than cash bribes. This one sealed both his own support for her and his heirs' support for her successors. No Roman likes paying tax. They are not used to it. This will be one of many such signatures in preparation for the conflict that will determine so much.

Canidius commands the army with which she and Antony are going to conquer Octavian. Egypt's is the finest fleet. Octavian, for all his posturing diplomacy, is weak, inexperienced, often sick, seasick always it is said. The war has begun. A battle is coming. After her victory the bribes that she is paying now will be money well spent. Octavian will be as dead as Pompey. Octavia? She will soon be fortunate if divorce is her only fate. Plancus? He will either be dead or suddenly remembering with pride all his services for Antony and Cleopatra.

After the death of Caesar's fake son, Caesar's real son, Caesarion, her own son, will be undisputed heir to the world, truly the King of Kings. Obelisks from all over Egypt are being gathered to make the gates of his temple, with places of honour too for Alexander the Sun, the boy whom his father Antony has just crowned King of the Persians, and his twin sister, Cleopatra the Moon, who, for the present, is Queen only of Libya.

Those were the best of coronation days, occasions for triumphal parties that pleasured even the most jaded tastes. Everywhere she goes in Greece, there are banquets and dances in her honour. In Rome, she hears, Octavian is mocking the 'Donations of Alexandria' as illegal gifts of Roman property to foreign bastards. Plancus, it is said, describes every detail of their dances in the Greek islands, an outrage, he claims, when the world is on the brink of war.

Ridiculous. And Plancus knows it. What seems an oriental orgy to the hypocrites of Rome is mere religious homage for her Hellenic hosts. Let her critics mock Cleopatra's piety if they will. Let Octavian's admiral, Agrippa, do his utmost to persuade the uncertain and disloyal. Let him try to secure the open ports of Greece, threatening, bribing and persuading. Every traitor has his reason. Meanwhile in Athens she has set up her court beside the Acropolis. She has revisited the temples that she last saw with her father when she was a child.

17.1.11

Rue Nebi Danial

Six hours ago I was imagining Cleopatra, a task I have intended many times. Two hours ago I saw her room, an experience not intended at all. It was precisely 4.00 a.m. when I awoke as though somewhere else. Those numbers alone, on the red lights on the clock in Room 114, proved that I was awake, still inside that hotel room, on the bed between the close yellow walls with their Venice prints. I was not in an office of grey and black although I could clearly see that office and move myself around it.

Every few seconds, between dark desk and shelves, I stopped to check that the clock light was still on, that I was still in the Hotel Metropole where I knew I was attempting to sleep. But beyond the red numbers I saw only shadows in which the queen had been sitting, the high sides of her chair, a foot-stool, a black vase of white flowers, the travelling equipment of a Cleopatra on the move, the place where bribes were exchanged for pledges and promises for gold.

I could see her pen, the sloping letters she had written, the instructions that even without her name were unambiguous because she alone could give such commands. Everything of hers was without colour, built from towers of smoke but no less solid for that. The desk crushed the carpet. A pile of papyri was poised to fall. There were no figures in either of the two realms here, no one else with me in the yellow hotel room, no one serving, filing, writing and certainly not presiding over the grey office. There was nothing fearful or fantastic about it. I merely watched for a while until there was nothing new to watch.

Afterwards it somehow seemed wrong to try to sleep. Dreams disappear. I want to hold the scene. So I am the first customer in the first cafe past the dead fountain, the nearest one that is open for trade before dawn. The coffee is in a copper-bottomed glass. The pastry is reassuringly hard. Across the road there are puppies in glass tanks awaiting the trade of the day, snoozing on shredded newsprint. There is no dog shit to disturb potential buyers, not a damp shred of yesterday's news stories of Copts and Muslims and national unity.

How do the pet salesmen do that? Is there some pen in the back of their truck where dogs go to do what real dogs do? These are not false dogs. They shuffle their shoulders and lick their tails and exercise their eyes when they see they have a watcher. We breed dogs not only for the finest range of long hair and short, long ears and short, but for eyes that look more like we look, so that they look as though they are looking at us.

These dogs need badly to look their best if they are ever to get out of these fish tanks into the dirty realism of a human home. These are not real dogs until someone imagines them as their friend. Cleopatra had a dog as a god and the Romans despised her for that.

I do not feel well. I am not seeing well. I am not writing much. Maybe I should have gone to Athens after all. But Mahmoud did not ask me in order to make Cleopatra happen more quickly. He wanted to get me away. I wish I knew why. It is still a relief still to be here.

It would be a further relief to continue walking south on this street towards the lake, to the point where the Mareotis meets the waters of the sands. There are thousands of birds to see. But walking further is no good. While Julius Caesar could dictate and walk at the same time, that is one of the very many lessons that he did not pass on.

So I have stopped at this new cafe near the bus station, where swarms of men are now beginning to arrive for work in the city trades. Dawn has quickly come. There are steel tables beside a yellow kerb, a solidity shaken only from time to time by yellow taxis taking the shortest distance to their destination. These little encounters of car and concrete must happen every hour of every day and night. Twice already there has been a scrape, not quite a crash, and a layer of sunny paint has moved from stone to metal or metal to stone.

Maurice was only an occasional visitor to the pubs around *The Times*. For months I would never see him at all. I want now to describe my old friend as he was at this time; but, of all his times, this is the faintest in my mind. He wore pink shirts with grey ties. His shoes were soft and shiny. That much I do recall. There must be more than that.

His schoolboy face survived intact above his collar, a little redder but the same face. I think so. Or perhaps I am just superimposing an older, stronger memory upon a newer, weaker one. It seems unjust to be describing him at all when he is not here to describe me. He would have taken that badly. He always gave as good as he got – and usually found in my sprawling suits and ill-cut curls some cause for cool critique.

He was a success in his own world. Twelve years after Oxford he was prospering in the promotion of pet food and perfume, the bright ad-lands of million-pound accounts and hundred-pound lunches into which he had briefly, and unsuccessfully, introduced me back in 1973. The Gray's Inn Road had journalists – but nothing much else to recommend it to him.

So I was surprised when he called and said we should meet at 7 p.m. in the Blue Lion. He had a business interest, he warned me. He remembered that my responsibilities at *The Times* now included some supervision of the diary column. Yes, I wrote worthy leading articles too – about politicians and policies. But a diary of gossip, he said, could do more harm than any diatribe about the court of Margaret Thatcher.

A few months ago the *Times* Diarist had run a comic campaign against one of his clients, the manufacturer of a male cologne called Drakkar Noir. It had been wholly trivial, funny sometimes he conceded, but not amusing to his client. This Drakkar Noir might indeed be 'pongy' and 'cheeselike', best used for confusing police dogs and poisoning house plants. But he had heard that the diarist was planning a return to his theme. Might I bring the man to meet him? Without being hugely optimistic, I said I would.

While we waited, Maurice consumed several large gins and a generous ladling of other newspaper gossip. Was *The Times* really going to have a Bicentenary Rout? Could I get him an invitation? Yes, I said. And yes, I would try. Our fellow Trinity man, Duke Hussey, was leading the case for a lavish event that would be remembered for decades to come. Charles Douglas-Home, the Editor and my boss, was taking a more stringent view.

It was not clear who would prevail. Duke had powerful support. CDH, as the Editor was always known, was younger but a nephew of both a former British prime minister and the playwright of *The Chiltern Hundreds*, the satire that V had so enjoyed at Brentwood. He had art and politics in his blood. Both men had their backers and critics in the Blue Lion and the Calthorpe.

Throughout 1985, as CDH saw it, *The Times* was already due to play host to the Queen, the Queen Mother and the Queen's sister on separate royal bicentenary occasions. Each event came with its own laboriously negotiated rules about whom the visitors should meet, what should be said to them and how many ice-cubes were needed for a gin-and-Dubonnet refresher. CDH thought this to be quite sufficient. His ambitions for the year were the collapse of the Soviet Union, the defeat of its British ally, the National Union of Mineworkers, the stiffening of Margaret Thatcher and an end to wasteful spending of all kinds.

Duke took a less Old Roman view of life. He argued that the Rout would be more public than the royal lunches, an opportunity for us to greet the Prince of Wales and the grandest of his future subjects at Hampton Court Palace, to impress advertisers and to remind them all with fireworks and acrobats of the glories of the Georgian age in which *The Times* had been born. A strict though substantial budget was agreed. The Bollinger Company promised generosity in the pricing of *Times* champagne: a thousand bottles were to be free. A royal 'fixer' was hired at an equally generous rate.

Duke promised precise attention to every problem. Would Elton John be a suitable entertainer? The Lord Chamberlain thought not. Would the guitar maestro, Julian Bream, go down better? Perhaps a little too quietly. Why did a juggler cost £200 for a night and a jester only £150? Should we have more jesters or risk an 'illusionist act with audience participation' (£350)? Was it possible to have Beefeaters instead of St John's Ambulance staff? The fixer was doubtful whether their skills were quite the same but Scots Guards, she knew, could be had for £25 a night.

Protracted negotiations ensured that everyone knew that smoking 'was permitted but not encouraged' and, more importantly, which flower vases in the Palace were suitable for water and which ones, given the exigencies of their inner glaze, would have to be filled with roses only at the very last minute. Perhaps we could also have a 'lady with a dove'. These were all details in which Duke, the Alexandrian of *The Times*, excelled.

Just as Maurice was newly anxious about his perfume, I was newly anxious about my responsibilities at *The Times*. I was somewhat surprised to be in charge of the leader writers. But these were strange days. I was a new arrival when novelty was suddenly a good thing. The newspaper was continually rolling from one crisis to the next. CDH was impatient of frivolity in part because he was dying of cancer, though few yet knew it.

Here in Egypt now, I am wondering whether this period almost thirty years ago is part of my 'last nights of Cleopatra' or not. Most of it is not; most of the serious troubles of that time are not. But some of it, for various and not always very connected reasons, earns its place. If that distorts the picture of a newspaper, an era and its people, so be it.

My main job was to be a writer of leading articles. This leader-writing is a peculiar kind of journalism. Its practitioners represent the editor and not themselves. They represent the views of the institution too, these deemed to be the same as those of the editor but not always at this time without a fight.

Great passion was spent on what should be the opinion of *The Times*. Occasionally there was a kind of holy warfare. The overt aim of leaders is to make things happen. On *The Times* in 1985 the leader writers were still called Cardinals, with a certain self-conscious irony, but with seriousness too. These were the anonymous men, almost wholly men, who advised the nation on its own good.

Acutely conscious of their place in history, they knew that the most famous leaders of their past were those that had called successfully for action. Demands for immediate resignation were best. Charles Douglas-Home's removal of a Foreign Secretary before the Falklands War in 1982 was still noted as a triumph even by those who hated him. But there was a creeping anxiety in our office that the best was behind us, that the importance of leaders was a conceit, or largely a conceit. It was an appearance of power that had too often been exaggerated and had to be very carefully maintained if any power at all were to remain.

There was division over how best to exercise this care. The Cardinals' most favoured tactic was to find out that a government policy was already agreed, or almost agreed, before demanding it themselves. The most artful leader writer liked to catch a moment just before something happened, to describe the javelin as it was poised to be thrown, and then to claim credit for its arc and its arrival at its target.

But *The Times* could not always be so well informed. So most leader writers preferred instead to argue both sides of a case, to make much use of 'on the one hand' or 'on the other', a habit made easier by the high proportion of leader writers who had read Greek at school and knew the power of '*men*' and '*de*' in constructing a fine sentence. This style disguised doubt beneath the appearance of rigour. It was also becoming a joke.

CDH, especially in his final days, was opposed to both kinds of caution. He was a stubborn individualist. He had old clothes and hard principles. He was monarchic in his instincts and a serious student of how monarchy worked. He hated communism and smoking, despised '*men*' and '*de*' and every other conventional wisdom. He did not mind being rebuffed. He wanted to write what, in his view, was right. *The Observer* newspaper, he often said, had lived successfully for almost three decades on its unsuccessful opposition to Eden's Suez war.

CDH knew about Egypt. He knew about the Ptolemies. We occasionally talked about Cleopatra. But his sole interest in ancient Alexandria was the way in which it was ruled. For its poetry, medicine, art or philosophy he cared nothing at all.

On our Drakkar Noir night, I left Maurice briefly in the Blue Lion and went back across the road to check that all was well in the office. I pushed against the Editor's door. There was no reply except for mutterings, murmurs and the sound of cloth crunching across carpet.

In a low light from the empty desk, CDH was on the floor with a young woman beside him, her body supported on one elbow and her arm flung lightly against his face. 'It's the Alexander Technique,' he said with a gritted smile as I backed into the outer (not far enough outer) office and the corridor beyond. The Alexander Technique? What was that?

Was this some joke at my expense? Was the Alexander Technique some sort of therapeutic massage? It seemed unlikely that in the wranglings between him and his staff about politics, between him and Duke about acrobats and dove-ladies, there would have been much space for Peter Stothard's feelings for Alexandria. I went back to my office. There was no real urgency to see the Editor that night. The next phase of his battles against the leader writers – over Arthur Scargill and the miners' strike, the Socialist Workers' threat, the Church of England, the Middle East and almost everything else bar the England cricket captaincy – could wait, and did wait, for another day.

I left to meet Maurice – and found him offering free Drakkar Noir samples to some youthful Welsh choristers. He was playful, happy, as happy as I had seen him in years. He had met his product's tormentor already, he said. He did not think there would be any further problems. The smell of journalism was disgusting (how dare we cast aspersions on any perfume?) but he appreciated the chance to check that I was still alive, that I was prospering in office life, and that the irrelevancies of Cleopatra were being supplanted by worthier ends.

We talked and drank for more than an hour, telling each other, as ever, what each thought the other should know. He loved the problems of the Rout. He was a natural impresario. He thought that £25 a night for a Scots Guardsman was particularly cheap. He hoped that the £200-a-night jugglers would at least be young. Then suddenly there was a crash of bodies through the door. No one looked up. A heavily bearded man, who spoke as though he was heavily entitled to be heard, began instantly abusing the Editor of *The Times*. His companions nodded. No one else took any notice.

Maurice stopped his pricing of the Rout and began playfully spraying from his little black bottle. Drinkers began moving away – both from the newcomers and from us. The combination of beer, sweat and Drakkar created an air like that of a small car in which teenagers have failed to enjoy sex. Maurice pointed. For the first time in years he made the shape of a big beard around his face. He made the same shape of a big beard around my face. Did I not know who the agitator was?

Did I not recognise him? Was I an expert on Cleopatra or not? Did I not remember our ill-fated, sherry-fuelled attempt at drama? This, he said floridly, was Canidius in Elizabeth Taylor's movie. Did I not recall the dumb messenger's sign? Did I not recognise the same man now?

I was still not sure. Maurice was absolutely sure. This was Canidius, the general who would get his *ginestho*, aka Andrew Faulds, actor, MP, Palestinian activist, hounder of Mrs Thatcher over the sinking of the Argentinian ship *Belgrano*, here in the Blue Lion with a noisy delegation. He had either just seen CDH – or was just about to see him. He was agitated, angry, leaning forward in a notably more confident way than when he had been booming bad news to Rex Harrison's Caesar. He was complaining most of all about the disgusting smell in the bar.

This same Andrew Faulds, Maurice hissed, had also been the radio voice of Jet Morgan, the Englishman in space to whom we listened on our home-made transistors when we were six. This man, this voice, was almost a family member. Perhaps we should introduce ourselves. I disagreed. In one weird way, from Cleopatra the First to Cleopatra the Eighth, the Member of Parliament for Warley East was the single thread that held the story together. In other ways, he was no part of it at all.

We moved to the back of the bar. Had I heard from V, Maurice asked, switching from Canidius to Rothmans, Brentwood and the cinema story we had talked about as we planned our Cuppers theatrical coup. No, I said. Then be grateful, he continued, waving a letter he had received from her about us both, attacking me for being part of the media-capitalist conspiracy and him for merely being a capitalist.

I felt guilty. I had never mentioned to him V's arrival on Gray's Inn Road during the shutdown nor the revelations about her role as a statue in his Red Tents. I could have discovered if she was telling the truth. I was not as frank with Maurice as I should have been. There was so much in our lives that was now not shared with the other.

Instead I let him gently pass on her taunts. According to V, he said, I had had 'ideals once'.

Maurice said he did not remember any of my ideals but, if he did remember one, he would let me know. He might also give V my address if I did not buy him another drink. He was being sympathetic in his own way. Much more importantly, he wanted to know everything about what was happening at *The Times*.

I tried to hold his attention, never an easy task for long. I described a lunch that CDH had held that week for Margaret Thatcher, the disapproval of the leader writers, the sycophancy of the executives, the courage of CDH himself who was in constant pain through every course. It seemed odd to me then how much Maurice wanted to know about our office politics, and how many people also wanted to know. We were a court of reporters and writers. We were attracting the attention of reporters and writers. It was like living between two mirrors.

For the next few weeks the office workers of *The Times* saw more of CDH than they were used to. Every few days he would limp around the corridors checking the cleanliness of carpets, the perils of half-removed partitions, the off-whiteness of paintwork and the fluorescence of bulbs. Sometimes he was accompanied by men with tape measures and attaché cases falling from languid wrists. Duke Hussey was almost always there too.

The Editor was a disciplined delegator but he could not delegate the marking of a royal progress around his newspaper. The protocols, the timetables, the receiving lines and even the redecoration – or rather the parts of the paper not chosen for redecoration – caused trouble. 'I hope that the paint-line at the beginning of our corridor does not mean that the monarch will miss Business News,' the Business Editor asked with a hostile smile. 'Having sat through two bicentennial television documentaries that did not mention me and my team at all, it would be too much to bear.' The reply was characteristically non-committal. 'I hear you,' the Editor said. When he wanted to register understanding without agreement, he often used this old Scots phrase.

A fortunate few, chosen to be introduced personally to the Queen, had to produce a three-line biography for the Palace briefing book. The Editor well knew the prolixity of his colleagues. But even he was amazed at the lengths to which these journalists would go to gain a few more lines of type. 'Do not in any circumstances cut the bit about my beagling,' said the Arts Editor. 'It's a shared interest, you know.' The Editor already knew.

According to the programme, the Queen and the Duke of Edinburgh were to arrive at 10.30 a.m., shake hands with the three-line-biography brigade, tour various departments, avoid Business News, attend morning conference and return home for lunch. In the evening they would be back to watch the printing of a special royal edition in which their day would be described with suitable respect.

At the appointed time the electricians outside the Editor's office were still fiddling with fluorescent bulbs. The corridor light was deemed too harsh for a woman of sixty. Fifteen minutes later she arrived. Her Rolls-Royce ceased its purring in the road between the twin newspaper buildings. The reception-line machinery – manned by well-polished reporters, new-suited executives and an Editor in a blue V-neck jumper and less-than-usually frayed cuffs – began its own smooth purr.

The Queen and her Duke shook their way down the first line in the

Editor's office. Everyone smiled back loyally. The royal party passed into the newsroom where the writers, sub-editors, photographers and diarists were clumped around pillars, propped against the glass cubicles and generally attempting the impression of an office at work. After witnessing an extraordinary variety of bows, extraordinary to me if not to her, she was seen speaking for several minutes with the Labour Editor, a proud Yorkshire man and probably the journalist closest to the then national bogeyman, victim of some of our most virulent leaders, the National Union of Mineworkers' leader, Arthur Scargill.

With a look of nearly-all-over on his face the Editor rested his back beside a grey metal desk. He had watched with satisfaction and barely concealed amusement as his newsroom staff imitated gymnasts, jack-knives and circus elephants in the depth and rigidity of their bows. He even had a friendly word for the hovering television and radio reporters who had been invited to present *The Times* in a favourable light in its bicentennial year.

I was a few feet away with nothing to do but watch what happened next. In a place that was briefly and unusually quiet and without stories, there were suddenly just two words, 'one' and 'man', one story.

The Queen and the Labour Editor, it seemed, had been noting the progress of the miners' strike, the bitter battle between Mrs Thatcher's government and Mr Scargill's union. Under harsh fluorescent light BBC reporters were talking to our Labour Editor; *Times* reporters were talking to the BBC reporters and *Times* executives were talking to each other. Heads were turning. CDH, for whom the war against Scargill was a personal crusade, kept his head still. He stared at Duke who stared at me.

The whispers accelerated. The Queen had said that the strike was 'all down to one man and very sad'. This 'one man' was Mr Scargill. She was thus backing the contention that the miners were good men led by a bad man. Quotes and misquotes spread, each amplified and extended to sharpen the criticism of the miners' leader, to align the Queen more closely with Mrs Thatcher's position and to improve the story for publication. The two words spread at epic speed. New arrivals asked me what had happened. Duke asked me what had happened. Somehow I was expected to know. I soon decided that I did know.

'One man', one queen, one way of thinking about why things happen: it was a respectable way of thinking were it not for the convention that the monarch does not think aloud on such matters. CDH, a cousin of Princess Diana as well as a nephew of a prime minister, was writing a book on royalty and politics in the modern age. He remained supremely indifferent to this 'stamping of media feet'. Within minutes we all moved off to the next stop on the tour, the safer zones of the diary column and the Arts Editor who shared our visitor's interest in beagling.

Eventually the morning was over. The planners slumped in the chairs in the Editor's office. The daily news and leader conferences – rarely witnessed by outsiders – had gone well. One of our leader writers had objected that his name on the seating plan was in the form of 'Ronnie', an over-familiar diminutive that he did not wish the Queen to see. Even this last, awkward detail was attended to in time, Her Majesty's copy being individually corrected to remove the abbreviation. To CDH someone's name was not a trivial thing.

The time was now almost one o'clock. The television was switched on. We anticipated perhaps a gentle coda to the bulletin in which the Queen would be shown in graceful pilgrimage to the most famous newspaper in the world.

Instead, 'our news' came before 'the news'. The Queen's 'unprece-dented attack' on Scargill was labelled the 'gaffe of her reign'. A swift call to the Palace found a team of courtiers congratulating themselves on a 'thoroughly natural and relaxed visit'. This was code, apparently, for a great success. So success had somehow to be restored.

It seemed an impossible task to me. This gaffe was already an event. It could not be disinvented. But I was naive and wrong. Everyone rapidly agreed that there had been a 'severe' distinction between what the Queen had said and how reporters had interpreted her views. Rumours of a tape recording of the conversation proved unfounded. After a few hours the story became a newspaper embarrassment – a comic interlude rather than a constitutional row. By the time the Queen returned in the evening, all was forgotten. CDH apologised to his guests for the 'nonsense' and was assured that it had all been noth-ing. The special edition flew off the presses in due order.

I made some notes for my Cleopatra files. What were the rules of a court where the Queen's words made things happen, whether she uttered them or not? Were Cleopatra's words made and unmade too? There was barely more than a single page before I had to stop and stuff what I had done into my desk drawer.

18.I.II

Hotel Metropole, Place Saad Zaghloul

In the following weeks of 1985 newspaper life continued with as much normality as it ever could at this time. On the first Sunday of May CDH telephoned me at home. I listened intently to compensate for the quietness, sometimes the blurring, that the painkillers now brought to his voice. He spoke instead with drugless clarity. He was going to be in hospital for the next two or three weeks, he said. There was no question of an 'acting editorship'. He was going to edit the paper via the telephone and a 'squawk box'. For most of the staff, he said, it would not make any difference.

The squawk box was a polished wooden loudspeaker case that in recent weeks had been sitting uncomfortably on the leader writers' table, as out of place as early television sets in drawing rooms. There would in future be another similar box by the Editor's hospital bed and he could bark orders into it or contributions to debate. In the leader writers' conference this object became a wild, unnatural talisman watching over us. Whenever it squawked into life, it was like an oracle, leaving its hearers either instructed or bemused. From the technology of this box, as well as from the Editor's character and mind, came that dying voice which friends saw as boldness and enemies as bombast.

Next morning the formal announcement of physical absence was posted on the noticeboards. It was described as an 'internal memorandum'. Politics swept by. Through the squawk box we denounced the plans for a US–Soviet summit. A leader, headlined 'The Heart of the Matter', blasted the stubborn evil of inflation. Next morning the squawk box said that it was time to call for the sacking of one minister and his replacement by another. Somewhat drowsily, these instructions dawdled their way into *The Times*.

Preparations for the Hampton Court 'Rout' meanwhile took some unpredicted turns. There was the problem of protocol and the African ambassadors. To put it tactfully, which Duke did not always do, there was the requirement that the longest-serving diplomats – 'some Communists, some cannibals and some of them both cannibals and Communists' – be deemed senior in the seating plan to newcomers from more important countries: thus Ethiopia might be better placed than the United States. This, said Duke, was a nightmare from which only venerable Luxembourg – 'a splendid fellow' – could save the day.

There was disagreement over how much the Prince of Wales should be made to act out the extravagance of his predecessor as heir to the throne in 1785. Prince Charles had rejected the 'Prince Regent' plan that he leave the Rout by carriage, escorted by flunkies for a mere few hundred yards until he reached his car. Duke thought this a shame.

Then there was the staff. The first impression among the reporters had been of a giant office party, reminiscent of the days when the proprietors took their workers away to country estate afternoons. There was always a certain readiness to deride such hospitality; but there was none for the revelation that this was to be no staff party at all. Maurice and a few friends of mine (designated as coming figures of influence) were sprinkled among the very great and very good on a secretly circulated list for invitations. Barely half a dozen *Times* writers or editors were going to see the dancers, escapologists and jugglers, to sup with the Prince and Princess of Wales, to be offered 'jellied borscht if the lobster cardinal was not to their taste'.

The journalists organised an unofficial rival 'Not The Hampton Court Gala' in the nearby Hampton Court pub. The Editor suggested, with sincere reluctance, that the newspaper would pay the costs. The damage, however, had already been done. When the invitations went out to a bicentenary staff party in the Domed Room of the Victoria and Albert Museum, the venue was immediately retitled 'the Doomed Room'. Worse, when some of the secretaries asked if they could have tickets for the 'Not the Hampton Court Gala' they were told that the event was for journalists only. Plans were then made by the secretaries for a 'Not the Not the Times Gala'.

News leaked out of a rehearsal at which the finger bowls had been deemed too small, the portions of potatoes too large and the asparagus too dull. Our advertising agency, the same one into which Maurice had pushed me a dozen years before, suggested spending some of the bicentenary party money on restarting 200 stopped clocks in public places.

For the big event itself, the Editor freed himself from hospital. It was a perfect summer night. There was the free *Times* champagne, the costly *Times* troubadours, almost everything that Duke had wanted except the illusionist, the Regency coachmen and the lady with the dove. There were Green Jackets instead of Scots Guards. The Editor's recourse was to grit his teeth, grab the lapels of his white jacket, grin and bear it as best he could.

While drinkers drank and thinkers drank and everyone but the Editor drank, Duke introduced the doyen of the diplomatic corps to the wife of the Lord Chief Justice – and performed a hundred other such acts. Royal attendants watched anxiously lest any liquid be poured on porous pottery or any elbow pierce a piece of canvas. Duke seemed to have endless time, enough to point out a faraway picture from the palace collection. 'The banquet of Antony and Cleopatra', he declared rotundly. It was a portrait of a Dutch lady taking an earring from her ear, modest, severe, surrounded by a smiling husband and seven children of assorted ages around a small table.

I was unprepared. 'Have you never seen it before?' he said again, before another ambassador tore him away. I gave an empty nod. I did not want to admit that I had not seen it before. We few hosts had to concentrate on our acrobats, fireworks and examples of living royalty. Anyway, it was a very odd picture. Antony and Cleopatra looked like actors in a pantomime.

Afterwards I had to describe it all to Maurice. His own invitation, along with those of all my influential 'businessmen of the future', had been culled. Maurice's place had been taken by a Moroccan who held higher seniority than the Papal Nuncio. That was what I told him. If he had not been invited in the first instance, he would not have cared at all. But, once whetted, his appetite for information, like all his appetites, was high.

On a Sunday at the end of September the Editor telephoned to say that he had nothing to write that night. He asked me to call the senior leader writers but gave no idea of what I should tell them to say. Anything new, even a matter as simple as a massive earthquake in Mexico, was too much to consider. His telephone voice, which for so long had been his badge and tool of editorship, was frail and rasping, like paper rubbed on paper.

Leaders became ever more difficult. At the same time the journalists' union at *The Times* was threatening a strike over pay, computer typesetting, a four-night week and whether a writer covering an

African famine should be allowed to take photographs without a photographer being present.

On Wednesday the Editor presided over the news and leader conferences in person. The strain was patent. The corners of his mouth turned down into dark chasms. As he listened to limp talk of monetary reform, his eyes were deep in his temples. At that time I had never before seen a brave man dying.

Soon CDH was in hospital again. We had just taken delivery of a new improved squawk box which was so sensitive, he boasted, that he could even hear in his bed when a leader writer's eyebrow was raised. The sense of vacuum was now oppressive. Journalists want even bad things to happen quickly – as though some phantom edition of the newspaper is waiting for the news. Or they become bored while waiting. Or they want a new story, a new Editor to tell stories about, or anything new at all. Within a day we had all that we wanted. On the morning of Tuesday, 29 October 1985 there came the stately sadness – and the arrangements: 'the funeral will be on Friday; the memorial service, attended by the Prince of Wales, will be at St Paul's'.

The death of the Editor was the chief item on the news conference list. Behind his empty desk, somehow invisible before, were photographs of coffee beans, the proof of a new book on constitutional monarchy in Spain, a child's picture of a goldfish in the weeds, a painted boat against a large round sun and a *Thank You for Not Smoking* sign. They were joined, at around six o'clock, by a small carton from the hospital, a radio, a colour TV and a bright new wooden squawk box.

Duke was prominent at the funeral alongside the Prince of Wales. Two decades later the Prince, like many others of the same mourners, was at Duke's last service too.

The old world of newspapers did not last much longer. New technology required a new place. Outside the Blue Lion, the Calthorpe and the Pakenham Arms there was this time a decisive industrial battle. The journalists moved eastwards, and to drinking places unknown. I left the *Times* building on its last night with nothing but a portrait of a Victorian foreign correspondent and a case of wine. Crowds gathered in the street, spilling out from all the bars. All printing machinery had stopped. Order was temporarily fragile. Security was provided by competing forces of management and labour. Later seemed time enough to collect any last possessions, the various bits of my Cleopatras inside my locked desk drawers. Next day the desk was still there but the drawers were gone.

A loss? Probably not. I was only briefly even angry. Biographies of ancient characters are always bolstered by background information that is only indirectly relevant. In studies of Cleopatra these usually include Alexandrian obstetrics and fashion, the ethics of vivisection, the

properties of extinct herbs, the propagation of corn in mud and the superstition (a favourite of Octavian's too) that seals protected sailors against lightning. Chapters and paragraphs on all of those and more were in that desk – alongside easy musings on the links between past and present, too easy thoughts that were best left unsaid.

Khat Rashid

For two hours the lorries of vegetables and soldiers have been thundering past this desert service station, far out east beyond Montaza. The ground is scattered with rubbish sacks. There are wrecked cars that not even the keenest pimp could use. This is where Socratis said that I should stay for a day or two. Zaghloul Square was once again a problem. The police were picking up Sudanese and Tunisians. Who knew where they might stop?

I was not convinced. The view from the Metropole seemed calm enough to me. But Socratis insisted. When arrests began, it was never clear when the arresting would end.

So I have come here to a desert petrol station that is also a motel, a shop and a place for repairing lorries. I am in the corner of the car mechanic's store. It is not as bad as it sounds. The exact location is a little obscure: Khat Rashid was the last sign I saw before we stopped. But to be 'left alone' is still what I want most. In my mind is an oil painting that is 350 years old. Mahmoud objects to visitors projecting upon modern Alexandria their images of the past. But to replace a dirty garage window with a Dutch master requires no one else, offends no one and does no possible harm.

The picture is Jan de Bray's dark family portrait, *Banquet of Mark Antony and Cleopatra*. I did not know it when it first appeared as one of the damp picture cards that Lew crossly crumpled in the Calthorpe Arms. But since its second appearance, on the wall of Hampton Court Palace during the Rout, it has been always with me. It looks very much at home in Khat Rashid – as in one way it should.

A puzzled man, a pugnacious woman and a bright white pearl are as though freshly painted on the wall in this soldiers' garage. The still life on the dinner table is alive, glowering, glowing, indestructible. This mysterious banquet scene can assemble itself anywhere for me – in hotel rooms, airport lounges and hospitals, on advertisement hoardings on Al Hurreya or the Gray's Inn Road, in place of poster invitations to buy beer and soap, to vote Mubarak or Conservative.

It fits neatly here now, merging its painted parts with the windows, ledges and walls. The grey of army uniforms and spanners behind the sand-smeared panes becomes Cleopatra's oyster supper, the meal that Antony thinks so strangely modest. A Koranic exhortation to military mechanics is the tablecloth, freshly unfolded, ready to be smoothed by a final touch. A fading spot of neon is the pearl. Anywhere and at any time in the past twenty-five years I have been able to summon Antony as a red-cheeked bearded man, almost Christ-like in wonder, and the sterner face of Cleopatra, defiant, dominant, holding her right hand to her left ear and a wine glass in her left hand. Their children look puzzled and playful, the servants serene and there is Plancus, the dark man with an axe who supervises the revels.

Jan de Bray was a Dutch artist of the seventeenth century. In Haarlem, just after 1650, he portrayed this bourgeois Antony and Cleopatra at the decisive point of their notorious competition over which of them can provide the costliest banquet. Antony is confident that he can outdo the miserable plate of shells at Cleopatra's table – until she takes from her ear the world's largest pearl, sits straight-backed, staring back, poised to crush it, dissolve it and drink it. The moment is absolutely still. The morality of the tale is untold, left to tell itself. The steadiness in the surrounding faces is intense, as if they are watchers at an execution.

The picture has been in a palace of British kings and queens since it was purchased by Charles II. It might be thought an odd subject for any but the merriest monarch, the extravagance of a doomed queen of dubious reputation who ground down a pearl worth fifteen cities. Before coming to Hampton Court, it hung in the Queen's Drawing Room at Windsor for two hundred years.

The models were the painter's parents, a mother who was wealthy, impetuous maybe, and a father from whom the young Jan was trying to break away. His brothers and sisters played the parts of the little Moon and Sun, of Caesarion, and their extended family and retainers. The Sun is querulous, the Moon is pleased to be allowed up late. The painter himself takes the part of Plancus, the axe-man who will decide the winner and who protects the second earring from a similar destruction.

No one knows precisely how this part of Cleopatra's story matched the life of the De Brays, Catholic stalwarts of Haarlem, pillars of the painters' guild of St Luke's, courtly collectors of Turkish carpets, peacocks, gold, glass, Delft-ware and devoted servants. The family members were surely more than mere models for a classical scene. This is a story set truthfully in two ages, two places, two worlds.

Seventeen years after its completion, everyone in the picture except the painter and two of his siblings would be dead – from the plague that ravaged Haarlem as it ravaged London at around the same time before the Great Fire. Jan de Bray later painted the whole scene again as a theatrical tableau on an even grander scale, adding his own first wife who had also died. The story of Antony and Cleopatra was a play in which his family twice could star, filmed for posterity in roles of curiosity and wonder which, however anyone judged the original subjects, had survived for almost seventeen centuries. If Cleopatra could define and intertwine with the good burghers of Haarlem, she could fit almost anywhere.

What then were Lew's other postcards, the result of that half-hearted picture research for the *Big Oil Times*? Some of them were traditional court portraits, the type more routinely to Charles II's taste, available aristocratic wives with pearls and snakes painted by lesser-known Italians. The model with the black stare to match her stockings and the marble matron looking down on her tiny tuft of pubic hair? She was the subject for a southern German classicist called Georg Scholz, working somewhat later in 1927. It is one of his best-known works.

For the titillators of the Restoration the heroes of ancient history enliven and promote the present. For other artists they show how dead is the past. Scholz preferred flesh to marble, his now to his then. Picture research produces sometimes peculiar results. His model did not represent Cleopatra at all – except in the sense that the most sensual opposition to Roman virtue always has.

It is late at night in the room above the garage, time for some more traditional ancient history, for Actium, the name for one of those battles deemed decisive in the history of the world, September, 31 BC, on a sandy outcrop on the eastern shore of Greece, East vs West. Antony and Cleopatra vs Octavian and Rome, one truth vs another.

I will start with Dellius, Antony's pimp historian. It was he who betrayed the battle plans. Dellius and Cleopatra had quarrelled over wine. Her officers at Actium, he jibed, had been reduced to drinking vinegar, vintages fit only for destroying jewellery. Octavian's men meanwhile had the best of everything. So Dellius had no option but to change sides. Plancus had been right. The sailors with the best wine would surely prevail.

All the auguries and odds were switching fast. That was only too true. Agrippa, Octavian's admiral, had seized so many ports so very quickly that the Romans could now land their troops almost anywhere. Antony's massive forces meanwhile were penned up, hemmed in by sand and shallows, suffering from plague and bad alcohol.

Canidius wanted to lead the army back inland and lure Octavian to follow. A land battle would still have been Antony's best chance if Cleopatra had permitted it. Antony was still the more experienced commander on open ground, while Agrippa was proving himself an ever more potent master at sea.

But Cleopatra said no. The navy was hers. Her treasury was held by her navy. If they were to retreat to fight another day, it would be safer to escape by sea to Alexandria. Canidius could be left behind in Greece with their miserable, complaining army to prove that he was as good as he had always claimed. Those were her orders, the final orders.

So Dellius's defection was a fact. But it did not matter. Cleopatra's orders were simple: as soon as the Egyptian captains saw an opening in the Roman lines, they were to burst through and sail away home. It was not much of a plan to betray. Octavian must have worked out most of it for himself. But it was all that Dellius had.

19. I. 11

TEWFIK EL HAKIM

THÉATRE
DE
NOTRE TEMPS

* * *

DEMAIN - MORT OU AMOUR
J'AI CHOISI
(Traduit de l'Arabe)

LES MAITRES ÉTRANGERS

NOUVELLES ÉDITIONS LATINES
1, rue Palatine — Paris

Khat Rashid

The wooden clock in this depot for armed men and carrot-sellers records 4.00 a.m. Dawn is fast approaching while the night stays sleepless and charcoal black. From the flat lands between here and the city the closest light comes from patches of faraway neon, the whiteness of invading stars. The advertisement hoardings are under repair. Across each square, from corner to corner, crawl small black figures, electricians jerking like tiny frogs, painful to look at too long. Posters would normally protect our eyes. But this is the hidden part of an advertising display, the glare that we are not supposed to see.

These bare fluorescent tubes ought to be behind invitations to buy a Coca-Cola or to vote for the son of the President. But on this nineteenth night of the new decade there is reduced demand to tell Alexandrians or their visitors what new delights they can have for their money. The election is over. The Mubarak family has won everything again. There has been a bombing. Egypt, the President claims, needs support for its fight against terrorists. There is the uncertainty of empty space.

Meanwhile, preparing for better economic times, the neon-tube repair men are in harness, in sticky-footed shoes, scrambling slowly across screens that are impossibly white. These hoardings will soon be wrapped in new posters, 'buy-me' pictures, buy my cigarettes, buy my bathroom furniture, buy my houses by the sea. But on this night the empty neon taunts the eyes. Look too long and the screens become columns of giant type, seven across a newspaper page, occasional dark spaces, a pair of broken bulbs that need to be replaced, a tablet where once there was a picture of an apartment or a politician.

Look harder, till the eyes hurt. In the vacant dark the site of the sometime lighthouse is shining too, many miles and two thousand years away. The sky is the colour of bruises, a punched cheek, a prayer-beaten forehead, an eye becoming black. This is not where I wanted to spend the night. But it is a fine place to look back at Alexandria and consider the last hours of Mark Antony, the time when he knew he had lost, when he was abandoned by the city's gods. Any biography of Cleopatra is now in its final phase.

The problem for the queen after Actium was to write the story of what had happened before her enemies wrote it. The parties to celebrate her success had to begin in Alexandria even before the killings did. Both celebrations and assassinations were essential. Actium had been only a skirmish. The danger was that it might be seen as a defeat. It was for her and her alone to define what a battle was – and when or if it had taken place.

Actium had absolutely not been a defeat. Her supporters understood that. It was barely even a setback, and only a diplomatic setback at that. There had never been a battle of Actium. For so many reasons it was no shame to have left Canidius and his army to win on land, to do what he had wanted to do from the start.

Yes, a land campaign had seemed unattractive at first. To leave the coast would have meant leaving her ships and her treasure and any possibility, even in victory, of returning quickly to Egypt. But she had not betrayed Canidius. She had allowed him his chance as soon as it had seemed impossible to win at sea. This was going to be a long game. Nothing had been decided yet.

Yes, there was some small risk now that Alexandrian opponents (there were always a few) would present her strategic retreat as a rout. The best retort to that would be to invite them to parties, to cull their numbers, to take their property and to plan the next phase of the war as soon as Antony could rejoin her in the city.

As a precaution she would slaughter some of the prisoners taken in Antony's Persian campaigns. No one in that war, indeed in most wars, could agree what had definitely been a battle and what had not. This time she was the one who would draw the lines. She would kill the Persian survivors now so as to make her own distinctions a little clearer.

Then she would kill some of her less reliable Alexandrian friends. With the money from their confiscated estates she would move some of her fleet south and overland to the Red Sea. A ship could move across the desert on rollers as easily as her granite pillars from Aswan. If she or her Caesarion, or the Sun and Moon twins needed to open a new front against Octavian, she could deepen her retreat as far as India or widen it to Spain, always as long as her treasure, the world's greatest concentration of wealth, went with her.

Socratis has sent a messenger. His driver in the yellow suit, for the first time cleansed of mud, asks if I mind being here for the rest of the morning. It is good, he mumbles, that I have stayed here. The news is confusing. There are all sorts of troubles coming. He hopes that I have been able to spend the time well. Before I can nod my head in assent he turns away and is gone.

Optimism did not last long in Alexandria after Canidius returned, reporting the story of Actium as it had been told to Antony's army, of how the legions had been ruthlessly betrayed, sailors preferred to soldiers for Cleopatra's sake alone. Plancus had moved fast, telling Antony's Greek allies that while they should have already changed sides they were still free to do so. The men of Ephesus had followed his advice. Others too. Canidius's army had surrendered – and it too had been allowed to join Octavian. Canidius himself, Octavian claimed with persuasive effect, was a traitor to Rome.

Cleopatra's response was to declare Caesarion to be Egypt's male ruler. The Sun and Moon were rising by his side.

Low in the pale-blue sky the neon patches have turned to fading stars, a constellation connected by a low-flying plane in a continuous line of white air. A few minutes after 7.00 a.m. the first bus stopped by the petrol pumps. No one stepped off or on until a second followed and then a third. Five black-hooded crows, dancing around the dusty ground, scattered only when the first feet of the soldiers kicked out of the doors. From the second bus streamed a rabble of schoolboys. The third disgorged three mechanics, four women with fruit baskets and Mahmoud, screwing his eyes against the lights and limping. Every new bus – eleven of them now – has brought only soldiers until there is nothing but the grey of metal and uniform in every direction.

For all her stratagems, Cleopatra could do little more than kill. Plans to sail a fleet across the desert to the Red Sea were foiled by the unforgiving tribesmen whose bitumen business she had disrupted in better times. She succeeded only in sending Caesarion away with his tutor on the route to India. She sent messages to Octavian, embassies

and bribes, gold to pay his armies in exchange for guarantees that her children could rule in Egypt after she had gone. Octavian responded with silence, threats and the sending of his own emissary, a poet whose charm and eloquence with the Queen pushed Antony into depression without achieving any other purpose.

Their parties took on a new tone. In the past they had created a club called the 'inimitable livers'. Now they called themselves by a new name, 'those who would die together'. Cleopatra built herself a mausoleum into which she brought her treasure of emeralds, pearls and gold. Inexorably the news came that Octavian was advancing on Alexandria.

Antony roused himself for a cavalry charge which won a modest and much celebrated victory. But that was his last success. Alexandrians later described the following night as the one in which the gods of Greece led a procession out of Alexandria. This was when Antony was abandoned by his protective deities. Dionysus led Isis away into Octavian's camp.

Antony's response was to bluster and bribe, challenging Octavian to single combat as though they were heroes at Troy, offering money to

Octavian's troops to change sides as though he were a captain of mercenaries. He sent a fleet to meet Octavian, the ships of both sides shadowing their armies along the coast. Then suddenly the Egyptian navy defected to Octavian, just as everyone and everything else was defecting.

It is now 9.00 a.m. in the troop depot that was once a service station. There is a clock at a table beside a coin-operated roundabout of camels. Mahmoud did not approach me immediately. We had not spoken since he climbed into the back of a black car at the Montaza Palace, saying that we would meet again on his return from Athens. He limped towards the metal shelters full of officers. After ten minutes he emerged smiling, waving his glasses. He was still walking awkwardly like a much older man.

He did not stay long. He did not mention Athens. He did not explain why he was here. He did seem pleased to see me. He said only that he and Socratis had a surprise which they were sure I would like. He asked politely about my literary progress. I said that it had almost ceased. Then he left on the same local bus that had brought him, the sole passenger now that the mechanics and basket carriers had reached the end of their journey.

I am suddenly more sleepless and confused than at any time since I arrived in this city. Uncertainty now seems as normal as exhaustion. The ancient story tumbles into a chaos of its own. Antony accuses Cleopatra of ordering her fleet to betray him. She flees to her mausoleum. He thinks she is dead and tries to kill himself with a sword. In fact (inasmuch as there any facts here), she is not dead and he is hauled up to her for a bloody reconciliation, and then a lengthy process of dying. Many years of scholarship and literary invention have been since deployed in establishing – or not – who was betraying whom.

Sharia Yousef

I am back now in the city. The three of us were to meet again at 4.00 p.m. at the Roman Theatre, in the archaeological gardens on the other side of Nebi Danial Street from the Dead Fountain cafe. That was the driver's first instruction when he collected me at Khat Rashid and his last before he left me at the hotel. Socratis was going to bring his mother. This was to be a great privilege, a rare appearance. So I had to be punctual, and to be waiting precisely when requested on the steps in front of the ancient heads.

Mahmoud was the first to arrive, just after 4.30, still limping, stroking fondly the smooth surface of the eyeless granite as though for comfort. Socratis himself appeared next, without either his mother or his driver, arriving suddenly from a hut beside the wall to the barracks. He looked past us toward the tourist gate, smiling first at Mahmoud and then at me. The absence of his driver seemed to be a good sign that his mother too might be with us soon.

No one spoke. Mahmoud seemed lightly dazed. The peace was like the moment before the firing of a gun. Behind us were the stone goddesses in their drapery, rows of silent survivors of so many saltwater centuries.

I asked about the investigation into the bombing. Normally a question about that could draw an answer from Mahmoud, even if only his usual answer that the plotters were foreigners and fortunately dead: and that the good fortune was their own as well as that of Egypt, the

337

hollow-eyed phone pictures of their faces suggesting hideous last hours. This afternoon he said nothing at all.

The only tourists were far away by the outer walls. The Roman stage was empty except for the skinny shadows of trees. From the Villa of the Birds there came suddenly a high note of opera, a trill, a pause and a repeat. The sequence was repeated as though it were a summons, again and again, until Socratis rose and gestured for us to follow. We crossed some hundred feet of Polish masonry and imperial mosaic until we were only a few steps from the singer, to whom he politely bowed.

This was Socratis's mother, she of the personal relationships claimed with Cleopatra, King Farouk, all the little Farouks and every other leader of eternal Alexandria. She was standing in the villa behind an open glass door. At her feet were the brightly coloured floors, the mosaic birds, somehow brighter than I had seen them before, washed stone feathers of a purple water-hen, a peacock, a duck and dove. The dove was flying, the duck staring at the sun, and the water-hen was stretching its red legs. Behind her were rosettes and a panther and the rough-cut stones of what was once one of the finest houses in the city.

I looked up at her before Socratis did. She was disappointingly normal, wearing a thin black dress and a shawl weighted with pearls sewn as stars. Around her neck were golden fishes, their scales and tails shaped as crescent moons, their eyes in turquoise. Around her left wrist was a bracelet of charms, a silver cucumber and glass beads in the shape of Africa. Her feet were fixed on the wings of a purple gallinule.

Certainly, she was a very privileged visitor. Paying tourists were kept away high on glass walkways. There was no sign of the attendant now. The singer seemed as relaxed and commanding as if she were at home, continuing to look out over our heads and back to where we had met.

She sounded her note again. This time it echoed around both of the theatres, the new and the old, a bouncing syllable of an unknown song. Mahmoud looked at me expectantly. I was clearly expected to recognise what she was singing. Socratis produced a blue silk sheet and placed it over a low stone wall so that his mother could more easily lean back and project her notes into the outer air.

She smiled like a cat. This was the woman who saw history as a single flat plate, a non-stop now, within which the big players lived simultaneously and for ever. This was the woman who wished that Jesus had never come to Alexandria, who thought, her son had said, that Cleopatra was still available for dinners. This was the witness to the aftermath of the New Year bombing, the mother whose grief had caused her son such concern and her son's friend such suspicion.

She did not seem in any way abnormal today, no madder than any woman would seem while singing an unknown aria into an empty archaeological site. She looked like a gracious, wealthy Egyptian with dark-set eyes, greeting one of her son's friends who had travelled from afar. She stopped for breath. Socratis, much the more deranged of the two men, introduced us with a whisper. I began to commiserate with her about the carnage in the church but Mahmoud broke in to say that this was unimportant now.

They knew that I had questions, he added. I was not sure what to say. It seemed an age since we had first failed to meet. She began quietly to speak in English. She hardly seemed a possessor of exotic beliefs. Had I not recognised her songs from Handel? Surely Handel had been from England? Did I not know his *Giulio Caesare*? That was the very best of parts for a Cleopatra.

She trilled again into the outer theatre, triggering a long, metallic echo, like that of a bullet against a pack of distant tanks. But even this Cleopatra, she said, stopping suddenly in her song, was not as good as the one she had once played here long ago, forty years ago. She whispered the words as though her character were still breathing, a baby asleep, not yet to be woken. Cleopatra would always be in Alexandria, she said, when she was needed the most.

Mahmoud and Socratis lowered their eyes. The whispering singer took no notice of them, looking only outwards and over the Odeon seats towards the marble heads from the sea. This time she did not sing. She spoke softly in Arabic in rhythmic, rasping beats. And then she recited in a language that was probably still Arabic but in syllables which were sour as though mingled with smoke. For the next five minutes the words grew wilder and the skin lightened under her eyes. It was as if she were younger and slighter, manically remembering.

When she stopped, she sat down on the blue silk cloth. That was a wonderful speech, she said, 'a Cleopatra with a happy ending'. She had played this part in this very theatre soon after it was found by the

Poles. It was easy to play here then. This was the play that proved the 'unconquerable power of Egypt'. Cleopatra was dead. That had been her death scene. In truth, the Romans were the ones defeated. It was easy, she said, to believe that then.

Socratis began to speak. He looked as though he were about to shout, smoothing his hair in futile gestures. His mother motioned him to be quiet. She had been five years old, she said, when Egypt had had its last true victory over its enemies, when Nasser had taken back the Suez Canal, when Britain and France were humiliated by those they had occupied so long. It was the first event she could remember. Did I too remember it? How old had I been? Five too, I told her. After the triumph there had been constant celebrations. Under Nasser and Sadat there had always been celebrations.

Had I been to Alexandria's opera house? It had soft leather doors in purple and bronze; and there was an altar on the ceiling to all the great composers. She had never sung her Cleopatra there. She would have loved to do that. She was a singer but not a good enough singer. She would have loved to play her stage part there too. But she had only ever played it here. Soon Cleopatra would be at the opera house again. The Queen had never disappointed.

Then slowly, as though instructed by some ghostly director, she rose from her silk-draped wall and walked out into the ancient rooms behind the stage. These were the caves of arches where she and her friends had kept their costumes, she said. Was there to be an encore? There was not. She walked out onto the flat sand with her son, past the smooth heads of the gods, past Mahmoud, pausing only to collect the plastic-wrapped chauffeur.

Socratis looked at me. I had seen enough and should make of it what I could. Within minutes the attendant had returned to enforce

341

the house rules of the Birds. Two French women were standing idly with Tutankhamun postcards in their hands.

Bibliotheca Alexandrina

I want to find the play I have just heard. Neither Mahmoud nor Socratis knows its name. To them it is just 'the Cleopatra play'. I ask at the desk if anyone can help. After a few hours a small pile of books arrives.

The topmost shabby volume is entitled *Théatre de Notre Temps*. It contains a surprise, or a possible joke, or a bizarre coincidence, certainly a shock. If Mahmoud and Socratis have organised this they are smarter than I see them.

Neatly marked with a library card is *Mort ou Amour*, an Egyptian dialogue, a French translation, in which an historian in an Alexandrian hotel room is struggling to write a book about Cleopatra. The dramatic hero does most of the things that I have done here since I arrived, ruefully recalling past efforts, weighing fact against fiction, realism against romance, 'la politique ou le coeur' as motivation for peace and war. He complains that 'le nom de Cleopatra m'a suivi toute ma vie'. He admits that the name has often haunted him more than the Queen herself. He remembers hangovers and nights of 'insomnies'.

Troubled by past and future cancers, he talks for three acts about his life to a visiting friend called Cleopatra. This woman knows the story only from the film that she last saw as a sixteen-year-old. The two argue about the Elizabeth Taylor version – 'une femme splendide' – and what should and should not have been in it. She smokes; he drinks. There are more sleepless nights. He argues that ancient and modern history are the same, that his two Cleopatras are the same. The historian is not quite deranged but neither is he quite himself.

This is almost a threat – or a fortunate escape. If I had known earlier of Tawfik al-Hakim's *Mort ou Amour* I could hardly have written this year what I already have. But I do not want to read any more of it. I have already read more than is good for me. It is not a joke. It is a coincidence. But sometimes the two can seem the same.

Mort ou Amour is also not what I have been looking for. This oddity from the catalogue cannot be the iconic hit that Socratis's mother performed, the one whose 'happy ending' I have just watched from the Roman villa. The only good omen from Tawfik al-Hakim is that at the beginning of Act Three his historian has completed 200 pages, his muse is encouraging – 'Deux cent pages en un mois? Pas mal' – and the end is in sight.

The second work in the library pile is *The Downfall of Cleopatra* by Ahmed Shawqi, a book from a rather more distinguished figure, a politician as well as a writer, an ally of Mr Zaghloul against British rule

in Egypt. Shawqi wrote it in 1927, the same year in which he was hailed as the Prince of Poets, a laureate of Arab aspiration. The text is in English although the translation here is no triumph of rhyme: 'the great are concerned in many ways/about how they are destined to end their days'.

As in *Mort ou Amour* there is little action. But this earlier play is written in salon verse not bedroom prose. It is set in 31 BC instead of the present and has a high patriotic tone. The louche Alexandrias of Plutarch, Shakespeare and the Victorian erotic are all equally far away.

The first scene begins in the private royal part of the Library where gloomy young scholars listen to cheers in the street outside for the victory at Actium. The celebrants cry that Alexandria's monarch, like its lighthouse, is queen of the seas. But this, the scholars know, is a trick. The fleet has returned by night so that its broken masts and sails can be repaired by morning. The mob is like a parrot; its mind is in its ears. Their heroes are traitors, whose crown is a wine goblet and whose throne is a bed of lust.

Shawqi's Cleopatra blames others for spreading the falsehoods and false hopes. She must accept that Actium had not been a victory. But neither had it been a defeat. It was an opportunity to let the two Roman sides destroy themselves, leaving Egypt to become the big victor in the end. Shawqi's Antony is a useless sot while this Cleopatra is a cunning Egyptian liberator, a national unifier who ruthlessly betrays her lover in the better interests of her country.

After lengthy acts of partying and prophecy, the Queen recognises that she herself is doomed. Death by snakebite must ensue. But in the long run she knows that Rome is the more doomed. She has no interest in an afterlife with Antony. She cares only for the future of Egypt. Its enslavers will be enslaved. The invader has opened for itself a grave. One bad rhyme after another: better in Arabic perhaps. After the uprisings of the 1920s it was a national call to arms.

Shawqi's play had many revivals in the 1960s and was a popular staple for concert performances in Alexandria and Cairo. After the military disasters and deceptions for Egypt that followed, it seems, quite reasonably, to have fallen out of favour. Perhaps Socratis's mother was merely reviving her own youth. Perhaps she saw some imminent chance of a new revival.

I was not going to find out more. Some parts of a story can be neatly tied. Others cannot. Ahmed Shawqi himself, after writing six plays on historical themes and a comedy set in a harem, died in 1932, a respected rebel comrade of the even more celebrated Mr Zaghloul, whose high statue tonight is guarded closely.

20.I.11

Place Saad Zaghloul

So what did happen to Cleopatra in the end? Maurice was asking the question. It was June 2010 and we were back in the Blue Lion, the first time we had been there together for twenty-five years, the first since the night of Drakkar Noir and Andrew Faulds MP. The place had changed according to the pattern of the intervening time, more salad-eaters, fewer beer-drinkers, more pistachios, fewer peanuts, lagers from implausible Dutch towns, light and heavy wines in small and large glasses.

It seemed easy and natural to be back. We were continuing to slip in and out of each other's lives as we had for all of our lives, noting the progress of his marriage (initially good, latterly poor), his boyfriends (the best of them away east of Suez), his sons (one of them at Trinity), the peculiarities of different cancers, the curability of some, the inexorability of others, including the one that was beginning to bring Maurice's life to an end.

When we were last on the Gray's Inn Road the Editor of *The Times* was dying of cancer. Maurice reminded me (as though I needed reminding) that ten years ago, when I was editing *The Times* myself, and in my eighth year of the job, I too was told that a rapid cancer death lay ahead for me. What kind of cancer had I had? It was pancreatic, like Maurice's, but a different pancreatic, the neuro-endocrine variety, sometimes the kinder sort. He knew that. He just wanted me

349

to say it again. But if the topic is the wrong kind of cancer, it is hard to sustain an honest optimistic conversation for long. Maurice had given up alcohol. And he did not speak of that for long either.

Within minutes we were back in the past, I recalling the sherry decanters of Oxford and he the Red Tents, the higher life, the champagne and pills that produced better sex with mermaids. The tents had been his finest creation. Okay, yes, it had been a development of others' efforts. But the gauze, the gods, the questions in Greek, those were wholly his own. Dear Frog, the flying suicide, would never have had the inspiration. The sea-creatures in the inner sancta had almost always been men (no, always, all of them). Did I know that until the late Middle ages the 'mermaids' of art and poetry had been mermen to a man?

He smiled. I wanted to press him more but did not. I avoided V's employment as a statue. I recalled instead his Nubian teacher in the red dress. We looked, too, at his later life. Maurice used his money now to help anonymous addicts in need. He had long ago given up advertising and finance.

His eyes were still bright. His hair and skin were not. What was this peculiar organ called the pancreas? It was a tiny fish-tailed thing, 'an inner mermaid', he mocked. Why in different ways had it bitten us both? Had we shared something nasty in the Essex water, some rays from the Moscow-watching radars of the Rothmans estate, or a blight in the Oxford sherry? It was hard to be light, although Maurice liked, when he could, to make light of everything.

So what did happen to Cleopatra in the end? He asked the question again. I was feeling defensive. It was absurd that I had never finished my book. I began a defence of how Big Oil, Mrs Thatcher, the 1986 print revolution for the press, the editing of *The Times* and *The Times*

Literary Supplement (now, oddly, back in the same office opposite the Blue Lion where *The Times* had once been), and other books about Tony Blair and Spartacus, had all found a higher priority.

No, he said. What had happened to the real Cleopatra? That was what he suddenly wanted to know. It was as though we were back in our shared set of rooms, dressed from Marks & Spencer and Chelmsford Market, planning to plagiarise Charles Marowitz to the sound of a reel-to-reel tape recorder.

After Antony's death Octavian wanted Cleopatra stripped immediately of her treasure. It was too easy to destroy an army's wages by fire. Metals might be melted into different shapes and saved; but ivory, pearls and precious stones would be dust. Cleopatra could not be allowed to immolate herself like an oriental martyr. Paying the victorious soldiers was the victor's immediate priority. Nothing mattered more than that.

Octavian sent Rome's most glamorous poet and soldier, Cornelius Gallus, to be his envoy. Gallus was that most Alexandrian of Romans, literary innovator, glorious elitist, lover of Antony's own favourite actress in Rome and commander now of Antony's four African legions. While Gallus distracted the Queen with art and gossip, a junior officer was tasked with climbing up to the back window of her mausoleum, to burst in from behind and take her captive.

The manoeuvre succeeded perfectly. After that there was only the lesser, but still significant, question of Cleopatra's personal fate. Octavian allowed her request to leave and prepare Antony's body for burial. She beat herself almost to death, feverish, refusing food, but relieved to learn that her Caesarion was still free and on his way east and south. Most of Cleopatra's remaining interest was in the fate of her children.

Maurice nodded, pouring a little water on the wound on his wrist through which the chemotherapy came.

Octavian then came to see Cleopatra himself. He found her either as a feverish captive or an unbowed queen, depending on which of the main ancient versions we prefer.

As always when there was doubt in the air, Maurice began to look combative. Perhaps I would like to make up my mind, he suggested sourly, turning over a dirty ashtray.

The dignified and unbowed was the better of the two pictures, the one from Plutarch's *Life of Mark Antony*, the main source for Shakespeare, the one that Shawqi hoped to contradict. One of Plutarch's best sources was Cleopatra's doctor. At times Plutarch, masterly observer of eclipses, writes like a doctor himself.

Octavian was uncertain what end for Cleopatra would suit him best. He wanted the option of taking her to Rome in his triumph. But there was the memory of her sister, Arsinoe, in Caesar's parade. The Romans had wept for little Arsinoe. It was impossible to be certain of how a queen might be seen by the people.

Cleopatra herself had clearer requests. She wanted the best life for Ptolemy Caesarion, for Alexander the Sun and Cleopatra the Moon. She wanted guarantees for them and the option of suicide for herself, but on her own terms, when and how she wanted to make it happen.

While both sides weighed their choices Cleopatra made a last visit to Antony's tomb. Afterwards she sat on a straw bed and tried to persuade Octavian that she had acted against him only from fear of Antony. Octavian did not believe her. She replied with prayers and fists and arguments over the inventory of personal trinkets missing from her treasure trove.

Four months later, when the summer was over, Maurice and I were back in the same Blue Lion seats. He had some points that he hoped I might say at his funeral. But the listing of his achievements in advertising, finance and charities did not detain him beyond the first glass of Evian.

We sat after that as though with those blue plastic boxes of Agfa colour slides, the ones that were fashionable for our parents in our schooldays. In the 1950s most photographs were of happy scenes, or scenes made happy, scenes that the photographer wanted to remember. So too were these colour-slide memories, memories of mud and rugby, sports days and concerts even though neither of us had succeeded with ball or recorder except in our own minds. We remembered how both of us had been 'groaners' at Rothmans Primary, and we remembered the Brentwood book-burning.

Did I remember Miss Leake and the children's parties at his house in front of the chicken farm? Yes, I remembered most of all the parquet floor and the find-your-partner games and the time Maurice almost smashed the china cabinet. How did I know that I was not imagining the parquet floor – or that he was not imagining the cabinet? We did not absolutely know. But there were magic cushions and wooden lakes. I was sure about that.

If Maurice were still in touch with V, perhaps he could ask her whether we were right? He was not in touch, he said firmly. It had been years since her last attack on us for betraying political beliefs that neither of us thought we had ever possessed. There had been no more complaints that I was failing to make a difference, failing to make things happen, always preferring to name things than change them. Once this had been a refrain, Maurice said. Now it had long ago stopped. And anyway, V had not been at his fifth birthday party.

Did I remember his performance from the Trinity bell tower? He reminded me eloquently of this lest I had forgotten, adding details, like the names of the loudly listed underground stations that I had indeed forgotten. His voice was fixed back in the past. Even the ravages on his skin could not destroy the images of how he had been long ago, slightly reddened cheeks, slightly slackened vowels, a glass in his hand so differently filled.

We talked of how acts of memory are useful for the dying. There were Greek and Roman philosophers who warned against the fear of death and taught the power of shared recollections to keep fear at bay. In that lost pub of *The Times* we pictured the winter of 1963, our shiverings as useless wing three-quarters on a rugby ground that was the coldest since the restoration of Charles II. We watched again Maurice's Duncan in the Brentwood School *Macbeth*. He thought that the doomed Scottish king lacked any good lines and wanted most to have been Banquo.

Then how did she die? Maurice's question was suddenly almost urgent. Beneath the tight skin of his jaw, tiny muscles were still moving after his words had ceased. He was like a singer listening to one of his own records, knowing what he had heard before, what he wanted to hear.

Painlessly.

Painlessly is good, he replied.

Cleopatra discovered that Octavian was about to send her to Rome by ship. She had little remaining time to decide.

So how does she die?

By the quietest poison, I said. Ignore the stories of asps or cobras or any other kind of snakes hiding in fig baskets. With the knowledge from human experiments that the Ptolemies possessed, no queen would leave her suicide to the whim of a reptile. Cleopatra was an aficionado of painlessness and pain. She had seen the agony caused by the snakes of Egypt, signed many a *ginestho* for the experiments and executions that proved why no one would want to die that way if other ways were available.

Painless is good, Maurice repeated and ordered coffee. It was good that she had deceived her tormentor and died as she intended to die. That seemed much the best version of events.

We moved away again to the times we had spent by the cold North Sea watching birds on the waves, the wheeling, wailing and gangling that were the same when we were five and fifteen as when we were fifty-five. We recalled grey gulls massing on the beaches as the mud dried. He seemed suddenly tired. It was hard to hold these thoughts. He pouted – as he had used to do when his cheeks were fatter. It was still a very recognisable pout.

We spoke of E.M. Forster. Maurice particularly liked the scandalous late novel that bore his name. The author of *Maurice* had shown little interest in his Alexandrian books, *Pharos and Pharillon*, after he had written them. But he had given his only speech about Cleopatra's city in the east-coast town of Aldeburgh, where for a while Maurice had owned a house.

I brought with me a copy of this speech. The novelist had drawn desperate comparisons between Aldeburgh and Alexandria, between different scapes of sea and sky, nuanced brown and unbelievable blue. He had tried hard but had found nothing in common to mark the two places 'beyond the first two letters of their name and the occasional visitations of fish'.

Maurice smiled and recalled the Aldeburgh seals that looked so human when they stared. Were seals man's first inspiration for mermaids? He wanted to know how what we imagined intersected with our memories. He already knew how cancer can trigger the imagination, the desire to be somewhere else being so strong as the disease takes its grip.

And James Holladay? Was it true that he had died of a heart attack in a plane flying over the Bermuda Triangle, a most unlikely end for a man who must so much more likely have collapsed in the back bar of the King's Arms? Yes, it was true. He died twenty-two years ago, New Year's Day 1989, and was buried under a marble slab in a forest of mahogany and coconut.

The coffee arrived, and then a cab, and the evening was over. Maurice died a month later. A part of me departed too.

21.1.11

Rue Nebi Danial

While Cleopatra was beginning her immortality in Alexandria, Plancus was in Rome taking smaller steps along the road to being remembered. He was being practical, helpful, ingratiating to the victor who was now undisputed leader of the Roman world. Gradually the great survivor became cautiously optimistic. He began to see a new future for himself.

He saw some of the letters he would eventually want on his tomb, the ancient pillbox that Duke was to contemplate on his way to Anzio. There would be the COS for his consulship back in 42 BC. To have taken that post had been his decent duty after the death of Julius Caesar – to hold the fort, to stabilise, to do good if he could. There would be a word or two on his foundation of the Roman colonies 'Lugdunum et Rauricam', places that would become Lyons and Basle. There would be room left on the lintel for other offices he might hold, temples he might build, but none for any references to his services for Antony and Cleopatra. There would be no more mention, except by his enemies, of his slitherings on palace floors in a sea-creature outfit or his judicial role while Cleopatra turned pearls into the world's most expensive wine.

Plancus wanted to be a player again. Dutiful constitutional service was to be his epitaph. Beyond the record of his virtuous offices there would also be space for his heirs and for any honours that they might gain from his example. Caieta, close to his family home, was his chosen burial site by the sea. This had also been the burial place of Aeneas's nurse, a minor but significant character in the myth of Rome's foundation. Perhaps Plancus was pleased by that coincidence. Perhaps it was no coincidence at all.

Words would last longer even than tombs. That was what civilised people were beginning to think. If a tomb were somehow linked to art, the chance of survival might be higher still. His marble memorial might, with appropriate encouragement to Virgil, take its place discreetly (but not too discreetly) in the epic of the great new order. It would match the first lines of the second half of Rome's greatest poem. To any young reader who had only the second half in his hand it might be the very beginning of the *Aeneid*.

Poets were useful. That much Plancus knew. But poets were not always as clear as marble and concrete. Virgil was maybe the most reliable, a public poet who knew his place. But there was Horace too, a younger genius of the new age, equally revered by the new regime, a master of the more personal style. Horace was Plancus's friend. But he was tricky. He was Alexandrian in his way although he did not always like to admit it. No one who received a poem as a gift from Horace ever knew quite what it meant, still less what others later might think it meant.

In the four weeks between Maurice's last visit to the Blue Lion and his last breath, we met and spoke whenever we could. Much of our shared memories in this book are his own memories, retained by him, released by his dying and merely reinforced by my own. His present then presupposed his death. His present revived his past. I wish I had been with him even more.

I had other appointments to keep, the kind of appointments that come to an Editor of the *TLS* with interests in the ancient world. One of these, and of all the chances in this story it seems still the strangest, required a Sunday morning reading in Gloucestershire of that most peculiar and subtle poem which Horace addressed to Plancus. This was the one known by its first words *Laudabunt alii*, the beginning of thirty-two lines which, while Maurice was dying, and thus so very eerily as it seemed to me, my task was to explain, word by word, on stage, to an audience in the West of England countryside.

Plancus's long afterlife arrived in Cheltenham on the occasion of a literary festival, a temporary village of tented bookshops, libraries and halls, a virtually unknown event in the calendars of the 1970s and 1980s but in 2010 as common as a game of cricket. The aim of the event was to help readers who had never read a Latin poem before to read one for the first time.

I had agreed to chair the meeting. The choice of poem was not mine. Plancus followed me by purest chance. '*Laudabunt alii*' we all began at 10.00 a.m. A light-pointer identified each word: 'will praise' was followed by 'other men'. *Laudabunt alii claram Rhodon aut Mytilenen Aut Ephesum bimarisve Corinthi moenia*: Others will praise bright Rhodes, or Mytilene, or Ephesus or the walls of Corinth on its two seas. The audience had come to read it in Latin – and it was my task to help them do just that.

V was sitting in the second row from the front, between two blocks of schoolchildren and their teachers. She had a boyish face, not much older than I remembered but larger, her pale cheeks framed by dark, shoulder-length hair, a tattoo on her left shoulder and what I would once have called an Alice-band to keep her forehead clear. I knew immediately who she was. She smiled up while another member of our panel was explaining *Laudabunt alii*, how the second word is the plural subject of the verb in the future tense that precedes it, and what comes next, what precisely it was that 'other men will praise'.

V was taking notes. My colleagues were beginning to explain what the words might mean. I remembered the problems. Is Horace about to praise Plancus? Or is Horace not as straightforward as that? Are the words already a warning to Plancus? If 'other people' are handing out the bouquets, this may suggest that Horace is not going to give any himself. Perhaps Plancus will not like his ode.

Perhaps no one will be praised. The subjects are not, it turns out, even people. They are places, Greek places, tourist sites that were also controversial places, names which any educated soldier of the past decade would know well, in Plancus's case much too well. The light-pointer moved jerkily over the words.

> *Laudabunt alii claram Rhodon aut Mytilenen*
> *Aut Ephesum bimarisve Corinthi moenia.*

Why did Horace choose Rhodes? Was it as beauty spot or naval dockyard island? Why Mytilene? As a peaceful town of poets, protected by Crinagoras, gentle poet and diplomat? Or as a ruin pillaged by Roman armies? Ephesus was the city where Arsinoe was strangled, where Antony and Cleopatra danced on their way to Actium. Corinth was the port with a mouth on two strategic seas. Both welcomed wealthy tourists all the time. Sometimes desperate generals came instead.

My colleagues posed their questions. I concentrated on the answers. In one sense this is a simple drinking song, a request to

Plancus to cheer up and enjoy some wine while he can. But little in Horace means what it seems to mean. We must look at what is omitted as well as what is there. The stresses are within the lines and within the names. Even readers finding this poem for the first time have to take a view of the distant unknown.

V did not seem to have any young charges of her own. While the other adults in the row checked whether their pupils were taking down the translation correctly, she alternated careful note-taking with looking straight ahead. When she caught my eye, she did not smile but held up the back of the exercise book on her lap. On it was a V, in Quink-blue ink, lest I might not have recognised her face.

I was doing my best but I was drifting. My eyes scanned around and around the circular hall. There were polite questions and from my colleagues beside me came answers equally polite.

Sunt quibus unum opus est ... celebrare: There are some people who do nothing but celebrate ...

In the following lines, we learn, Horace does hand out a little praise of his own, not to Plancus but to another place, to Tibur, Rome's summer suburb of tinkling water gardens, temples and facades – a bit like Cheltenham perhaps – where Plancus and Horace both have pleasant houses.

This was not a helpful direction for Plancus. He may have felt a little guilty about Tibur. The means by which homes there had gained their owners were rarely as pleasant as the houses themselves. Horace's own retreat had been a reward for loyalty from the new regime. Plancus's place had been gained a little earlier and in much nastier circumstances, it was said. It had belonged to his brother whom he had betrayed to Mark Antony after Caesar's death. The pursuers had caught him because they knew in advance the perfume he was wearing. Perfume was as great a slur on a Roman man as any betrayal.

There was much here in Tibur that would ideally be forgotten – by Horace, by Plancus, by everyone. But Horace has simultaneously both a message for Plancus and a description of him. Have a few drinks, adapt and survive, subtly, not by changing sides any more but by changing the past. Many of their friends were dead. Cleopatra and Antony were dead. Crimes were still crimes. Let them fade rather than be erased. To continue was the key and to be a Continuator was to be a king.

Others will say the good things.
Come to sunny Rhodes, to Ephesus by the sea.
Come to magical Mytilene, to Corinth beside two seas, to drink-
       drenched Thebes and Thessaly and Delphi too!
The holiday list goes on and on.

Some will always like to praise.
In Athens every olive tree is a garland-in-waiting.
Some go for Argos (so good for horses) or Mycenae.
Every one of them a delight.

But not I, Plancus. There is too much else to say.
Rhodes, Ephesus, Corinth, Athens, all those names.
A bit like a map of your war, don't you think?
OK, my war, our war.

If I must say good things about somewhere, let me praise little Tibur instead, where the streams tumble by the orchards, where our beautiful homes, ours at least for now, are calmed by whispering caves. Perhaps you prefer that, Plancus. Perhaps you do not.

Enough, enough. Remember just three thoughts that are true.
There will always be darkness behind the sun.
A good glass of wine clears any darkness away.
And your wars are not quite over yet.

So time for a Trojan War story. Teucer. Remember him? Smarter brother of the mad, drunk Ajax who died of failure.

Teucer was a realist. He could never have saved Ajax. But when he sailed home alone, was his father pleased to see him? Was he hell!

Teucer had to turn right around. He made a speech to his followers. 'Nil desperandum. Trust me.

There is a new home for us in a new world. Have a drink. Have another drink. Tomorrow we will set off once again upon the sea.'

Ninety minutes later, when 'How to Read a Latin Poem' was over, V was sitting on a wall outside, smoking a grey cigarette and rolling a second between her fingers. She had not stayed to the end. The book with her initial on the back was on top of a canvas briefcase.

She apologised for walking out. Our first words after more than twenty years were about how she needed a nicotine injection. Otherwise it was as though we were still circling warily around the evils of private schools and the inadequacies of Elizabeth Taylor's director. She was never one for pleasantries.

'So what did I miss?'

'A story, an *Odyssey* story, an *Aeneid* story. Horace wants to tell Plancus a story.'

'It is the weirdest ending. I don't get it.'

She snapped at me like Mr W at a student of German.

'Teucer's is not a famous story now. It is one of the lesser known odysseys that began with the fall of Troy. There were hundreds of them.'

She screwed up her face into an ancient scowl. 'Remember that your thinking about Plancus was my idea.'

Alexandria's librarians kept a careful catalogue of all the odysseys they knew. There was the long journey of Odysseus himself who took a decade to reach home from Troy, kill his rivals and reclaim his wife. There was the shorter trip by Agamemnon who came home quickly to be killed quickly too. Helen, whose abduction had caused the war, was delayed with her husband Menelaus on Pharos, and escaped their captors only by wrestling with a god of the sea. Aeneas, a minor Trojan prince, copied the best adventures of Odysseus and rose to be the founder of the Roman race. Those were just the best-known stories.

Horace rarely chose the obvious when the obscure was available. He preferred the oblique, the tangential. That was what the Alexandrians had taught him.

'Horace tells Plancus the story of a man called Teucer, the brother of the giant Ajax, one small hero of the Greeks at Troy and another much greater one.

'... *Teucer Salamina patremque Cum fugeret, tamen uda Lyaeao*

Tempora populea fertur vinxisse corona, Sic tristis affatus amicos: When Teucer was fleeing Salamis and his father, he became drunk with wine, tied a poplar wreath to his brow and spoke to his sad friends.'

'What was the point of that?' V posed the question as sharply as before and pulled at her cigarette like a teenager.

Teucer was a minor player in the war. He was like Plancus. He was trying to make a fresh start. Teucer, too, did not have much choice. His father, king of Salamis, was angry at his son's return from Troy without his beloved elder brother.

There was no reason in this. The reception was unfair. Everyone in Salamis said so. Teucer had been loyal and devoted to his crazy kinsman. Both of them had served the Greeks loyally until Achilles had been killed and Ajax had lost the battle for his beautiful armour.

Then there was chaos. Nothing can be done about chaos except wait for it to end. Ajax confused animals with Trojan enemies, slaughtered cattle instead of fellow heroes and finally killed himself, leaving Teucer behind to go home alone, to face their father's wrath and be forced out of Salamis again in permanent exile.

None of this was Teucer's fault. He could not have saved the mad brute, Ajax. Neither he nor his bigger brother could have saved Achilles. So there was no option but that of a new start.

'*Nil desperandum*', he told his comrades, the phrase in the poem that James Holladay long ago commended.

The future had to begin with new loyalties and new trust.

'*Mecum saepe viri, nunc vino pellite curas; Cras ingens iterabimus aequor*: You brave men who have often suffered much worse with me. Drive away your cares with wine. Tomorrow we will set out again upon the mighty sea.'

'So what was the point?'

Teucer's final speech to his friends is not directly about the cast of the Cleopatra story. Nor is it even precisely about Plancus himself. It is merely an artful reminder of them all. *Nil desperandum* is its most famous phrase. *Despair of nothing.*

Plancus needed to forget his previous employers, how he had raised Greek ships and money for them, how he had solemnly discussed whether little Selene, the Moon twin, should rule over Libya or which of hundreds of eastern towns her brother, Helios the Sun, should have as his domains. Together he and Horace should find quieter times, calmer waters, whatever words their politics and poetry required.

Just as Plancus is a classic Roman, '*Laudabunt alii*' is a classic Latin poem.

'Are you sure?'

'Well, not absolutely sure, no. Nothing is absolutely sure.'

'How long did you go on writing about Cleopatra?'

'Off and on for a while. More off than on. And not for a long while.'

V nodded. She was pleased, she said drily, that I made so much progress. There was a pause – and a long procession of teachers, pupils and other festival-goers who by now had slaked their Sunday morning curiosity among the white tents.

She was also pleased, she said, that she had seen the event announced in the Cheltenham guide and been bothered to come. It was good to see that I was still alive.

'Have you been to Alexandria?'

She asked her question in a high monotone, as though we had never met. She said she had been once with her first husband. She still sometimes found cheap souvenirs around the house. There was not much ancient to see but I still might do better in the place where it all had happened.

'No,' I said. I had not been and I did not think it would help.

How were her parents?

'Fine. Still in Essex, still complaining about the clay in the garden (not the same garden but the same clay) and making balsa-wood models of planes, boats, trains and radar masts.'

She knew that Max Stothard had died (was it about ten years ago?) because her father had mentioned it on one of her rare returns to Rothmans. But she did not know about Maurice.

'How is he? It has been quite a few years.'

She did not seem shocked by the answer. She was surprised he had survived so well so long.

This has to be Cleopatra's very last night. Socratis for the first time leaves a written message. He reports rumblings from Tunis, the country that had once been Carthage and which the Romans knew simply as Africa. There is lightning over Pharos and thunder threatening for miles. There is already a scouring storm.

The square is almost empty. The horses and cars have gone. Even the police are under shelter. The trash of the pavements is bobbing in a river towards the Corniche. The waiters are as troubled as the waters. The concierge is especially agitated. The Polish drug addict and windscreen-wiper is tonight allowed to shelter in the hotel doorway.

22.I.II

Place Saad Zaghloul

The mirror in Room 114 tells me I should shave. The stubble looks like stitches after a car crash. Long ago I did once wear a beard. There were pictures in Maurice's Oxford collection to prove it, him with the chin of a pink-billed bird, me like a fat, brown nut. But it is not a good look now. I start, stop the blade, stop again until every last stiff hair has gone.

Socratis offers to drive me to Cairo. It will be no trouble, he insists, and a chance for him to check the state of his parked cars. There have been deep floods and few Egyptians have experience of floods. Even the Dead Sea fountain is filled with water. The military men are on 'high alert', he says, and speed-traps can become road-blocks. Road-blocks are places where the unwary do not want to be.

This is tempting. But it still seems better to book a driver whose sense of timing is more attuned to the discipline of airlines, one with less of a record for leaving me with the time to write this story.

In Room 114 the wastepaper basket overflows. The rough-book scraps, the Big Oil letterhead and the reporter's flip-pads have finally served their purpose. Keep the Roman map? Mauretania, Africa, Numidia, Cyrenaica, Aegyptus and the names of all the deserts and tribes between them? Yes, keep the map.

I wish I had bought the Alexandria carpet. Is there time to go back? Without Socratis I would never find the shop.

Mahmoud calls. He has to return urgently to Athens. Can he share my airport car? Yes, he can. We will be leaving the Metropole at noon. So these will have to be the very last words.

Last words on Canidius: the general whose *ginestho* gave me my new beginning was one of the few who did not change sides after Actium. He was executed in Alexandria on the orders of Octavian. Neither he nor his heirs in perpetuity could claim on their agreement for tax-free wheat and wine.

Last words on the Big Oil men: Lew died not long after we last met. Mr Antony Brown was a useful fiction, just as the chain-smoking lobbyist had said. Lew said he had always known. The Ferrari-owning art director works in a garden centre in Wales. His boss, the book-collector, is a spiritualist on the Essex coast.

Last words on Plancus: Consul, Censor, Twice Victorious General, Builder of the Temple of Saturn, Divider of Lands in Beneventum, Man of Distinction, Founder of Basle and Lyons. These are just the words he would have liked.

There is no time to buy a souvenir from Alexandria to take home. If there were, I would like a French clock from Lyons, authentic Louis Farouk from Rue Zaghloul, a flock of blue china birds around golden Roman numbers. Every clock here seems to be from Lyons.

Last words on Mr W: still alive, I think, and living in Cornwall. We have not spoken since I began to remember our time together. We would never have remembered the same things. Sir Anthony Browne's Brentwood School is calm, civilised and successful today, a credit to his memory. Equally thriving is the Calthorpe Arms, regularly welcoming the *TLS*'s classicists and critics through its doors.

Last words on Horace: Horace's response to Cleopatra's defeat remains one of his most quoted odes, its first words and lofty rhythms often repeated, over two thousand years, at Mermaid clubs and other clubs when men (mostly men) have gathered for a drink. *Nunc est bibendum, nunc pede libero, Pulsanda tellus, nunc Saliaribus Ornare pulvinar deorum:* Now is for drinking, now time for freedom's feet to pound the earth, now for feasts to pile upon the tables of the gods. The first line is borrowed from Alcaeus, the freedom-fighter of Mytilene. Most of the rest is Horace's own.

Almost everyone has liked Horace's poem. It both praises the new regime and its victim. *Nunc est bibendum* is as subtle in its way as *Laudabunt alii*. It is sympathetic as well as triumphal, foreshadowing much of the later portrayal of Cleopatra, as a queen who took her poison like a true proud Ptolemy and refused to be humiliated by her conqueror.

This became the official version of the Augustan age. She was a worthy adversary: '*Saevis Liburnis scilicet invidens Privata deduci superbo Non humilis mulier triumpho:* As though scorning to be led away in her enemy's ships, no longer a queen, a mere woman in a triumph.' Cleopatra had been an evil foe but a worthy one.

Last words on Virgil: in the eighth book of the *Aeneid*, when Aeneas has buried his nurse and is preparing for his battles to found Rome, he is given a shield by his goddess mother, Venus. Actium is at its centre and Augustus is high on his ship above the foaming waves, light pouring from his eyes. Cleopatra, blind to the snakes that await her, is attended by a god dog.

Last and strangest words on Cornelius Gallus: after Cleopatra's death, this poet, persuader and general became the new ruler of Egypt on Augustus's behalf. Gallus was a much-venerated Alexandrian in his day. He became equally fascinating to later scholars even though, until the end of the 1970s, we possessed only that elegant single line about the river that separated Europe from Asia: *uno tellures dividit amne duas*.

He did not, however, prosper in his Egyptian role. The office workers of the Ptolemies were used to working for a royal autocrat; and a royal autocrat is what Gallus became, attaching his *ginestho* to the erection of gold-tipped obelisks in his own honour and golden statues of himself. Bureaucracies pass on their rule books regardless of their ruler. After five tolerant years, the emperor demanded and got a decent suicide.

Rather worse for Gallus's reputation was the discovery of more of his poetry. In 1978, from a ditch near Aswan, there emerged nine lines of lumpy love poems and pious praise of Caesar, none of it befitting either what his ancient admirers had claimed or the more modern had imagined. This was in one way as rare a discovery as the *ginestho*. It was the oldest Latin text in the world, a book that Virgil or Octavian might have held. This was not enough to stem the decline in its writer's repute.

Socratis calls. He sounds excited but he is brief. Mahmoud will not be coming with me to the airport. All Egyptians must stay here now. The Tunisians have set off an explosion. I ought to stay, to study my Roman map, to listen.

Finally, last words on Cleopatra's children: Caesarion was still on his way to India when he was betrayed and executed. Or, alternatively, he was brought back to Alexandria on the promise that he would rule Egypt; and then was killed on arrival. No story about Caesarion is without its 'either', its 'or' or its 'alternatively'.

In 1997, the head of a sixteen-foot statue was pulled from the harbour; it is in grey granite and shows an elegant young man, without a nose, with a worn and down-turned mouth, and hair showing, unconventionally, beneath an Egyptian headdress. This might have once represented Caesarion. It might even have been planned to stand beside Cleopatra's Needles outside the Metropole Hotel.

Whether or not Caesarion was genuinely Julius Caesar's son was never clear and ceased to matter. Octavian had the advice of an Alexandrian scholar called Arius Didymus who professed it unwise that there be even the possibility of two Caesars. Following best local practice Arius cited two lines from Homer's *Iliad* to support his case for execution.

Little Sun and Moon fared better. They went to Rome where, unlike their mother, they marched in Octavian's triumph. From there they were taken not to some underground cell but into the new imperial family where Octavia, Antony's widow and the new ruler's sister, was their guardian.

Of the two, Cleopatra Selene was the preferred. Like her mother, the Moon was a serious student. Of all the Cleopatras she is the most likely owner of a glowing amethyst inscribed with the advice that a Cleopatra should be 'sober when drunk'. She was later permitted to marry another royal North African prisoner, another veteran of a Roman triumph, whom Augustus made King of Mauretania. This young King Juba became a renowned historian and scholar of his realms. The last Cleopatra to reign as queen over a great library did so in Morocco.

When Cleopatra Selene died she inspired a poem on the subject of an eclipse, a night when the moon rose and then grew dark, hiding her sorrow as the beauty who shared her name lost her life and descended to the world below. 'With her', the poet wrote, 'she had shared her light; and with her death she had shared her darkness.' Even in his old age, Crinagoras, pale successor to Alcaeus and elegist of gift-wrapped roses, could put his pen to a perfect quick Alexandrian poem of departure.

Epilogue

During those last nights of Cleopatra in January 2011 the 'Arab Spring' began. While I was sitting in Khat Rashid and Place Saad Zaghloul, President Ben Ali of Tunisia, a man not well known outside his country despite his dictatorship there for a quarter of a century, was packing for Saudi Arabia with a jet full of gold. Any military anxiety on the road out of King Farouk's palace was well justified. A few days later, the streets of Cairo and Alexandria were filled with protesters demanding that Hosni Mubarak too should leave his palaces for the last time, ideally leaving the national treasure behind but, if that were impossible after thirty years in power, he should simply leave.

Eventually and reluctantly, Mubarak obeyed. His friends told him he had lost. In Libya there were already the first protests against President Gaddafi. Commentators speculated on which of his own closest allies would abandon him first. There were newspaper articles daily from Benghazi, Greek Cyrene as once it was, a place more freedom-loving than the rest, or so it was said.

The Spring was spreading into Syria and Arabia. Back in London I felt a mild guilt that I had left the story just as it was about to happen. But I was no longer a foreign correspondent or newspaper editor. Any journalist could go to Alexandria and many did. I had been pursuing a different story and, in the peace of ignorance, had completed it.

For days I watched the Al Jazeera pictures from the Corniche, the banner-wavers who passed by the Metropole and Cecil Hotels, wondering if I would spot Mahmoud or Socratis and, if I did, what side they would be on. There was one time when I thought I saw the yellow-suited driver. If it was the right man he was definitely on the demonstrators' side, but I could not be sure. It was possible, even

likely, that if my two Alexandrians had a choice they would be on different sides.

There was a news report that the New Year church bombing had been planned by the interior ministry in order to bolster international support against al-Qaeda. This was close to Socratis's own suggestion although, in those last winter days, he had not expressed himself quite so firmly. Both men would eventually want to be on the winning side, Mahmoud the more so.

On 23 March Elizabeth Taylor died. For one night only there were news images on television of another Alexandria, the place of silver and ivory, of gold, bright blue sky and the massive application of cosmetics.

Two days later a battered postcard of Hosni Mubarak arrived at the offices of the *Times Literary Supplement*. It showed the former Egyptian president in black-haired youth and black-suited severity, just the sort of picture that a rejected dictator in a closely guarded hospital bed would have distributed himself if he had been able to. It carried both an Egyptian and an English stamp. It was hard to read the postmark. It smelt as though it had been pulled from a drawer of mothballs.

The message read: 'RIP Cleopatra. All best to you and her for another thirty years, V.'

ACKNOWLEDGEMENTS

To all those who read the text: to Mary Beard and Paul Webb. To Raphael Cormack for Egyptian research and photographs. To Jo Evans for picture editing. To Sigrid Rausing, publisher and editor, to Ed Victor, my agent, and to Maureen Allen, my assistant at the *TLS*.

Keep in touch with
Granta Books:

Visit grantabooks.com to discover more.

GRANTA